The Gods Arrive

TAUCHNITZ EDITION.

By the same Author,

THE YEARS THAT THE LOCUST HATH EATEN   1 vol.

.

THE GODS ARRIVE

BY

ANNIE E. HOLDSWORTH,

AUTHOR OF "THE YEARS THAT THE LOCUST HATH EATEN."

COPYRIGHT EDITION.

LEIPZIG

BERNHARD TAUCHNITZ

1898.

MY FRIEND.

July 20, 1897.

CONTENTS.

PART I

Page

Chapter I. When Half-Gods go 9

— II. The Voice of the People 18

— III. Katherine stands in the Wings 27

— IV. The Key of the Spring 42

— V. And behold! it was a Dream 52

— VI. The Horsehair pricks 61

— VII. "To Katherine, on Leaving" . . . 74

— VIII. A-foot to Great Lowlands 84

— IX. A Return to Nature 97

— X. Peggy at the Fair 107

— XI. The Ethics of the Situation . . 115

— XII. Gods or Mortals? 132

PART II

Chapter I. Oh, what a Plague is Love! 140

— II. Woman's Independence 156

— III. Katherine claims her Friend 166

— IV. There is always a Way out 179

			Page
CHAPTER	V.	On the Eve of Defeat	195
—	VI.	The White Gate	204
—	VII.	A Man's Love	211
—	VIII.	Reapers	221
....	IX.	Shall we taste this wonderful Wine . . .	325
—	X.	Martha's Advice is sound	231
....	XI.	Vigil	247
—	XII.	Where two love true	258
....	XIII.	A Mecca-window in the Temple	264
—	XIV.	The Book is a Masterpiece	271
....	XV.	The Gods arrive!	281

THE GODS ARRIVE.

PART I.

CHAPTER I.

WHEN HALF-GODS GO.

"STILL, the end spells triumph," said Franklin, gloomily. His voice roused the girl, huddled up, asleep, in the chair beside the window. In a minute she was wide awake, but she did not move or speak. She smiled to herself.

"If I were so certain of triumph I should at least have the gaiety of my convictions," she thought. "They win who laugh, yet he has won already, in spite of his seriousness." Tender lines gathered round her mouth as she thought of the story that had first attracted her to Richard Franklin. He had beggared himself to feed the starving women and children in a great dock-strike. A book-lover, he had sacrificed his library for them; his furniture, his savings, even his clothes had been offered up. Finally, to save himself from starvation he had been forced to take a humble post in the Labour movement.

The story made him a hero and even a saint in Katherine Fleming's eyes.

In the dim light she could not see his face, but she knew the look that in his present mood it would wear.

By a quick turn of thought she threw his profile against the dusk: the sharp outline that expressed the eagerness and dissatisfaction of the enthusiast; the straight forehead, the nose clear-cut and powerful, the firm lips above the firmer chin. And seeing her idea of him only half complete, her glance wandered to the man himself. But twilight had fallen between them, and the dying fire showed neither her brother's friend nor her brother.

"Your triumph will be the 'victory of the vanquished,'" laughed Mark Fleming.

There was as little prophecy of success in his mirth as in Franklin's melancholy, but it pricked the other man's mood. He sat up sharply, and the edge in his voice cut like a knife through Katherine's musing.

'We *must* triumph!" he cried. "The next century will see the end of the aristocracy, and then—"

He stopped, knit his brows, and finished his sentence in a lower key.

"And then,

> "'Heartily know,
> When half-gods go
> The gods arrive!'"

"Meanwhile," said Mark, discontentedly, "we are face to face with a crisis like this; and the people—you would say the gods—are powerless."

"'Powerless to be born,'" said Franklin, sadly, in the slow voice that contrasted so oddly with the eagerness of his face. "But it can't be always so! If we only had a historian. . . . You see," he went on more quickly, "we have no book that has ever brought the subject before the thinking world.   Our story is yet on the knees of the gods—   If it were only written. . . ."

His fingers drummed impatiently on the arm of his chair. . . . "But there isn't a man among us who could write it!" he finished.

"There isn't a man," said Mark; "but there might be a woman,—Katherine, for instance."

"Your sister!" Franklin said incredulously; and his tone sent the blood galloping in Katherine's veins.

She opened her lips to tell them she could hear what they were saying, but she remained silent. What did it matter?   They knew she was there. . . . If they chose to discuss her. . . . She shrugged her shoulders and did not speak.

"Your sister?" Franklin repeated, but in a more guarded tone, throwing a glance at the figure beside the window.

"She is asleep,—she won't hear," said Mark, also lowering his voice. "Yes, I mean Kit—Why shouldn't she write this book? She has heart and brains; she is clever and enthusiastic."

"Cleverness and enthusiasm; humph!" said Franklin, disparagingly.   "It is easy to be an enthusiast when one feels the grip of a movement.   That does not imply power to grasp its details and its meaning. . . . As to cleverness, that is an easy feminine virtue. . . ."

His eyes darkened; he was silent a minute. "Let me see; how long has your sister been in town?" he added suddenly.

"Three years," Mark answered.

"And she came fresh from Newnham.   What can she know of life, let alone the problems of life?"

"Oh, come, old man, as much at any rate as you.

shut up among your books for twenty years! A girl can't be a journalist without learning something of life; and as to problems, it's women who make the problems of life. . . . Besides, Kit's clever, successful too; and success is not an easy feminine virtue. Did you see that article of hers in 'The Flight'? . . . Coates says she will get on. Newnham has given her balance and a trained mind. You might do worse than suggest that she should write the History of the Labour movement."

Franklin pursed up his lips: "A trained mind is not necessarily a strong mind. The science tripos won't solve the problems of existence. Your sister looks at things from the sentimental side; and sentimentalists weaken the force of great movements."

"They make 'em popular though," said Mark.

"We must have knowledge," Franklin returned. He bent his brows toward the end of the room, where Katherine made a patch of deeper shadow on the shadow. The light from a lamp outside streamed through the window, and showed her eyes on him, scornful and indignant.

She sprang up, and crossed the room and faced Franklin, her figure drawn to full height.

"So this is your opinion of me!" she cried passionately. "And all the time I thought. . . . I thought. . . . But you are wrong! I am not a sentimental enthusiast. The people's cause is everything to me. . . . I would give all I have to make a better life for them. . . ."

Her voice broke. She steadied herself against the table, twisting the corner of the table-cloth in shaking fingers. "And I thought you believed in me . . . understood me. . . ." Her eyes appealed to Franklin.

"Yes?" he said.

The interrogation in his voice was maddening. It lashed the girl.

"Ah! you don't believe in me?" she gasped. "But I will make you. . . . I will become a power in the Labour movement. . . . I will write that book. You shall see I am not a weak-minded woman. You think I haven't balance and judgment—I will make you own your mistake."

"I am always obliged to anybody who makes me do anything," said Franklin, gravely, stroking his moustache to hide his amusement. The kindly gleam in his grey eyes was lost on Katherine. She amused him by her independence and spirit, though these were not in his category of feminine virtues. He had only studied woman through the medium of Schopenhauer; and he had no wish to study her for himself.

But Katherine intruded on his thoughts—he told himself that her type was objectionable; nevertheless, he listened to her frank utterances, and approved of her life with her brother. He kept his eyes on her now till the anger died out of her face and left it only resolute.

"You doubt if I have the power?" she said quietly. "You shall see. The end will spell triumph for me, too."

"We thought you were asleep, Kit," said Mark, with a halting apology in his voice.

"I was dreaming," she said; "but Mr. Franklin woke me. How cold and dark it is! . . . Is it you who have let the fire go out, Mr. Franklin?"

She turned to him with a casual, indifferent manner.

"It is not out," he answered; and he dug his heel into the coal, and sent the flames roaring up the chimney.

Katherine kneeled down and held her fingers to the

blaze, her attitude almost inviting the criticism Franklin
was giving her. He had never thought about her seriously
enough to be critical. Her enthusiasm for the people
was only a phase; she supported herself by journalism,——
and a woman must be ambitious, clever, unscrupulous, to
succeed there. Was there a strong side to her character?
He looked at her curiously.

The flames showed him a girl with a strained, passionate face, and a mass of bright hair on a small
head. His eyes wandered to the hands she held to the
fire.

They were so slight and thin they touched his pity;
but his eyes remained critical.

"Her brain is not solid enough, her nature is not
large enough for real work," he said to himself. "She
can feel, but she hasn't begun to feel. She thinks she
is thinking, but she doesn't even know when other people
are thinking. If she were not so young she would not
take herself so seriously, and then she might be a nice
little thing." His severity relaxed; the gentler expression came back to his eyes. "After all, she is very
young," he added, from the standpoint of his two-score
years.

Mark lighted the gas, and Franklin realised that at
least twenty-five years must have gone to the moulding
of Katherine's face.

"You are looking haggard, Kit," said Mark. "Too
much work, as usual. How much have you done to-
day?"

"I have reported a wedding, the opening of Mary-
lebone Concert-hall, and Mrs. Bland's reception," she answered, in a voice whose evenness was a glove thrown
down to Franklin.

"Great Scott! and she calls that work!" he said to himself. "And does it pay, Miss Katherine?" he asked cynically.

"It pays so that I can dress well enough to make Mrs. Bland's footman take me for one of the guests," she answered, glancing at her smart green frock.

"And is that worth doing?"

"Anything is worth doing that gives power;" looking up, her eyes met his steadily.

She rose slowly and stood beside the mantelpiece, her figure slim and straight, ambition in the set of her head. Her attitude irritated as much as it amused Franklin. To hide his vexation he walked to the window and stood in silence while Mark and Katherine talked together.

Out in the night the people kept the carnival of want. Goodge Street was ablaze with light; over the stalls that edged the pavement, the naphtha flames flashed and flared, shaming the steadier glow of the lamps. On the stalls Plenty lay rioting, mocking the hungry crowd that hustled each other on the pavement.

It was Saturday night, when the curtain is lifted on the tragedy of the poor; and Franklin knew that Katherine was used to make one of the spectators of the drama.

On Saturday night she sat at the window to take notes of all she saw. The scenes stirred imagination and pity, waking comprehension of the struggle of life. They had turned her thoughts to the problem of the people. It was this that had coloured her writing so that a red glow in her articles flashed strange lights across the society news and gossip. Now and then a deeper red betrayed heart. The tinge was unusual, and

attracted notice.   Katherine Fleming began to be known
as a daring and original journalist.   But Franklin had
never read her articles.   He gave her credit only for the
fashionable chronicle.   He stood looking out with darkened
eyes.

The streams of people flowed steadily along the street.
The cry of the salesmen at the stalls rose shrilly; the
murmurs of those that bought struck the lower keys of
sound.   A child's cry pierced through the noise and
broke on the upper silence.   In the middle of the road
a quarrel blazed and spluttered.   A woman went past, a
despairing figure swaying to her doom. . . .

The man noticed nothing.   He was annoyed that
Katherine had heard his criticism of her.   He did not
like modern women, and had no faith in their pretensions;
but he had never let Katherine see that.   She was bright
and clever, and he had come to take Mark's opinion of
her, and to share Mark's comradeship with her.   They
had been good friends, and he had not meant to quarrel
with her.   In fact, he had liked the girl.   But to-night
she had disappointed him.   A woman who loved power
and sought it invariably became unsexed.   He did not
wish to think of Katherine as unsexed.   He turned suddenly round and caught her in the act of kissing Mark's
head.   She lifted herself and gave him a defiant look,
while she reddened.

He lounged across the room, as if he had seen nothing.   "And what will you do with your power if you
should ever get it, Miss Katherine?" he said carelessly.

"I will make you recognise it," she answered.

"I think you would not be so cruel," he laughed.

His teasing fired her resentment.

"Good-night," she said coldly, and swept from the

room. In her bedroom her self-control failed. She paced the floor, hurt, angry, indignant.

"He doubted her power. He said her love for the people was all a matter of sentiment with her!"

The word sentiment bit into her thoughts like acid on steel. Was it true? Had she never touched modern questions on their practical side? She listened to the ideas round her and gave them currency when she talked or wrote her articles. But were they any more than the small change of her interests by which she paid her way among the workers? She was ready with sympathy for the people's cause; but was it for the cause or for the sake of Franklin, to whom it was life? She thrust the thought from her. No, it had not been for his sake! She had studied the subject for itself, and because it opened a new world to her. She had given it the same interest she had given to her Newnham studies. . . . She drew herself up sharply. . . . Those absorbing studies no longer interested her. Was her interest in social questions only another phase to be lived through? Would it follow her interest in Franklin, which the last hour had killed?

Shallow, incapable, insincere! This was his idea of her, while she had thought him impressed and attracted by her qualities. . . . All these months she had been sharing his interests, consulting his opinion, deferring to him on all points, showing openly her admiration of him; and for what? To find that she was nothing to him but a sentimental woman, probably a bore!

Her heart sank. She tasted the bitterness of the woman's lot,—to wait in silence while love passed by; to make no sign while happiness stumbled past blindfolded.

She clinched her hands as she paced the room. Then she lifted her head proudly.

The Gods Arrive.   2

Well, so much the better that she knew it; so much the better that he should go before he had made himself necessary to her life. Now she could prove to him and to herself that she had joined the Labour Movement for the sake of the people. She would give herself to it with no weak womanish desire to share Franklin's work. . . .

Yes! let him go. What was it he had said?

> "When half-gods go
> The gods arrive!"

CHAPTER II.

THE VOICE OF THE PEOPLE.

THE next day was Sunday. Katherine woke feeling sore and bruised. Conscious of a strange misery, she stayed for a moment in the borderland between sleeping and waking. Then she opened her eyes, and the outer world clashed into the world of dreams.

She was in her own room, surrounded by the pictures and books that told of her success. She spent a good part of each year's income on books, and her library was growing. That, and the etchings, were eloquent of the phases through which she had passed.

In art, beginning with the dawn of Dante, Rossetti, and the other pre-Raphaelites, through the noonday of Botticelli and the Masters, she had travelled into the twilight of Impressionism. And the same movement could be traced in her religious life. It had passed from the "De Imitatione" through High-Churchism into the desert of the Materialist. The path she had travelled was strewn with relics,—the well-worn Thomas à Kempis, the shrines and rosary, the crucifix over her desk, the works of Comte and Frederic Harrison.

It was a curious collection of past moods, and characteristic. Even her furniture betrayed progress, from the sofa-bed and oak of Newnham days to the luxurious cushions and rugs of a later date. Her eyes went round the room, but found nothing to account for her wretchedness. Success shouted a contradiction of Franklin's estimate of her abilities.

Then she remembered what had happened, and forgot her misery in disdain of his opinion.

She was to address a Labour meeting in the Park that afternoon; and she sprang from her bed, eager for the hour that should show him what she could do. The tingling cold of her bath braced her still further; and by the time she had dressed, her face had lost the haggard look it had worn the night before. Her eyes were bright and alert, her face was full of movement and charm. While she dressed, the colour had come rosily to her cheeks.

She stood before the glass, twisting the heavy coils of hair about her head, and she nodded and smiled at the face that looked at her.

"There is nothing of the lovelorn woman in you, Katherine Fleming. I even begin to doubt that it was love you felt. Thank goodness! the modern woman is not dependent on the emotions for interest in life. Power is a greater thing than love."

She finished her dressing hurriedly, and walked up and down, repeating aloud her speech for the afternoon. It was true there was nothing of the lovelorn woman in her appearance.

2 *

She was disturbed by Sarah the maid. Would Miss Fleming be so kind as to let her do the bed-room now?

Katherine was scarcely conscious that she spoke. "Come in after breakfast, Sarah; I don't want to go into the sitting-room yet."

Sarah looked appealingly at her.

"If you please, miss, I'm going with my young man to 'Ampton, and Mrs. Gumtion says I can't go without the rooms is all done; and the boat starts at nine, and it's gone eight now. . . ."

Katherine had not listened at all. "Don't interrupt me now," she said impatiently. "Go away, Sarah, I'm busy." She was walking up and down, muttering to herself, and Sarah dared not speak again. She knew that Miss Fleming had a temper.

A few hours later, and Katherine, grave and self-possessed, stood on the platform in Hyde Park, listening to the applause that greeted her name. Above the clapping she could hear the women's voices: "That's our Miss Fleming!" "Kitty Fleming, bless her sweet face!" "She's the friend of the workingwoman, she is!"

"The voice of the people is the voice of God," Katherine thought, hearing them. Franklin was on the platform close to her. Would this convince him?

She breathed fast; her face flushed, and her eyes grew soft. She could not speak at once, and there was a minute's silence. Then she leaned forward and stretched out her hands to the crowd.

"Dear hearts!" she said, "God bless you, God bless you!"

The directness and unexpectedness of the words, the little graceful gesture, were charming. She was always popular; to-day she had touched the people's hearts, and while she spoke she held them.

Her triumph was fitly set in the twilight of the wintry afternoon, among leafless trees spectral in mist. The picture itself, the platform with its group of workingmen, the girl, the massed faces like a key-board swept by her voice,—this was real enough, and stood out in the foreground in living impressionism. Franklin sat on the platform, his scholarly air marking him out among the Labour leaders. His lips were pursed; his eyes, apparently seeing nothing, raked the faces below the platform. He was listening to Katherine, wondering at her graciousness and earnestness Was this the girl who had defied him last night? Where were her pride and her passion? She was speaking simply, earnestly, effectively.

"She is doing pioneer work," he said to himself. "She inspires faith in the cause, makes it popular, as Mark said. It is true she has no grip of the movement; but the movement has taken hold of her. And what a clever little face it is!" Her closing words interrupted his thoughts. His eyes brightened with cynical amusement; he leaned forward, listening with a half-smile to her elaborate peroration.

"I ask you to believe that the Labour movement is leavening the nations," she was saying. "A strong force working silently for the lifting of the masses; a complex power, far-reaching and inevitable, stirring peoples still unborn; a life uncrusted by the tyranny of wealth, untrammelled by the bands of property. The movement, an unseen tide, is carrying its healing waters to every shore, bearing life to the nations far off; and with irresistible force—a mighty current of God—is laving our shores with the first onset of a wide industrial peace."

She stopped, threw out her arms, and her voice rose
to a cry, ringing and passionate.

"Yes, the tide is coming in. But oh, dear men and
women, are we waiting for it to lift us into new conditions? But the new conditions are within us; and the
movement will only raise the individual when the life
within the individual has touched the movement."

She sat down, trembling and breathless.

Franklin was the next speaker, but he came too late.
His voice, following Katherine's, was like a cold mist after
a glowing sunrise. It was useless for him to expound his
pet theory,—a policy of alliance with constituent movements, in vain to show the impossibility of trades-unionism
working unaided the miracle of the workingman. His
plea for co-operation and socialism was so much waste.
His facts were like sucked bones thrown to well-fed dogs.
In three minutes the audience had scattered, leaving one
or two of the hungrier sort to wrestle with the dry data
of Franklin's reasonableness. Katherine was still on the
platform, but she had forgotten that he was speaking.
She was intoxicated with her first taste of leadership.
She could not even recall the words that had moved the
people. At that near view memory was blurred and in-
distinct; but the "Bravo!" of the men round her, Franklin's "Hear, hear!" and the hands held out were high
lights in her remembrance. To-morrow she would see the
whole clearly; to-day she was content with the bare outline of the picture.

The fierce, hopeless faces seen through the veil of the
mist were but eyes into which she had brought a gleam
of hope. The human side of the question had touched
her. The workers were no longer mere mathematical
signs—noughts and crosses—for presenting the problem

of civilisation to the country. She saw in each unit the desperate, unquenched life of the whole; in each individual she imagined a lonely fight for the mere right of being, and she was honestly moved.

She did not doubt the sincerity of her feeling; she knew that it had told. The people listened to her, not to Franklin.

Her quick glance lighted on him, and on his poor handful of listeners, and her eyes sparkled. "So much for knowledge," she thought. "He hasn't learned that love counts. Brains? What are brains? To reach the people one only needs a heart."

Suddenly her mood changed to pity. How pale he looked! His face had lost its eagerness. He was speaking slowly and wearily, with that cynical intonation that marked his bitter moods. She understood how galling it must be to him to see that he could not hold his audience.

"I wish I had not spoken first," she thought with passionate regret; "I would have given up my success to see him succeed!"

The mood was quickly over. Her changing colour and excited air conquered the pity in her eyes. Mark laughed at the spring in her feet as she hung on his arm going through the Park homeward.

"Well, are you satisfied, Kit?" he smiled. "What do you think of your triumph?"

Her eyes brightened. "You call it a triumph?"

"Rather! Brace and Coates said we have had no speech like that since Mrs. Sturge left us."

"Did Franklin hear that?" she asked eagerly.

"Yes. He couldn't have been over-pleased after what he said last night."

"Did he seem vexed?"

"No; he isn't small. He told Brace your last sentence was worth the whole of what had gone before. That's his cussedness. I thought the end an anti-climax. You should have stopped at 'the first onset of a wide industrial peace.'"

Katherine lost what he was saying; her brows were puckered.

"I can't remember my last sentence. What was it, Mark?"

"Oh, ask Franklin! It didn't strike me. However, you did splendidly, Kit, and I am proud of you."

She gave his arm a grateful squeeze.

"Dear old boy! you are always so good to me. Mark, I wonder"—she hesitated— "Wouldn't it be splendid if some day we two led the whole movement?"

Mark shrugged his shoulders.

"That will never be so long as Franklin is in it. He's bound to come to the top. Besides, I don't hanker after leadership. I fancy someone has other ideas for my future."

Katherine looked up sharply. The tone of the last words was not Mark's usual tone.

"Other ideas for your future?" she echoed, staring at him. "To give up the people! You can't mean that mother wants you to go back to Great Lowlands? What *do* you mean, Mark?"

Mark flushed. His eyes dropped before Katherine's. He smiled vaguely, deliberated a moment, while he bit the end of his moustache, then decided to put off explanations till events forced them.

"What would be the use of my going home?" he asked; "my genius doesn't lie in farming, as the poor old dad saw when he made that ridiculous will of his. But I fancy they are in a bad way at home. That young Tom is a lazy beggar; the farm has done nothing since he has been on it. He wants a pushing person like you over him. You should have been the farmer, Kit."

Katherine made a grimace. "I a country farmer? Imagine it! No, thank you. I mean to be a Labour leader."

Mark laughed. "Well, stranger things have happened, but, you see, there's Franklin. You are an ambitious small person to want to rival him. Still, you scored over him to-day."

Her eyes flashed. "And yet he says I have no ability. Mark," she went on quickly, "I shall never rest until I have proved to Franklin that he was wrong."

Mark half stopped in his walk, and stared at her. Her mouth was set; there was a hard glitter in her eye. The glitter seemed to be in her voice, too; it rang like steel. Mark had never seen her in such a mood. He was proud of her ability, and her unlikeness to the rest of the family,—the weak mother, and the lazy brother on the farm at Great Lowlands. A sudden wonder at her seized him. They had lived together in the lodgings at Goodge Street for three years, and he had helped her in her journalism and watched her grow to self-reliance. She owed her career to him, and yet she seemed at once to have gone beyond him. This tone of hers made him almost uncomfortable, but her next words reassured him.

"Don't look so frightened, Mark," she laughed softly.

"I will triumph over him in fair fight. I can write that book, and I will do it. You believe in me, and I will prove that you are right and he is wrong. What a lot I owe to you! You helped me through Newnham, and now you give me an ideal life. I want nothing better than my life with you."

The very decision in her voice told of doubt. She looked before her and missed Mark's expression.

"That is all very well," he laughed uneasily. "But some day you will want another home, another comrade . . ."

"I shall never want anyone else," she interrupted fiercely; "I shall never love anyone else. I only want you."

He did not answer, but walked more quickly, impatient for the end of the conversation.

They had left the Park and were among the bricks and mortar of the streets, the mean-looking houses, the sordid life that fringed the wealthier neighbourhood. Over them rested the Sunday quiet like a sleeping strife. The fog touched them with chill fingers; the lamp-posts vanished in the distance, grim, and grey, and unstarred. There were no lights in Goodge Street.

CHAPTER III.

KATHERINE STANDS IN THE WINGS.

FROM that time Katherine set herself to forget that she had ever loved Franklin. Her heart was torn and wounded, but she hid her pain under an assumed indifference.

She was proud too, and when she met him nothing in her manner betrayed her. She was a little more casual perhaps, a little less friendly than before; but that was all. The change was so slight that neither Franklin nor Mark saw it. Only to Katherine it was a change from summer to winter, from dawn to midnight.

She knew it was his opinion of her that had altered her feeling. But she told herself, and partly believed it, that the change was due to discovering her mistaken estimate of him. He had weaknesses to match the strength that had first attracted her. His calmness was only indifference; his power self-assertion. His clever cynicism was a disguise for self-consciousness; his stability of purpose was sheer obstinacy.

She stirred the porcupine of Franklin's character, yet when the beast stood before her, roused and prickly, she took it again to her breast, forgetting her wounded fingers in disdain of the creature she loved.

To escape from her emotions she threw herself into a whirl of occupation. She was never idle a moment. She went here, there, and everywhere; reporting meetings, describing weddings, attending receptions, interviewing celebrities; tossed ceaselessly on the restless waves of modern civilisation.

She was living the life of the successful woman journalist, and it brought power of a sort. She met, no matter how, the men and women who had "arrived." She was sought by those who had not arrived, and who knew the value of newspaper paragraphs.

She was flattered at the notice they gave her, though she despised them for giving it. She saw the bare bones of the motive, but she did not shrink from the skeleton. She faced it gaily at every board to which she was invited. What did it matter to her that it was only human vanity that made her a person of consequence at the feast of life? She had not been long enough in journalism to savour it. It offered her life, and the zest of life intoxicated her. The bitterness was in the dregs of the cup, and as yet she had not drunk deeply.

Contrasting the rapidity of her life with the old days at the farm, or even at Newnham, Katherine told herself that she had only now begun to live.

She compared the theories that in Newnham days had seemed to be deepest philosophy with the theories of the men she met. And she gave to the latter a value that lay in difference of sex and an uncomprehended point of view—and not at all in the worth of the theories themselves.

She contrasted life seen through college gables, and actual contact with men and women; and she was glad that the maidenly outlook was no longer hers. She was close to the human drama, standing in the wings, an on-looker at the play that other women saw only from stall and gallery. Did it matter that from her standpoint there was little scope for imagination and less for pleasant illusion?

Was there not an end to imagination, an awakening from pleasant illusion?

She thought with a great bitterness of the awakening that had come to her; and her heart rose passionately against the conventions that made woman a modern Prometheus. Let her but touch the divine fire, and she must be chained to the rock to have her heart torn by vultures, a spectacle for gods and men.

Katherine hid her scarred palms and told herself proudly that she was glad she took part in the great human drama. From her place in the wings she watched the tragedy of her own heart, and so learned to understand the piece on the boards.

Once, wondering if she had chosen well in entering journalism, she had looked enviously at her Newnham friends,—high-school teachers, secretaries, literary women. But some of these same women had come to her to push them before the public, and she had scorned them. Her work needed no recognition for which she had to pray; they touched life from the outside, at one point; she was in the very heart of it, among the unseen forces that made their world.

Franklin had given her her first real dissatisfaction with journalism. He had been a frost biting the blossom of success; but the frost was bracing too. It had nerved her ambition, and set her seriously to work on a history of the Labour Movement. And since she had begun the work she had seen beyond Franklin a power ruling the future. Every hour she could spare from journalism she spent in the reading-room of the British Museum, gathering facts and data for the book. The study gave the articles she wrote solidity and weight, while it influenced her life with Mark.

She was rarely at the rooms in Goodge Street now; and missing her companionship, Mark hurried on what was to give the death-blow to Katherine's career in London.

She was too absorbed to notice his silence and pre-occupation. A year ago his absence night after night would have hurt her. Now she did not even know he was absent.

Sometimes Mark would look wistfully at her and open his lips for confession. Then the pucker on her forehead and her inward gaze would deter him. She was living furiously, he saw; booted and spurred for race, she had no eyes for the wayfarer plodding along the road. She had long ago out-distanced him; why should he check her pace?

Then he would shrug his shoulders with the relief of the man who has avoided a scene, and would attack his dinner with new appetite.

"It's a jolly good thing for Kit she is finding her own interests, and can go alone," he would think, under the whistle that silenced his uneasiness at the secret he kept.

Meanwhile Katherine's Museum study was making her knowledge of the Labour Question less superficial. She understood something of what she talked about, and would criticise the speakers and speeches in the Park with as much true inwardness as Franklin himself.

Franklin heard these criticisms with growing wonder. They made him question his idea of her shallowness; but they confirmed his detestation of public work for women. Katherine's self-assertiveness had always irritated while it amused him. Now, noticing that she grew hard, and had ceased to defer to him, he told himself that he disapproved of her.

"She is losing all softness and womanliness," he would say, biting savagely at his moustache. "Why can't she leave public questions to men?"

An irritated glance at her would show him that her nose was becoming pinched, her face sharp and eager; that there was no gentleness in her eyes, and that the absorbed pucker on her forehead was rarely smoothed out. Sometimes he met in her attitude the defiance of the woman-with-a-purpose, and he would sigh. There was nothing sweet or girlish in her appearance but the soft bright hair that stood out round her head halo-wise.

Franklin did not guess that he had had to do with the change. He had never suspected her feeling for him—his life had been lived altogether apart from women in the provincial town where he had kept his second-hand book shop, and avoided things feminine. A few portraits of women hung in his gallery of memories. They were neatly and solidly framed in the knotty oak of his prejudices. One was that of his housekeeper, who had tyrannised over him; another belonged to his stepmother, who had been a thorn in the flesh to his studious minister father; a third was a sketch of woman in the abstract as delineated by Schopenhauer; the fourth frame held Katherine. Because she was Mark's sister he had had a certain friendship for her. He would have been glad now to prevent her from taking a place in the car of the Labour Movement. He gave his life and heart to the Movement, but he saw that it suffered from its friends. It would never advance on the lines of garrulous sentiment on which its supporters were pushing it into notice.

To Franklin the question of the poor was too urgent,

too bitingly insistent to be answered by young and ill-informed women. He abhorred the modern woman, and especially the platform woman with her cheap echo of second-hand opinions.

He watched the development of Katherine ironically. The change vexed him. She seemed to be compacted of faults. There was none of the shyness of the girl about her; none of that dainty mystery which is woman's subtlest charm. She did not rouse his curiosity,—he saw all her nature at one view:—there was no other side to her. She was like a map of womanhood on Mercator's projection,—an expanse of qualities. There was no suggestion of roundedness, of unseen lands and unknown continents; no poles of passion, no zones of change. There was nothing but the flat extension of sex. And not even this last; for she had laid it aside, and in face and bearing and manner was simply a journalist, an individual that is common as to gender.

His office was in Fleet Street,—the girl's necessary haunt,—and he often saw her pushing along the pavement with her eager air, openly impatient of the men who lounged and gossiped, obstructing the footway, and hindering busy women who had work to do. Or perhaps she was catching an omnibus, running after it, springing on the footboard, like any printer's devil whose educated heel did service for his uneducated head.

He met her at all hours of the night going home from newspaper offices, or saw her hanging about the box offices of theatres, waiting for a stray returned ticket. He watched her in a crowd, elbowing her way to the front, wherever place was possible by reason of push getting it.

He knew that her paragraphs arrived first in the

editor's room. Whenever a specially audacious or catching report appeared in "The Flight", he recognised her hand in it.

All this was hateful; and his detestation of the modern woman grew with his annoyance that Katherine of all women should be in the frenzy of public affairs.

One day he had been lunching with Mark at Ludgate Circus. They were standing outside the restaurant when a shouting turned their gaze to Farringdon Street. Dashing down towards Memorial Hall came a runaway hansom, heading straight for the river of traffic that flowed across the Circus. There was no driver on the box. A woman's face stared wildly from under the hood. "God help her!" Franklin exclaimed, springing forward.

"Don't be a fool. You can't save her!" said Mark.

Just in time he swung Franklin back by the collar from under the nose of a carter's van.

Franklin shook him off. "Let me go!" he said, breathing hard.

"You can't do impossibilities," said Mark, coolly. "But you can kill yourself."

Franklin saw he could not reach the horse in time. His face whitened. His eyes were on the woman in the hansom. They stood on the Fleet Street side of the Circus, and the horse was on the brink of the traffic. . . . Suddenly, into the middle of the road, right before the galloping feet, sprang a girl. . . . With a sickening horror Mark saw that it was Katherine.

Franklin had recognised her, too, and his heart stopped beating. His fascinated eyes were glued to the figure in the very pathway of the maddened horse! . . . It was on her! . . . No, it had swerved and half stopped. . . .

In that moment Katherine leaped up and locked her arms round its neck. . . .

The horse reared, lifting her from her feet, and Franklin fell back giddily against a window. But Katherine held on, and came safely to the ground. . . . She had checked the speed. . . . Another instant a dozen men were with her, and the horse, quivering and foam-flecked, had been stopped on the very edge of the stream. Neither Mark nor Franklin could move. But when Katherine shook herself free of the crowd and crossed towards Fleet Street, Mark swallowed a lump in his throat and went to meet her.

"What do you mean by trying to commit suicide?" he said roughly; but his face was grey.

She stared at his frightened eyes. Then, with a strong effort, she controlled her own excitement, and laughed nervously.

"What are you frightened at, Mark? It was no worse than catching the horses in the meadow at home."

"It might have killed you, Kit;" his voice shook.

She laughed again. "How absurd! Well, I'm not going to stand here for the crowd to stare at. Good-bye."

She swung away from Mark and was face to face with Franklin.

"Are you quite safe, not hurt?" he said, catching her arm. "You must have had a shock. . . . Come into my office. . . . Let me get you something. . ."

His voice was strange and hoarse. Katherine gazed at him in amazement.

She saw his lips tremble under the heavy moustache, the nervous twitching of his face, his jerky manner. There was a new expression in his keen eyes,—pity,

terror, admiration. She noticed it all in a glad exultation. "He loves me! he loves me!" she said to herself.

Franklin saw her grow pale. He put his arm quickly
through hers. "You are faint; it has been too much . . ."
he cried anxiously.

His tone recalled her pride. She freed herself.

"Thank you," she said easily; "it was only for a
minute. I'm quite well now. I must get on to the
'Scribblers' to finish a report. This will work into
copy. . . . You and Mark are making a great fuss about
nothing."

"You are a plucky girl," he said, glancing at her
slight figure and delicate face.

The colour mounted prettily to her cheeks. "Certainly
a busy one," she smiled. "This is my 'bus. Good-bye."

On the top of the omnibus her self-control relaxed;
her knees trembled; her face grew white. A flickering
happiness came and went in her eyes. "He loves me!
he loves me!" her heart chimed like a peal of bells.
"Some day he will know it, too. . . . A plucky girl? Ah,
he will say more than that one of these days."

Franklin watched her disappear towards the Strand.
He drew a long sigh, passed his handkerchief over his
face, and shook off the terror that had unmanned him.
With a hurried word to Mark, he turned into his office.
But he could not take up his work again. A small white
face intruded among the ranks of figures. Its expression
changed with every instant. It was set, defiant, childish,
scornful, appealing, resolute. It eluded him, reminding
him in likeness and unlikeness of the girl he had just
left.

He dropped his *pince-nez* from his nose, and pushed
aside his papers with a short, embarrassed laugh. He

3 *

leaned back in his chair, and selected a cigar, after a precise study of those in his case. He watched the wreaths of smoke rise and curl about his head, and his thoughts twisted themselves into coherence.

"What is the girl to you? What is any woman to you?" The subject of Katherine was in the wooden frame of his prejudices; he saw the frame, and missed the picture. . . .

When his cigar had burnt to the end, he took up his pen again, his mouth set to a smile half regretful, half relieved. The girl was nothing to him;—he had never given her a thought. He adjusted his *pince-nez* and turned cheerfully to his work. A small white face in a wreath of smoke flitted mockingly among the figures.

Katherine had meanwhile alighted from the omnibus, and plunged down one of the streets leading from the Strand to the Embankment. In this street was the "Scribblers," a club for literary women,—journalists and the younger novelists.

She went directly to the reading-room, where she wrote her article. Then she wandered into a larger room. The prevailing tone here was green, palms and cushions and carpet echoing it. A flippant visitor—a man—had said that the green room and the blue women were responsible for the yellow that tinged the fiction of the day. Katherine threw herself into one of the big chairs, and leaned back with closed eyes, smiling. Her heart rested against the look she had surprised in Franklin's eyes.

A maid came in and out, preparing a table for tea; it was the day of the weekly At Home.

Katherine professed to think these functions a bore; but they supplied her with paragraphs. Scraps of literary talk, journalistic items, fashions, art gossip filled the room. She listened and found copy.

About four o'clock the rooms began to fill. One or two men dropped in for tea and mutual compliments. Well-dressed women with happy faces moved about. Handsomely dressed women with haggard faces and worn eyes filled lounge and chair. The women who looked happy were still on the road to success. The others were already there.

There was another class of women writers, those who wrote starving; but these were not members of the club. If, by chance invitation, one happened to be present, she might be known by her careful dress and careless gaiety.

Katherine had once taken an interest in one of these, —a bright little woman whose witticisms were quoted at the club a year after she had dropped over Waterloo Bridge. Since that time Miss Fleming had been careful not to probe through the merriment of any woman. She sat now in a corner behind a big india-rubber plant, but she was not long hidden. A plump lady with very red cheeks and very black eyes sat down beside her in a rollicking fashion, and rolled out a big hearty laugh.

"So here you are, Miss Fleming! I have been hunting everywhere for you. I wanted to congratulate you."

"Yes?" gasped Katherine, feeling as if the great voice had put arms round her and was choking her.

"Yes, those articles in 'The Flight,'—they are really excellent. . . . Such grasp! . . . And you lectured at South Place last week. . . . I heard all about it. . . . I ought to congratulate you again. . . ."

"We all want to congratulate Miss Fleming," said a thin elegant woman on the other side; "really I feel

quite proud of knowing such a distinguished person,—I
do really. . . ."

"Now then, Miss Vincent," rolled out the big voice,
"you are not to speak till I have finished my talk with
Miss Fleming. . . . It is so seldom. . . . And I have something very important. . . ."

"I will give you two minutes," said Miss Vincent,
playfully, withdrawing herself like a furtive shadow pursued
by the sun.

Katherine turned to the sun: "You had something
important? . . ."

"Yes, indeed. You know I hate log-rolling;—I think
it is immoral. . . . But a little dainty appreciation. . . .
Besides, if you don't roll the log you are rolled under
it. . . . I said that to my publisher to-day, and he quite
agreed with me. . . . And you know your things are
quoted everywhere;—yes, they are, don't look so modest....
I saw a man reading one in the train quite lately. Trust
a man for looking at the lady's letter in a newspaper. . . .
Two minutes up, Miss Vincent? Why, I haven't even
begun. . . . All I wanted to say to you was this. Couldn't
you give me a note or two about myself and my new
book—'Green Daffodils'? I hear it's the best thing I've
done yet. . . Say what you like about me—it can only do
good. Describe my figure;—my stays are thirty-six, but
you can say thirty. I don't mind *what* you say, so long
as you say it. . . . You will? Thank you so much. Are
you engaged for Sunday? Come to dinner, do. . . . Yes,
Miss Vincent; I've quite done."

The stout lady rose with difficulty from the low chair;
Miss Vincent slipped into it and sunk her voice.

"You are so influential, Miss Fleming, and you know
everybody. I wonder if you could get me some light

post. . . . On any paper, I don't mind which. . . . Politics, art criticism, or music, or a fashion column. I shouldn't mind writing up new plays; it's so nice to go to the theatre. I am sure I could do something of that sort. . . . In fact, I could do anything I was wanted to. . . . Don't you think I could?"

"Miss Vincent, the woman who can do anything usually can do nothing," said Katherine, brutally. "Adopt a political creed,—no matter if it is illegitimate—and specialise! specialise! specialise! After that you will help yourself."

Katherine rose as she spoke, but Miss Vincent put out a trembling hand and detained her.

"I read your articles in 'The Flight,'" she stammered. "And I thought you of all women would help a woman. . . "

"Miss Fleming, may I introduce Mr. Celandine Ambrose? You quoted him the other day in your clever paper on 'The Social Butterfly,' and he is longing to talk to you."

From Miss Vincent's plaintive appeal Katherine turned easily to the new-comers. Mr. Celandine Ambrose was a minor poet. If one had not known this, one would have thought he was a woman. He bowed gracefully over Katherine's hand, and murmured the verses she had quoted. Katherine forgot Miss Vincent while he spoke of his long hope of meeting her, his admiration of her writing, his happiness in realising his hope. . . .

He purred on contentedly, but he was not allowed to monopolise her. A crowd of eager women besieged the corner, and Katherine was flattered, congratulated, entreated. She felt proudly that she was a power in journalism. Even Franklin must have been impressed if he had been there to see her popularity.

Her half-god had gone, but the gods themselves were at the gates. Not even Mrs. Angel Harrington, whose novel was the talk of the town, had received so much attention. . . . Her cheeks burned, her eyes flashed. . . . She lifted her head and met the irony of Franklin's quiet amusement.

She returned his look with a change in her manner, a drop in her elation. He had touched the butterfly wing of her triumph, and it fluttered, maimed, to the ground. He came forward, pushing a way for a handsome girl whose eyes studied Katherine curiously.

"Miss Fleming," Franklin addressed her, "I have brought Mark's friend, Miss Rossetter—Miss Tonina Rossetter—to speak to you."

Katherine looked from the blushing face of the girl to the significance of the man's manner, and back again to the girl;—and her ease deserted her.

"Mark's friend, Miss Rossetter?" she echoed, stupidly.

"Hasn't he ever mentioned her?" Franklin asked, lifting his brows.

"No; but I am glad to meet any friend of Mark's," she said, regaining her composure, and holding out her hand to the girl with a smile.

"But he has told me of you. . . . He is so proud of the clever sister Katherine. . . . I know you quite well, oh! quite well," said Miss Rossetter, in a pretty foreign fashion. She took Katherine's hand in both hers, and looked smiling into her face.

But Katherine's eyes held a thundercloud. She turned stiffly to Franklin.

"Won't you take Miss Rossetter into the tea-room, Mr. Franklin?"

"There is no getting near the table," he laughed. "But you must have some tea too. You have been so surrounded you have not had a chance. And you look tired," he added kindly.

At his tone Katherine lifted her head quickly. Then he had seen her popularity! But her exultation was beaten back at the sight of the girl beside him.

Who was Miss Tonina Rossetter; and why was she Mark's friend? and what did Franklin's manner mean?

CHAPTER IV.

THE KEY OF THE SPRING.

ALL the week the thought of Miss Rossetter pressed heavily on Katherine; yet she would not force Mark's confidence by asking the meaning of his friendship. Franklin's manner had been significant. Was it possible that she was to lose her place with Mark, to step into the second after walking abreast with him in the first rank? There was a new strain on her face during the days following; but she bore the pain and doubt in proud silence, and soon even the dread was crushed down by work. It was the height of the season, and life was a rush from function to function. Thought was an impossibility. She was only conscious of impressions passing in quick and vivid succession.

She had to give up her Labour interests at the very time when indignation contrasted society London and its under-world. She burned to denounce the world, the flesh, and the devil in season and out of season; to paint the West-end lurid before the eyes of the East-end; to prove herself the workingman's friend by attacking her friend, the rich man.

In place of this she gathered the season's harvest,— with defiant eyes for the ironical fulness of her purse.

Every day found her chronicling fashionable weddings, making inventories of wardrobes. She saw drawn, white faces of pitiful women crushed under the piled silk and lace. She heard their sobs in the smiling silence of the bride; and she set her lips, and wrote rosily of bells and bridals. One marriage followed another till she loathed the rustle of satin, and longed for crape and death's realities. Her work was robbing life of all romance. It was not easy to spy sentiment in the crush at St. George's, or to gauge love by the number of shoes in the *trousseau*. And when Death struck its silence through the chimes, and her favourite poet died, she had no time for regret, nor even for a natural gravity. She heard under the slow tramp of the horses the galloping feet of the hours. In describing the greatness of his obsequies she forgot that a great man had passed. It was not possible to mourn while clamouring for the names of the distinguished mourners. Journalism barred the door to the emotions; but it let her into the grand circus of fashionable life.

She received invitations to "smart" houses, accepted them, and next day paid for them in paragraphs in society papers. Her reputation as an agitator also brought invitations from that set whose smartness lay in interest in the world farthest removed from its own.

It was fashionable this season to be earnest; and women, the cut of whose clothes betrayed the man, protested publicly against the sweating in tailors' dens; or, on the platform, harried the eight hours' question, regardless of the dressmaker fretting out her appointment at home.

Miss Gore of Park Lane was earning a reputation for seriousness by her ignorance of the Labour Movement, and she found a valuable ally in Katherine. The girl was in the movement. She knew celebrities abroad, and fashionables at home. She made remarks that could be quoted; and her capable air struck a new and original note in the crushes in Park Lane.

Katherine was going to one of Miss Gore's evenings. It would supply copy while she amused herself; and she could work it in with a reception at the Imperial Institute. It was after ten when her hansom pulled up before the door in Park Lane. Outside it was dark and raining, but the house was brilliantly lit. Under the canopy which stretched from door to pavement a crowd pushed and peered at the dresses and jewels that made sudden lights on the steps.

Among the faces straining in Katherine caught sight of two or three familiar ones. The women were journalists too. Note-book in hand, they stood with wet mackintoshes and damp hair, bedraggled and miserable, in the night and the rain. They were like a shadow cast by the happier crowd that climbed the steps and disappeared in the light.

As the guests passed, the journalists pressed forward to the footmen, begging for names, while making a mental inventory of the colours and style that had supplied the personality.

When the flunkeys condescended to answer, they patronised the newspaper women, who missed the insolence, made hasty notes, and appealed again for verification.

It was mere chance that Katherine did not make one of that voracious group hungry for detail, but the men did not know this. One of them hurried to meet her. As she alighted he protected her dress from the wheel.

"Who is she?" "What's her name?" "That gown is Jay's."

The whispers hissed past her, then ceased with a suddenness that told her she was recognised.

She stepped under the awning, her feet, daintily shod, sinking in the soft pile of the carpet. Then she stopped, and held out her hand to the nearest of her friends.

"How tired you look, Miss Rowe! . . . Are you writing this up? I am sure it is going to be very dull. . . . And such a night! Look here, don't stop in all this rain. I will get the names for you and leave them at Charles Street as I pass. . . . That will save your standing about."

"It's awfully good of you," said the girl, gratefully lifting a weary face. "I'm too tired for anything, and I've had nothing to eat since lunch. . . . May I tell the others you will come to Charles Street, that they may go home too?"

"Yes, of course," said Katherine; and she passed on, proudly conscious of her fall in the eyes of the footmen.

She found her hostess, and was given over to Celandine Ambrose, who swept her with the current into the drawing-room. He chose a seat for her, and hung over her, talking. She was thinking less of what he said than of the people round her. She was cynically watching beauty on sale, age masquerading as youth, the paint and the powder, the boredom, the second-hand culture.

But the scene fascinated too. The electric lights shrouded by silk-petalled flowers, the soft-rayed candles, subtle perfumes, the air heavy with wealth and ornament and luxury, touched her æsthetic sense, and led her naturally back to the accents of Celandine Ambrose.

He was talking softly of his new poems, and the flattery of her article on Social Butterflies.

"So you think quotation is the sincerest flattery?" said Katherine, laying aside her cynicism, and looking up at him with one of her brilliant smiles.

"When you quote," he said, and fell into a most tender silence.

High above the rustle of talk a violin had made itself heard, and the first notes of the Kreutzer Sonata shattered the meaningless hubbub.

With quick appreciation Katherine turned towards the sound, sat up sharply, and stared at the violinist,— a girl whose yellow dress flamed in the foreground near the piano.

"Who is that?" she asked in a voice suddenly eager.

"The girl playing? That's Tasma Railton. Haven't you heard her before? She is quite the rage this season. . . . has a good many engagements. . . ."

"Yes?" said Katherine, vaguely. "Then she is? . . . Of course I have heard of Tasma Railton."

"Of course you have; who hasn't? Yes, she is a professional; fine girl, if you admire bulk . . . I don't."

His sea-green eyes looked significantly at Katherine.

"Do you know much about her? What is her real name?" she asked, avoiding the look.

"Tonina Rossetter—father an Italian, or something. She is married, I think; if not, going to be, like every woman. . . . But I am not interested in Miss Railton. . . . Do you know you remind me of a rondel I wrote the other day? . . . May I say it? . . . It is called *Schlüssel- blume,* the key-flower that comes in the spring. . . .

"O Love, your fingers hold
　　The golden key of the spring;
　The meadows are dusted gold,
　　The lark is high on the wing;
　　And his song bright notes doth fling
　Like living stars on the wold;
　O Love, your fingers hold
　　The golden key of the spring.

"But the day is wintry cold
　　And the lark no more can sing;
　The meadows in mist are stoled,
　　Your heart is locked to its king;
　O Love, your fingers hold
　　The golden key of the spring."

"It rhymes well," said Katherine, letting her eyes fall in order not to betray her amusement; "and how finely it contrasted with the strength and passion of the sonata!" She looked innocently at him. "Is Miss Rossetter going to play again?"

"She never gives more than one performance in any place," he said coldly, suspecting her innocence. "That is the secret of her success; one never gets tired of her. . . . You are not leaving me already, Miss Fleming?"

He rearranged the loose bow that served him for neck-tie and distinction.

"I must; I too wish to be a successful woman," Katherine smiled. She had risen, and was eagerly looking after a yellow dress passing down the room. A sudden impulse had seized her. She would follow Miss Rossetter and find out. . . .

She shook off Ambrose with difficulty, found her cloak, and reached the hall-door in time to see Miss Rossetter drive away in a hansom with a man who might certainly have been Mark.

Katherine stood hesitating at the door, heedless of the footman's questions as to her carriage, when Richard Franklin ran up the steps with a quick offer to see her home.

In the surprise of meeting him there, she hesitated, and was lost.

Taking possession of her, he drew her arm in his, and she slowly went down the steps with him. The rain had ceased, and the air felt cool after the stifling rooms. The first note of Franklin's voice was like the fresh air after the artificial atmosphere of the poet's sentiment. She drew a long breath of happiness.

"I don't want a hansom; let us walk home. . . ."

He looked dubiously at her . . . "Your dress? . . ."

She laughed gaily. "It is all right, being black; and I will pull this hood over my head. Now, isn't that perfectly correct?" She lifted eyes sparkling under the hood, and Franklin's smile met hers.

He liked this confiding mood; the touch of her hand on his arm was pleasant. It did not occur to him that he had been thinking a good deal about her since the day when he had decided that he never gave her a thought.

"I came at the right time, it seems," he said shyly, by way of saying something.

"What were you doing in Park Lane?" she asked; "I didn't know you knew Miss Gore."

"I don't. Mark asked me to walk with him; he said you were here, but he had promised to see Miss Rossetter home."

"What is Miss Rossetter to Mark?"

He hesitated a moment—"If Mark has said nothing. . . ."

"Don't go on!" she cried sharply. "I don't wish to know. . . . But why should he take her home?"

"Miss Rossetter has not been a professional woman long enough to lose the womanly grace of dependence," he said soberly.

"You mean the feminine vice of helplessness," Katherine retorted.

Her gaiety vanished; the cloud was partly vexation at Mark, partly vexation at Franklin's allusion to professional women. It roused the sleeping grudge. She hardened again the heart that had softened at the contrast between his sincerity and Ambrose's hot-house sentiment.

Franklin felt vaguely uncomfortable at her changed manner, but he explained it as caused by Mark's secret. He talked on, but she answered curtly, and dismissed him in Mortimer Street.

"I intend to see you home." He looked at her with a quiet masterfulness.

"I am not going home."

"Where are you going then?"

"To Charlotte Buildings, to take an account of the reception to some girls who depend on it for their dinner to-morrow."

"I will go with you to Charles Street."

She stopped and faced him.

"But . . . You hate my work. . . . Why should you go out of your way to do me a service?" she asked hotly.

"I don't think I should go out of my way to do you a service." His manner held the balance between eagerness and indifference. It nettled the girl.

"I know that. Please don't emphasise it. . . . But I can take care of myself. Fortunately I have been a professional woman long enough to lose some feminine vices."

The Gods Arrive. 4

"And gain others," he suggested.

She would have taken her hand from his arm, but he laid his fingers over it and held her against her will.

"I mean to take care of Mark's sister," he said, with a pitying thought that the days when Mark would take care of his sister were at an end. "You could walk safely in Piccadilly in this dress, but not in Charles Street."

"A working-woman has no right to wear a dress that is not suitable everywhere," she burst out.

"I quite agree with you."

In spite of her rage, Katherine laughed, and Franklin joined her. At Charlotte Buildings she asked him meekly if he would wait downstairs, or come up to Miss Rowe's room. He said he would go with her; and they toiled up some two hundred steps to the top of the great block.

Miss Rowe herself opened the door, and they followed her into a sitting-room furnished with an evident desire to conceal its near relationship to a bedroom.

There were cups and saucers, some butter, and an empty sardine tin on the table. Near the gas-stove two girls crouched, shivering; a horrible smell from the paraffin lamp mixed with the horrible smell of the gas. It was all so poor, so mean, so unhomelike, that Franklin's heart rose in pity for the struggling women to whom life gave nothing better than this. He wondered if it was the sort of place in which Katherine would live by-and-by. . . . But no! she was too clever, too fine, too delicate to come to this. . . . He glanced at her. She stood before the girls, explaining with a gracious kindliness the points in the notes they had made, adding names, giving hints. Her manner was quite simple and girlish; there was not a trace in her of the Katherine who had quarrelled with him on the way. He noticed the deference the other girls gave to her, and he was pleased with it. They seemed to like her too.

"I wonder if there is another side to her nature," he said to himself; and the picture of a gentle woman helping less fortunate women took the place of some other pictures of her on which he had dwelt in irritation and disgust.

When they stood before the house in Goodge Street he took her hand very kindly.

"I have helped you in spite of yourself to-night, Miss Katherine. Will you let me help you again if ever you should need help?"

She gazed at him in surprise, and answered perversely, out of sheer gladness of heart: "I hope I shall never be so unfortunate as to need your help."

He lifted his hat in silence. Something in his manner showed Katherine that he was angry. Her fingers trembled as she turned the latch-key in the door. She thought of Ambrose's verses:

> "Your heart is locked to its king;
> O Love, your fingers hold
> The golden key of the spring."

CHAPTER V.

AND BEHOLD! IT WAS A DREAM.

KATHERINE climbed the lodging-house stairs in a tumult. She had swept the whole gamut of feeling during her walk from Park Lane with Franklin, and one by one she dwelt on her emotions. They pointed contrasts that she scarcely understood. His presence had given her freedom, yet enchained her. She had felt humiliation at his allusion to professional women; pride in his domination; fear that he could so easily move her; courage to move him. Beneath it all was the unplumbed depth of her love, and trust, and ignorance of life; and she paused in a sudden horror of self-distrust.

She stood before the sitting-room, the handle of the door in her hand, a shrinking girl, weak and fearful. Then she lifted her head resolutely and tossed off the weakness, and showed herself under the shrouding mood, a woman who faced the future confidently.

Some letters were on the table in the room. She opened the first,—a small pink feminine envelope covered it. Her eyes darkened, she frowned as she read, then threw the letter on the table and stamped her foot.

"He ought to have told me! He had no reason to hide it! He has treated me shamefully! He could tell Franklin, but his own sister! . . . Ah, I didn't deserve it." . . . Tears of disappointment and passion were in her eyes; but all at once a new expression flashed across her face. "After all, it makes my own way easier. . . . I

could not have left Mark. . . . But if he marries I shall
be free." . . . Gentle lines broke up the hardness of her
mouth; her eyes cleared, her brows grew smooth. She
thought a moment, whispering half under her breath:
"Yes, it is true. 'When half-gods go;—when half-gods
go!'"

In a dreamy abstraction she opened the next letter;
but her face awoke at the first sentence, and a vivid
triumph sent the blood to her cheeks.

"To represent the women workers at the Labour Congress?—how splendid!" she cried. "Success is nearer
than I thought—The gods arrive!"

Her air was radiant. . . . She saw her life opening
out, ever more and more successful; she saw her dreams
realised, her hopes fulfilled, success in her grasp, love at
her feet. "How good it is to live!" she said breathlessly.

She took up the last envelope. Her fingers shook,
though the interest was in the letter she had just read,
and not at all in this. She knew her mother's writing,
and before reading could tell the contents of every page
that came from Great Lowlands.

She toned down her mood now to meet the com-
plaints of Tom's laziness, the threatening failure, the want
of servants, the greater want of money. But she had not
read far before she began to frown. She put down the
letter scornfully. "Of course, that is utterly impossible,"
she said definitely. She laid aside her cloak in the
manner of a person who was laying aside also a subject
that she found cumbersome. Her thoughts went back to
the second letter. They lingered over its effect on Franklin,
He would see her growing influence. This would convince him. . . .

It was after one, but she was too excited for sleep. She would sit up for Mark.

She threw herself on the sofa, and dreamed of the future. Through the open door of success she saw the great procession of the gods,—Jove with starred forehead, Mercury speeding before him, Mars armed for fight, Saturn of gloomy brow, Apollo shining in white robes, Pan radiant in sunshine, and, last of all, Love himself.

They passed before her, her thoughts, like dancing maidens, clashing cymbal and striking lyre; and as Love came in and she saw beyond him an averted face, she sprang up with a cry.

Mark was beside the sofa, looking down at her, and laughing.

"You have been asleep, Kit. I am sorry I woke you; but you shouldn't have waited for me."

"I wasn't asleep," she answered, sitting up and blinking away the procession of the gods.

"Dreaming then," he said, throwing his gloves on the table. "Anything interesting?" he added bashfully, seeing the pink envelope.

"Well, yes!" she exclaimed. "Mark, imagine it! They want me to speak at the Labour Congress; to go as the women's representative. . . . And I never dreamed of such a thing for years to come!"

"Whew!" Mark whistled, looking delighted. "You are getting on, Kit. Do you think you are equal to it?"

She drew herself up, and stood before him, her black dress making her figure slighter even than usual, her bare arms and neck showing rigid muscles.

"Do you think I look equal to it?" she asked.

"I can't say that I see any signs of weakness," said Mark, laughing. "What strikes me more is the incongruity between your present appearance, and yourself as a representative of the working-woman."

Katherine's face clouded. "You think I am not in earnest because I don't wear the sackcloth and ashes of the woman with a purpose," she said bitterly.

"Well, really, Kit, my dear, if you think of it, you don't act like a woman whose heart is bleeding for the wrongs of the poor. You hobnob with Park Lane, and wear purple and fine linen."

"And why not?" she said simply. "Should I help the people by looking dowdy and never going out of Goodge Street?"

"You would prove your claim to be one of them; and that would be a first step towards helping them."

"I am helping them," she cried passionately. "I have begun the book that will be the first step towards a new life for them; and I am making friends for them among the rich. I shall take Miss Gore to see the match-girls. I mean to get her into the ranks; her money will help."

"I like your enterprise," said Mark. "If only Tom had some of it, there would be hope for Great Lowlands."

He eyed the little pink envelope as he spoke, but Katherine would not see the glance.

"Tom, oh, Tom!" she cried. "I don't know what is to be done about him,—such a list of his shortcomings in mother's letter to-day. She says they are on the verge of ruin. Now he is infatuated with some girl and spends his time with her, neglecting his work; and mother says . . . But there is the letter; read it for yourself."

Mark took the letter she handed to him. His brows knit as he read, then he looked up at Katherine.

"Mother is quite right, Kit; you will have to go down and pull them out of this rut."

Katherine jerked up her head. Her face was scarlet.

"*What!*" she gasped.

His eye dropped before her look. He fingered the letter nervously.

"Well, the fact is, Kit," he stammered, "there's no doubt they need you at home, if only to keep that young rascal from making a fool of himself. We don't want a country wench in the family, you know. Things are going to ruin; the mother is ill and worried. It's your clear duty to give up your work here and go."

"My — clear — duty— to — give — up — my — work — here—and —go?" Katherine echoed, pausing between every word.

"Why, of course it is," said Mark. "Someone must go; and who is there but you?"

"I am not the only person in the family," she said slowly. The colour had died out of her face, leaving it white and still. "There is, for instance, yourself."

Mark shook his head.

"That's quite out of the question now. I'm no farmer The poor old dad's will shows clearly that he thought you the best man of us all; and for his sake you ought to go. Besides, you are the only person who can do anything with Tom."

"And you would let me sacrifice my career to the farm and Tom?" she asked wonderingly.

Mark's eyes wavered when he saw the tragedy on her face. He was fond of Katherine, but she stood between him and his plans for the future. If she went to Great Lowlands his difficulty would be solved in the manner most easy for him. He fidgeted with the letters on the table. They were both silent.

"You see, it's a question of duty, not sacrifice," he said at last.

"But . . . to give up my profession?" Katherine interrupted, fighting with the lump in her throat.

She saw so clearly what it would mean to leave town just now; to give up success and fame and love.

Great Lowlands stretched before her bare and bleak and desert-like. Around her were the lights of London. Franklin's eyes shone among them.

Her own eyes were piteous.

"You needn't give up your profession," said Mark, encouragingly. "You could write articles at home."

"Between nursing mother, seeing to the maids, looking after Tom, working the farm. Oh, Mark, what chance would my writing have?"

"Come now, Kit, you don't give up so much," said Mark, coaxing. "You are fagged to death with this everlasting press-work. Franklin was saying only to-day he never saw anyone so changed. He said journalism was ruining your character."

"Stop!" said Katherine.

At her tone Mark looked up sharply. He turned away at once. He knew what it would cost her to leave town, and he could not bear to see her face.

"It is a pity you have showed so much of your prickly side to Franklin," he said, with a natural desire to find fault with someone. But Katherine stopped him again.

"Don't bring Franklin's name into the discussion. He has never given me credit for any character . . . or ability . . . or . . . or anything good." . . . She swallowed down her tears. . . . "We need not take him into con-

sideration at all.   You forget that I should not give up
journalism only. . . . There is the Labour Movement."

"As far as that goes, Kit, I begin to think the Labour
Movement is nothing more than an attempt to roll a
stone up a hill."

"Mark!"

Mark balanced himself on the edge of the table, and
did not meet her eyes.

"Fact, Kit," he said.   "What was it I heard the
other day? 'The movement will only raise the mass
when the life within the individual has touched the movement.'"

"Ah!" she cried, "I remember now.   I said those
very words myself in the Park long ago; and you said
they were worth nothing.   How you have changed!"

"Yes, I have changed.   It is the life within the individual that must touch the movement, and there is no
life in me for it. These questions are not to be answered
in a moment; they are a riddle that it will take all the
ages to read.   The poor will always be with us.   They
are the soil from which the flower of civilisation springs."

"And like the soil they are to be trampled on," she
said hotly; "only, unlike the soil, they feel the tread of
the cruel feet.   You think because a man is poor he has
no human feeling, no passion, no longing, no ideals, no
consciousness even of the beauty of the flower that rises
from the human soil he provides for its growth. . . . And
you call yourself a Socialist!"

"I am losing faith in the whole thing," said Mark.

"Well," she returned scornfully, "if you are leaving
the cause, that is all the more reason why I should remain here to help it on."

"You'll do no good, Kit.   Women are not made of

the stuff that makes a cause. They care more for raising themselves than for raising the people."

She threw out her hands with an appealing gesture.

"Mark, do you mean that I am like that?"

He laughed uneasily. "I don't; but other people do. And, Kit, I hate to hear them say it. I always thought you would do something big until Franklin . . ."

"Franklin again!" she cried passionately. "Oh, I begin to hate his very name!"

"It was not Franklin only," said Mark. "Look here, Kit, my dear, I do think this life is spoiling you. You are not a bit like the girl you were. What chums we used to be once! but we scarcely see one another now, you have so many things in hand. And you are growing nervous and over-strained. It will be the saving of you to go back to Great Lowlands."

"For which my Newnham career has so admirably prepared me," Katherine said, with a bitter laugh. "You wished me to go to Newnham, and now you wish me to lose all I have gained there. It is not like you, Mark, to want to sacrifice me to Tom. But I see no reason to sacrifice my future, just when success is in my reach, too." . . . Her voice bent as she thought of some elements that would be lacking in her success. Mark's words had wakened her from her dream of love. . . . "Tom must make his own life," she went on. "And as to Great Lowlands, if the farm fails mother can come and live with us, and Tom must emigrate."

"I hate to have you sit there so coolly discussing the ruin of the old home," Mark cried. "If mother were likely to marry again so that the place would come to you, you would not take it so easily. Franklin was right when he said public life made women heartless."

"I have nothing to do with Franklin," she said very coldly. "The question lies between you and me. Ought I to give up my prospects, my future, my home here,— to leave you alone?"

"That is just it," said Mark, hurriedly, overcoming his nervousness. "I intended to tell you before, only you never gave me a chance. I have just got engaged, and when I marry . . . You see, Kit, two is company . . ."

He stopped incoherently as he saw Katherine's face.

"Don't take it too hard, old girl," he said, laying his hand on her shoulder.

She gazed at him despairingly. "Mark, we have been everything to each other. Are you going to give me up now?"

"Why, no, Kit," he said awkwardly. "But one's wife must come first, and Tonina is a splendid girl. . . . You met at the Scribblers. . . . I asked her to tell you of our engagement."

"Yes, she has told me," said Katherine; "I suppose she is braver than you. . . ." Her voice broke. "I hate her for coming between us!" she added passionately.

"Kit," said Mark, quietly, "we have been good friends, but I shall not forgive you for hating my sweetheart."

His voice softened at the last word, and a little smile relaxed the set of his lips. The smile stung Katherine more than his words. She flung away from him, and ran from the room.

Mark stood where she had left him. His eyes darkened as he stroked his moustache.

"Poor old Kit, it's hard lines on her," he said to himself. "Of course she could live alone, and go on with her work, but the mother would never consent to that.

And I couldn't ask her to live with us. . . . This call to Great Lowlands has come in the nick of time. It's the best way out of the difficulty, and it's absolutely necessary that she should go."

But conscience stirred. Would he have thought it absolutely necessary for Katherine to go to the farm if her going had not removed an obstacle in his way?

Then he caught sight of the little pink envelope, and his face cleared. He flung himself into a chair, and forgot Katherine and her claims upon him.

CHAPTER VI.

THE HORSEHAIR PRICKS.

KATHERINE went to her work the next day, but there was no pleasure in it. The conversation with Mark had broken the springs of life.

She was exhausted by a sleepless night; but she had arranged to interview a professional optimist, and she was obliged to keep her appointment.

With interested deference she listened to his sunlit opinions on the future of the race, the extension of happiness, the greater capacity for enjoyment of humanity.

Within a stone's throw of his easy-chair one could hear the sob of the people, the wail of London's poor. The moans of those crushed under the wheels of the city were the background for his brave words.

Katherine questioned him in her turn, her charm of delicate sympathy fascinating him into confidences that gave local colour to her sketch when it appeared next day in "The Flight." Her brightness and animation con-

firmed him in his vicious optimism.   Here was a young
woman in the very teeth of the struggle of life,—gay,
well-dressed, self-reliant.   Surely the world went well
with her!   Yes, a younger generation was at the door,
dowered like this very interesting young person with the
wealth of a highly sensitised being, more and more
capable of discernment, enjoyment, intellectual appreciation. . . .

Outside the door the mask fell from Katherine's face.

"Fool!" she thought bitterly.   "It is like virtue sitting at home in slippers telling us there is no mud in the
streets."

She picked her way through the slush of the pavements, hardly conscious of the fog that clung to her, and
was like her mood taking form.

It was May in London; but in the streets through
which she passed there was no sign of the spring.   The
houses stood row upon row in gloomy ranks, wearing the
same dull faces that had greeted winter.   They were
dead things that could not feel the stir and tumult of the
year; that knew nothing of the sweet secrets of parting
earth and pushing bud.   There was not even a tree to
whisper May's name as Katherine went through the fog,
her muddy skirts clinging to her ankles in just the same
way as the fog was delaying the feet of the young spring
She dragged herself wearily into the lodgings in Goodge
Street.   She had had no lunch, and she rang the bell for
tea and a fire.   Sarah brought in the tea, but explained
that after spring-cleaning Mrs. Gumtion did not allow
fires.

Katherine's dispirited "It doesn't matter" made her
take a second look at the figure on the sofa.   She
hesitated.

"I could bring you a hot bottle, Miss Fleming. You do look cold and upset, to be sure."

The kindness made Katherine aware of her forlornness and misery. "I am awfully upset," she agreed; and with feminine desire for sympathy she plunged into her trouble. Her brother wished her to leave London and go to live in the country.

At the word country Sarah's eyes snapped.

"Oh, lor, Miss Fleming, you don't mean as you think that a trouble! I was on a farm before I comed here, and I'd give the eyes in my head to get back again, only there's Jim,—my young man, the milkman, miss."

"You don't understand," said Katherine, wearily. "I am working here to make a better and happier life for the poor. And I've been asked to speak at a great meeting. It is an honour to be asked, and . . ."

She stopped, vexed at the tears in her eyes.

"Well, and indeed, miss," said Sarah, sympathetically, "the first floor as was here before you, was one of them public ladies; and she went up and down the country speaking on Woman's Sufferings; and it couldn't have agreed with her, for she was that thin and peaked looking. . . . If it's only that as you're leaving, you hadn't ought to fret yourself about going. Jim and me was in the Park that Sunday you wouldn't let me get away to 'Ampton, and we heard you speaking about helping the poor. And Jim, he said as how it would ha' done more good to ha' helped two sweethearts to be happy together than all the talk about making the poor happy in a lump. Jim, he said as you can't swaller a can of milk in a mouthful, though you can get through it a gill at a time. . . . But I'll just get that hot bottle," she added hastily, seeing Miss Fleming's face.

Katherine turned her head on the horsehair cushion, and the prickly cloth fretted her cheek as Jim's criticism fretted her mood. But she would not let the ignorant words of a servant disturb her. What did Sarah know about modern problems? How could Jim understand the questions that puzzled educated minds?

But she was very miserable. She forgot the tea while she thought of Franklin's misunderstanding of her aims, her capabilities, her ideals. He could not love a girl of whom he disapproved. . . . He thought her ambitious, while all the time it was for him . . .

A knock came at the door, and expecting only the hot bottle Katherine did not turn her head. But a sudden lightening of the atmosphere, a sense of stir and freshness and perfume startled her attention. She sat up frowning.

The dingy room was all at once bright. There was a warmth of red drapery,—the colour was repeated in the cheeks and lips of the girl before her,—a gleam of white teeth, the flash of great dark eyes, and a light of daffodils.

Tonina Rossetter pressed forward, holding out her hand while concern shadowed her face.

"Oh, you are ill! And you have been crying! I am so sorry; you must tell me what is wrong."

She flung the daffodils on the table and knelt down beside the couch. She took Katherine's hand, and looked pitifully at the face, haggard with weariness and disappointment.

"Won't you sit down?" said Katherine, drawing away her hand.

"Ah, no!" Tonina cried. "I want to comfort you; I want you to love me. . . . See, I have had your naughty letter; and you will not visit me, so I come to you. That big stupid Mark has made everything wrong. . . ." She laughed, blushing at Mark's name. . . . "And so . . ." She stopped again, and her eyes sparkled as they darted about the room. . . . "You have tea all ready, and I . . . Oh, I am very thirsty. . . ."

It was impossible to resist the appeal in the dancing eyes; impossible for Katherine to maintain her grudging humour. She looked toward the tray.

"You will let me give you some tea?" she said, relenting.

Tonina laughed with delight. "Ah, no, no! But I will give myself some, and you also. How cold you look! and you have no fire, though the day outside—it is wicked with your London fog. See, I will make the fire."

She sprang to her feet, crossed the room, removed the screen from the grate, and showed coals and sticks laid ready. Then she took a silver match-box from her pocket, lighted a match, and kindled the sticks; Katherine thinking meanwhile of the change in Mrs. Gumtion's laws against fires.

A gleam of amusement came into her eyes when Tonina's gaiety bubbled over at the sight of Mark's moustache cup on the tray. She insisted on taking it herself while she gave Katherine the smaller cup; and in the quarrel over this detail, the last of Katherine's coldness vanished. The tea thawed her reserve, and Tonina fascinated her. In wondering at her foreign graces, her friendliness and abandon she forgot that this was the woman who was taking her place in Mark's love.

Finishing her tea, Tonina took up the daffodils and brought them to Katherine.

"I brought you some daffodils, for they are like you.

Yes, I told Mark, 'Your sister is a daffodil in her funny
green frock with her pale face and the yellow hair over
her brown eyes;' and so I brought you the daffodils. . . .
What do you say?—Sweets to the sweet?"

She looked admiringly at Katherine, who could not
resist the admiration though her thoughts were bitter.

"You bring me asphodel, the flower of my dead
hopes."

Her silence touched Tonina wistfully; her mouth
drooped a little as she felt Katherine's bitterness.

"Ah, you are grieved!" she cried; "and I—I am very
sorry because Mark has made trouble. He wishes that
you should go from London to the dull country, but it is
not my wish."

Katherine's eyes flashed dangerously.

"Mark only wishes it because you wish it," she said.

Tonina sprang up from her chair and knelt down
again beside the couch.

"Ah, but Mark is stupid!" she cried passionately. "I
did but tell him, 'Katherine is so clever; she has a *salon*
with clever women; she works with her head and despises
me, who have but clever fingers. She is cold because
she thinks me not worthy of her brother. . . .'"

Tonina stopped, her big eyes grown pathetic, and
Katherine was touched. She was also softened by that
idea of herself holding a *salon;* and she put out her hand
and stroked the fingers Tonina had knitted together. The
touch enraptured Tonina. She caught the thin fingers and
kissed them.

"Ah! you will love me!" she cried. "You will stay
with us; and you will make me clever like you and Mark;
and the three, we shall be very happy."

"Yes, I will love you," said Katherine, slowly. "You

are like a flower too,—the japonica.   It will be nice to
have a sister. . . .   And if I live with you . . ."

She broke off thoughtfully and was silent a minute.
The knowledge that she would not be first with Mark
embittered her welcome. . . .   But she liked Tonina's
brilliance and her appreciation.   It would be quite easy
to have her own way with that profuse southern nature.
. . . She lifted her face smiling; and Tonina with a little
happy cry flung her arms round her and gathered her to
her heart.

When Franklin, after a repeated knock, opened the
door and looked in, he saw Katherine's face lying
like a white flower against Tonina's dark beauty.   He
felt a quick impatience with Mark.   Katherine looked so
frail; she ought not to be turned adrift to care for herself
while Mark sheltered and tended the stronger woman.

He slowly came forward, drawing off his glove, and
receiving the gushing warmth of Tonina's greeting with a
forgiving smile.

At his entrance she had got up from the floor, laughing
and blushing. She shook hands with him, and hurried away.

Katherine lifted herself from the sofa, but Franklin
stopped her.

"Don't move,—you look so very tired.   I came in to
see Mark;—he said six o'clock."

"It is not quite six," said Katherine.   Her voice
was very low, stopped by the furious throbbing of her
heart.   "Won't you sit down and wait?" she added
hoarsely, conscious of the searching look in the eyes bent
on her.

Franklin drew a chair near the sofa.

"You are certainly overworking," he said bluntly.   "Or
perhaps you have some trouble?"

5*

Her fingers plucked at a button in the sofa. She reminded herself that Franklin had criticised her to Mark, and she controlled her agitation and met his eyes steadily.

"I have no trouble, and I am not overworking."

"No?" His glance touched her shaking fingers and pointed the question. He adjusted his *pince-nez* and gave her a long keen look that ended illogically in a sigh.

"Well," he said, turning away his eyes, "if you were my sister, Miss Katherine, I would not let you remain a day longer in town. I would send you into the country."

His words were like gunpowder on fire.

"I thought I had you to thank for it," Katherine blazed up. "I knew Mark would never have wanted to send me away. *He* has some faith in me;—it is you . . ."

"Yes," he said gravely, waiting for her to finish the sentence.

"Oh, it is too bad!" She dashed her hand across her eyes. "We were so happy;—and Mark believed in me. He thought everything of me till you . . . till you said . . ."

"What did I say?" said Franklin, keeping from his eyes the amusement that he felt. He stooped forward to see her face, and her glance cut through him with the coldness and sharpness of steel. She mastered her anger and spoke quietly.

"You said that I was a mere sentimentalist—I was doing no good in the Movement. . . . And . . . and you have no faith in me. Even my character you say is deteriorating, and you never counted it very high."

She tried to smile, but her mouth trembled. Across her passion a flickering weakness played. He did not understand her eyes.

There was no amusement in his glance now. He had never before seen in her a sign of weakness; she had seemed unwomanly—even hard—in her self-reliance. The trembling mouth appealed to his strength.

He looked away from her, wondering if he had ever the true Katherine. He had a curious wish to vindicate himself in her eyes. "Tell me all about it, Miss Katherine."

The gentleness of his voice was like the wind that shakes rain from overcharged clouds. The tears that no harshness would have called forth came at the first kind word. She covered her face with her hands, sobbing.

Franklin coloured. Then he rose and walked to the window, where, moved and bewildered, he stayed looking out on the street while only conscious of the girl sobbing on the sofa. When he turned again she was staring before her; but there were no hard lines on her face, and she could not keep her lips from trembling.

He moved nearer, and stood looking down at her, a hand in his pocket, twisting into pellets an envelope that was there.

"I think you must have misunderstood me; I could never have wished to pain you like this."

He paused. Neither of them spoke.

"You have no faith in my work," she faltered at last.

"For any woman to enter your sort of journalism is a mistake," he said. "The work is fatal to womanliness. . . . You will not misunderstand me? It is a sad thing to see a noble nature warped by work that is ignoble."

"It is not only journalism. . . . You oppose my work for the people—you think it is only ambition that makes me work for them. . . ." She stopped, breathing with difficulty.

"Do you think there has been no ambition in it?" he asked.

She flushed, but went on in a carefully controlled voice,—

"And you said I was not equal to writing the History of the Movement. . . ."

"I still think so," he said quietly.

"You were wrong!" she exclaimed, starting up. "I told you I should write it; and I have begun it already. . . ."

His silence made her feel he was still of the same mind. She fell back on the sofa, white and trembling.

"Was I not right that you have been overworking, Miss Katherine?"

The tears poured down her face. She was too angry now to conceal them from the eyes that gazed at her with a new expression. Katherine in a helpless fury was more attractive to Franklin than she had ever been. She was no longer the intellectual woman, calm and balanced in judgment, but a wilful child; and she needed to be soothed and constrained like a child. He sat down again beside her.

"Listen," he said firmly. "You are wrong if you think I have ever acted in an unfriendly manner to you. I wanted to be your friend. Will you treat me as a friend now, and tell me what has happened? Why does Mark wish to send you away?"

"They want me at home," she said brokenly. "Great Lowlands, the farm, is going to ruin, and my mother is ill. Mark will be married, and he says I am to give up my career and go home." She bit her lips.

"And you don't want to go?"

Franklin hastily thought out the case. If Mark married and Katherine left him, there was nothing before her but the life lived by so many working-women, — loneliness, late hours, insufficient meals; life without its amenities.

He thought of her in Charlotte Buildings, coming home at midnight, wet and tired, to sardines and tea, and the wretched comfort of the gas-stove; and his heart revolted. Even in good conditions, with Mark's care, she felt the strain of the life. What would it be when she joined the ranks of women like Miss Rowe?

It was infinitely better for her to go to the healthy, out-door life at the farm.

"Why don't you want to go?" he changed his question.

She blinked away her tears.

"To bury myself in a place like Plimpton!" she cried. "To see the end of my dreams . . . all my hopes . . . To leave London—in the season, too!"

"My good child," said Franklin, repressing a smile, "Plimpton has its season too, when all the country beauties come out: the hawthorn, the cherry-trees, the apple-blossom; you will see them at their gayest. . . . Every tuft of lichen in the orchard will be in merry green or dainty pink. And if you are needed at home, a sick mother, and work to be done—surely it is no hardship to go. . . ."

"I lose everything if I go!" she cried despairingly. "And . . . and . . . you are not even sorry . . ." Her voice failed under the burden of her pain.

He shook his head, looking at her kindly.

"No, Miss Katherine, you lose nothing that is worth keeping. I shall not be sorry to see you go from the life that is hurting you."

Katherine dropped her eyes. Her heart fell, stunned to death by the words.

"He doesn't care! it is nothing to him whether I go or stay," she said to herself, very miserably.

Her silence spurred Franklin's thoughts. Galloping, they overtook his last sentence. Was it true? Would he not be sorry if she went away? He would miss the pleasant evenings in Goodge Street. . . . She was the only woman with whom he had had any friendship at all. . . . Would her absence not cause a blank? . . . He looked at her face closely. It bore the marks of hysterical overstrain, and he shook his head a second time.

No, she would cause no blank that work could not fill. She was too highly-strung and nervous—not the sort of woman that could ever influence his life. . . .

"You will lose nothing by going away," he said, with a sudden definiteness that startled Katherine. She lifted herself.

"I lose everything by going," she answered passionately. "I had a future before me, success, useful work, and recognition. What do I get if I leave them? I only lose what I have gained. Does it need intellect to see after sheep? Is the science tripos adapted to the needs of the potato-bed?"

"I should think you might adapt it to the needs of the potato-bed," he said, with a laugh. "The cultured spade will make an impression even on uncultivated ground. . . . Come now, Miss Katherine, things are not so bad. You ought to go away from town; and you can leave Mark, knowing he will be looked after. . ."

Katherine sat up stiffly and gazed at him wide-eyed. "You mean that I ought to go to Plimpton? . . . that I ought to give up my career for the farm?" she cried.

"But you said your mother was ill! I thought they needed you! . . ." he said, surprised.

"But I must consider myself," Katherine said quickly. "Spinoza says, 'Man's happiness consists in the preservation of his own essence.' I could not be happy at Great Lowlands, and they can do without me."

"I have heard somewhere that there is something better than happiness," Franklin said half shyly. The allusion to Spinoza had taken him back to the little dissenting chapel of his boyhood where his father had preached another philosophy.

"You mean duty," said Katherine. "Duty? What is duty?" she laughed.

The laugh jarred through his mood, and almost made him return to his first idea of her.

"And yet—and yet she is not a heartless and selfish girl," he thought; and a real fear for the loss of the gentler Katherine that had moved him made his manner unusually brusque. He got up suddenly and looked for his hat.

"Mark must have met Miss Rossetter, and gone home with her. It is no use waiting for him," he said.

Katherine saw the door close upon him. Then she turned passionately and buried her face in the horsehair cushion. She did not notice the prick and scratch of the little sharp points.

CHAPTER VII.

"TO KATHERINE, ON LEAVING."

MARK did not come in to dinner, and Katherine was too miserable to make any pretence at eating. She would have liked to nurse her sorrows, to brood over the loss of Mark, to scourge herself for having given her love to a man who despised her; but there was no time for this.

Her interview must be ready that night; and from seven to nine o'clock she wrote, the optimism of her celebrity giving ironical value to her own despair.

When the work was done, she dragged herself to the office of "The Flight," gave in her copy, and turned wearily home.

Mark was still absent. That was good. She did not wish him to see her when she was weak from that scene with Franklin. She would need all her strength to hold her own against that absurd idea that it was her duty to go home.

"Duty? What is duty?" she said to herself as she crept into bed. She had no answer ready, but in the silence she heard Franklin's voice: "I have heard somewhere that there is something better than happiness."

"Yes," she said eagerly to herself, "work is better than happiness: it never fails. . . . And if I go home, I give up my work for the people."

Across this thought flashed a voice: "We heard you

talk of helping the poor, and Jim said as how it would be a better thing to help two sweethearts to be happy together . . ."

"But I shall do that;" she silenced the voice. "I shall help Mark and Tonina when I live with them. . . ."

But the words were interrupted by Mark's voice, "Two is company . . ."

"And three is trumpery," she finished the sentence dismally. "He meant that he didn't want me. I am nothing to him, and I used to be everything . . . And how selfish he has grown; he doesn't consider me at all. Even Franklin was more considerate. . . ."

Her thoughts hung about Franklin's manner when he had soothed her unreasoning passion, and she softened towards him.

"He is a strong man. . . . If only he had cared for me, he would have made me a better woman. . . . I would do anything for love. . . . But he doesn't love me, else he would not have wished me to go away. . . . I am nothing to him. He doesn't care! he doesn't care! . . And he is all the world to me. . . ."

She lay moaning. The tears gathered in her eyes but could not fall. In her heart was a great longing, and silence that was pain.

.   .   .   .   .

Mark came whistling in to breakfast, threw a glance at the table, and walked by force of habit to the fireplace, where he stood with his back propped against the mantelpiece.

Katherine gave him a glance that made him uncomfortable.

"You needn't try to warm yourself there, Mark," she

said. "The fire Miss Rossetter lighted burnt out very
soon. There is nothing but cinders left to-day."

Mark ignored the words, but he came over to the
table.

"Is the bacon quite cold, Kit? I'm awfully late this
morning."

"I have kept it warm for you," said Katherine, lifting
the cover from a hot-water dish. "You were awfully late
last night," she went on. "Franklin waited here for you
a long time."

"Did he?" said Mark. "I met Tonina, and went
home with her . . . How did you get on with her?" he
added bashfully.

"I liked her," said Katherine, shortly. "She has
little foreign ways that amuse me. She won't be difficult to live with. I think we shall get on together very
well."

Mark took up a letter and broke the envelope.
Then he sat down carelessly. "So you liked Tonina?
. . . By the way, I must tell you, Kit. . . . Tonina said
she wanted you to live with us; and of course that
would have been very nice, but don't you see it won't
do? Someone must go to Great Lowlands;—and, Kit,
you ought to go."

"Why should I go?" she asked.

Mark attacked an egg, to which he gave his attention
while he spoke.

"Well, you see I am moving into a flat, and it
will be expensive. I've taken one of those in Ridgmont
Gardens."

Katherine's face became very still. Was there, then,
no place in his life for her?

"He doesn't want me," she thought. "He is driving

me away. No one wants me,—no one but Tom and
Great Lowlands. Well, I will go to the farm. If I have
no love according to Franklin, and no home according to
Mark, I have little enough to sacrifice. If Great Lowlands
offers me dust and ashes, has my life here given anything
more?"

"Pray say no more, Mark," she said aloud, quietly.
"I will not inflict myself upon you and your wife. I have
made up my mind to go home."

She winced as she saw the relief in his face.

"You are a brick, Kit," he said heartily. "I always
knew you would do the right thing."

He threw himself back in his chair and beamed
on her.

"It is not a question of the right thing," she said
coldly. "It is the only thing. You give me no alter-
native."

"Well, you ought to go for the mother's sake, and
I am glad you are going; though, of course, I shall miss
you."

"Don't take the trouble to say polite nothings," she
burst out. "We have been everything to each other, all
our lives, and now I am nothing to you! . . ."

"My dear girl, that is ridiculous. Marriage is not the
awful change you make it out to be. . . ."

"It kills me to think of the change it means for me!"
she cried fiercely.

Mark took up his cup and buried his face in it. The
action was very different from that of Tonina the day
before. Katherine thought of the merry eyes that had
danced across the rim of that self-same cup; and seeing
Mark's down-dropped and cowardly a sudden scorn of
him seized her. This was not the brother she had wor-

shipped. The man before her cringed meanly, and had not the courage of right deeds. It was not the attitude of Franklin, who had looked her in the face, and told her that her duty was at Great Lowlands. Was Mark selfish?

"I'll write and tell mother you are going," he said, his face still eclipsed.

"You needn't write. I'll wire."

"But that is not necessary. A letter will reach them soon enough."

"I start to-morrow," said Katherine, rising from the table. He put down the cup and looked at her. The expression on her face was unpleasant.

"Look here, Kit," he said coaxingly. "It'll do no good for you to go off in a huff. You only make yourself wretched. Then there's your work; that will have to be arranged."

"Oh, that is easy," she said cynically. "In journalism there are fifty pairs of feet waiting for one pair of shoes. I take off the shoes now and Miss Rowe puts them on to-night. Poor soul, she'll be glad enough of the chance. You see, Mark, you have stepped out of the Labour world only to find work for the unemployed."

"And there is your packing," Mark went on; "and the furniture in your room."

"That can be warehoused, and my packing is a slight matter."

"Ah, don't go to-morrow, Kit," he exclaimed. "Why should you? There is no earthly reason for it."

Now that it was settled and Katherine was leaving him, Mark saw what was passing out of his life. He was going to lose his sister, an influence that had ruled the past years. But with the memory of those years came

the remembrance of Katherine's intensity, her strength
and enthusiasm that had dominated his aims, the tyranny
of her earnestness. His thoughts sank back with relief
on the softness of Tonina's womanhood.

"You need not go off in such a hurry," he said, less
warmly. "I have to go to the office to-night; and to-
morrow I must go down to a meeting at Luton. You
may as well stop till next week, Kit."

"'What thou doest, do quickly,'" she answered.

She would not give herself time to repent. She would
not risk meeting Franklin, and breaking down before him.
She turned, and Mark looked regretfully at the door she
closed behind her.

"Franklin was quite right," he said to himself. "This
life is ruining her. It's the best thing that could happen.
. . . I wonder . . ." He drummed on the table. "It's
just possible they might have got on together," he said
thoughtfully. "But she is better away, and in any case
they want her at home."

In her bedroom Katherine with shaking fingers was
putting on her hat. She scarcely knew the face that met
her from the glass, it was so changed and old. She
smiled, seeing it.

"It is the face of the woman who buries her dead,"
she whispered. She had no time for reflections. Her
day would be crammed and running over with affairs.
She must go from office to office, giving up her work,
finding those who would replace her at a moment's notice.

Under the haste she was very bitter against Mark.
Yet she knew that it was not he but Franklin who had
decided her action. His wishes still had power with her.
And he had wished her to leave town. She hurried into

Tottenhamcourt-Road, where she waited for a 'bus. One after another went by, full inside and out. "There seems to be no room in the world for me to-day," she said to herself.

At last there was a vacant seat. She climbed to the top, and her tired eyes looked on the sordid scenes about her with a passion of regret.

The street was in the undress of the early morning; pieces of paper, dead flowers, bits of orange peel, the ashes of yesterday, gave it the unkempt air of a late reveller.

The people taking down the shutters were still half-asleep. They loitered on the pavements. Underfoot it was muddy; overhead a tattered curtain of fog was drawn across a sickly sun. The fog brightened the radishes and lettuces piled before the greengrocer's window. Katherine remembered it was springtime.

Reaching the Strand, she was again reminded of the spring. In the highways and byways leading from Covent Garden there flowed a stream of colour,—hyacinths, daffodils, narcissus, roses,—glad waves of flowers that flushed the dingy streets and swept the spring upon the flood.

Katherine's eyes brightened and saddened again. "I have to leave all this. I have to leave it all," she moaned.

She climbed the stairs to the office of "The Flight." The bustle up and down, the printer's boys ascending and descending, the sharp footsteps, the keen faces stirred her pulses. This was life, and the force of life, and she was leaving it. She caught her breath. To-morrow she would drift into the backwash of the current where she would not feel even the flow of the tide of events. She did her business without delay and without sentiment, though her suggestion that Miss Vincent should fill her place bordered on the latter.

It was flattering to see the editor's reluctance to accept her resignation.

"Called suddenly into the country, Miss Fleming? Well, we shall miss your pars.; they were smart, uncommonly smart. We could always rely on you to hit the bull's eye. Good day, good day. . . . Simmons, wire Miss Vincent, 17 North Crescent, Westminster, and ask her to look round to-day."

Everywhere it was the same thing. There was little time for regret or personal feeling. The same hand that helped her down from her seat helped her successor into it. Katherine learned that her place was easily filled. It opened her eyes to the value of the power she had vaunted. But she had time neither to think nor to feel; —not even at the office of "The People," where with unfeigned relief the editor heard that she could supply no more articles on Labour topics.

"The fact is, Miss Fleming, your style is becoming too technical. Those last articles were heavy, very. We don't want facts, you know; we have plenty of those. What we want is a popular style; it tells more."

"And means less," Katherine added brightly, that he should not see her pain. Here also she suggested Miss Vincent as her successor. The veiled satire pleased her.

All day through the streets she went, one of the crowd hurrying from place to place, not resting, not pausing even to eat. She used her luncheon time in a hurried visit to Westminster, where she gave Miss Vincent hints and directions that afterwards impressed the editor, and gained her appointment on the staff of "The Flight."

When she came out of the house Katherine gazed round her, hesitating. Then her face took on its resolute air.

The underground railway would set her down at the Temple, where she would be within a minute's walk of the Scribblers' Club. It was Friday,—the day of the weekly crush. She would run in, have tea, say good-bye, hold her *salon* once more, for the last time.

She did not notice that her appearance proclaimed the change in her fortunes. She was haggard, her face marked by fatigue; her dress was less carefully arranged than usual. She did not look like the brilliant Miss Fleming. The news that she was leaving town had arrived before her. It was being eagerly talked over by women anxious to fill the gap she was making.

After listening to some hurried regrets and many entreaties for introductions to her editors, Katherine saw that her day was past. There were no offerings of compliment and congratulation, she sat alone in her corner behind the india-rubber plant. There a late arrival, Celandine Ambrose, found her; and his delight soothed her cynical humour.

She allowed him to lead her again into the land of self-esteem, and his wail at her news kept her patient while he struck off a rondel "To Katherine, on Leaving."

He read it to her, and Katherine was pleased and touched.

> "I made a wreath of snow
>   To crown my fair Delight,
> 'T was wrought where torrents flow,
>   And winter binds the night.

"Love's brow with youth was bright;
 Her eyes were stars aglow;
I made a wreath of snow
 To crown my fair Delight.

"The snow is gone; and lo!
 With spring the crags are dight.
Love, where the roses blow,
 Twines roses red and white.
I made a wreath of snow
 To crown my fair Delight."

At the last lines he took Katherine's hand: "May I come and see you some day at Great Lowlands, where the roses blow?" he asked softly.

Katherine's heart was sore. She had been tossing all day on the waves of a cruel strife, battered in the tossing against the flotsam and jetsam of human nature. The tender words and look were like a sunny haven into which she had drifted.

For a second she thought of Franklin, dwelling resentfully on his criticism of her. Ambrose appreciated her; he believed in her.

Her face flushed when she told him she would look forward to seeing him at Great Lowlands.

There was no one to disturb her in her packing at Goodge Street. Mark did not return to dinner; there were no callers. It was her last evening in town, and she spent it alone. With a bitter disdain she tossed her clothes into the trunks. She packed the manuscript of her book on the Labour Movement among them.

"I shall write it yet," she said, setting her lips.

CHAPTER VIII.

A-FOOT TO GREAT LOWLANDS.

THERE was still half-an-hour before the cab would come. Mark had left early for Luton and would not be able to see Katherine off.

She sat down in her bedroom and looked at the dismantled walls, the empty bookcases. The room figured her life, from which all meaning, and culture, and art had been snatched. Philosophy, the religion of humanity, had gone. The relics of her old faith, the shrines and rosaries, had been packed among the things to be warehoused. She was taking nothing of her life with her. She would not be reminded at Great Lowlands of what she had lost. With a morbid pleasure she saw the empty room. A white cross on the dirty wall-paper showed where the crucifix had hung.

She was in a cynical mood. She had made the great sacrifice, and there were no spectators to applaud. She was taking the chief part in a tragedy, and no one saw in it anything but comedy.

Mark had given her a gay kiss, and told her not to fret. "Of course it is hard lines to leave town, but Plimpton's not a bad sort of place, you know, Kit. You'll be the chief person in the village; that will suit you."

Katherine had smiled bitterly. Yes, she would be the chief person in the village. Great Lowlands was the only house of any pretension. The rector was unmarried; the doctor's wife was an invalid; there was no other society in the place; and Mark said gaily it was "not bad."

That was the farewell she had earned after three years of devotion to him. He did not understand her feeling at all. He cast her off so soon as he had no use for her. How selfish men were! And now she was going away, and there was no one to bid her good-bye; not even Mrs. Gumtion, who had gone marketing.

Sarah came to say the cab was at the door. She looked half-frightened at Katherine's hard face. Then, from under her apron, she brought a bookmark: "And would you accept this, miss, to remember me with?"

Katherine took it from her. There was a "posy" in fancy stitches: "When this you See, Remember Me," framed in a device of hearts and love-knots.

"Oh, Sarah, how kind!" she exclaimed. "I won't forget you." She ran downstairs and sat in the cab while her boxes were taken out. She did not want to break down before the girl; and by the time she reached the station she had controlled her tears, and was lashing herself with scorn that a foolish thing like that should have upset her. She did not know that it had relaxed the tension of her mood. In the train she took out the bookmark and looked at it again. The hearts and love-knots were very funny, "A return to Nature," she called them. She could not help smiling at the crude senti-ment. It reminded her of Martha Collop, the old cow-man's wife at the farm. There was a wreath of forget-me-nots, too, bluer forget-me-nots than those in the pond before Martha's cottage.

She remembered the last spring she had spent at home, when Tom had waded knee-deep into the water to get her the flowers that Martha said bound the water like a blue sash-ribbon. She thought of the handsome, reckless fellow with a wistful longing. Tom had always been fond of her; and she had always ignored him for Mark. And now Mark had cast her off . . . Memory dwelt on the contrast between the brothers: Mark, the more intellectual, thin and dark and wiry, pursuing his aims with a relentlessness that she had admired until now, when she had seen the cloven foot of selfishness. She turned with relief to Tom's fair, good-humoured face, his merry blue eyes. His loose build, mental and physical, seemed just now more attractive than Mark's unbending-ness. Tom would never have cast her adrift in order to rent a fashionable flat. . . .

Her thoughts swung round to Mark. The lines gathered again about her mouth; her eyes became cold. She fixed them on the past, and missed the compensations the hour offered. The train had left London, and was speeding along through cuttings, the banks embroidered with daisies and primroses. Larch and willow trees made delicate tracery against a blue sky. Here and there a cluster of pines struck a deep note of green, and blossoms hung in white knots on the blackened boles of the cherry-trees. But Katherine missed it all.

She alighted at the station for Plimpton, her eyes searching eagerly for Tom. There was no one to meet her; not even a cart to take her boxes to Great Low-lands. She thought with dismay of the four miles' up-hill tramp, but she would have to walk. No conveyance was to be had at the station, and the nearest inn was two miles away in the opposite direction.

Leaving her luggage with the porter she set out for

Plimpton, her feet weighted by disappointment and weariness.

The road, winding among trees, rose higher and higher to the table-land on which the village rested. The silence of the country, after the roar of the London streets, struck her with a sense of loneliness. She had no eyes to see the blazing sunlight that was itself like sound outspread, no ears for the thousand tiny noises of wood and field and growing corn; and she dragged her way up the steep road, indignant with Tom, indignant with her mother, indignant with fate. It was a hot afternoon. She was wearing the winter clothes that had been necessary in town, and the heavy serge was a pain and a weariness.

She looked about for a seat, but the banks were wet, soaked by recent rain. While she hesitated to sit down, a sound of wheels came nearer and nearer and a dog-cart overtook her.

"What a pretty boy!" Katherine thought, till she saw that the driver wore a skirt. The girl in the cart stopped her horse.

"You look just awfully tired," she said with frank directness. "Are you going to Plimpton? Do let me take you up."

"Thank you," said Katherine, soberly.

She was too tired to be independent, and she clambered into the cart and sat down beside the young woman.

"Awfully jolly country, ain't it?" said this person. "You can't beat it for scenery."

"It is very pretty," said Katherine.

The young woman carefully and scientifically whipped off two flies from the horse's neck, then turned good-humouredly to Katherine.

"From London, ain't you?"

"Yes," said Miss Fleming, stiffly.

"I thought so; and yet there's a cut of Cambridge about you, too. I never saw a green serge made like that except at Newnham."

"Have you been to Newnham?" Katherine asked quickly, her face waking up.

The grey eyes twinkled with amusement. From under the brim of her bowler the girl shot a shrewd glance at her.

"My goodness, you are easy to draw!" she laughed. "I am Girton, that is to say, I was. I came down after a year at classics. I got tired of them, and took to cycling instead, and my uncle said it was less expensive for me to rotate at home. He's a good old thing; he only laughed when I gave up the bike for horses."

"And you are living with him here?" Katherine asked.

"Good gracious, no! I found a business; and he bought me a cottage, out of gratitude that I left him to his old bachelor life."

"And you drive about alone like this?" Katherine looked surprised.

The young woman laughed, showing a row of strong white teeth.

"Don't you think I look as if I could take care of myself?"

The words invited scrutiny. Katherine glanced at her companion, taking in at a flash the short hair and jaunty set of the hat, the tailor-made gown, shirt, collar, and horsey pin. Certainly the skirt was the only concession to the woman.

"Since you ask me, I think you look as if you might,"

she said smiling, her ill-humour passing before the disco-
very of a Girton girl in the neighbourhood of Great Lowlands.

The young woman tossed her head till, the short curls
danced.

"I can look after myself, you bet! Are you staying
in Plimpton?"

"I have not decided what to do," said Katherine,
coldly.

"Oh, not sure of lodgings? There's only The Three
Soldiers, and I don't think that will suit you. I wonder . . ." She stopped, bit the handle of her whip, and
considered. "Look here," she said unexpectedly, "I know
the loveliest old farm-house, Great Lowlands. They don't
take lodgers, but they are friends of mine, and they might
—if I asked them—put you up till you were suited. It's
a nice earwiggy old place, with a pond and a boat and
apple-trees,—perfectly heavenly. Or there's Milkmaid
Cottage; it's only the cowman's; but his wife, Martha
Collop, is a perfect old pagan, and you would love her.
I'd ask you to my place, but I have only one bedroom.
Well, if you are in a box, just ask for Laburnum Drive
and Miss Saunders, and I'll fix it somehow."

"You are very good," said Katherine, with an inward
amusement at being offered rooms in her own house. "I
don't know why you should wish to do me a service, I
am sure."

"Nor I!" laughed the other; "only you look sort of
worn-out; and your face reminds me of a person who
has been good to me; so I suppose I want to be good to
you."

The young woman smiled deprecatingly, and Katherine
noticed that her ear had grown pink.

"I suppose there is very little going on in Plimpton," she said, to break the silence. "How do you amuse yourself?"

"Amuse myself? Good gracious! I amuse myself by working. I am a professional woman. What do you think of Girton as a preparation for horse-training?"

"Horse-training?" Katherine echoed.

"Exactly," the girl laughed. "I am a horse-trainer. I wish you could see the muscles on my arm! This colt now, I broke him in myself."

"Seriously?" said Katherine.

"My goodness, yes. I could always do what I liked with uncle's horses; and when I got bored living with him I thought it would amuse me to have a profession. And it does. The profession makes the life."

"Professions are danger-signals," said Katherine.

"Danger is stimulating," answered the girl.

They were driving slowly past a green lane closed at the end by a gate. The horse shied at the white bars of the gate. The girl managed him smartly, and a stroke from the whip sent him dashing past the turn.

"You needn't be frightened; he always shies at that gate," she said to Katherine, who had clutched the side of the cart. "When I was breaking him in for riding I used to try and make him take it, but he wouldn't. There's a nasty dip in the field beyond, and I saw it would be sheer suicide to make him go over, so I gave it up. But he may have to do it yet. . . . When life gets too hard for me I shall make him take the leap."

She set her face with a grim expression, and Katherine smiled.

"I should think the horse will be dead long before that happens."

"Goodness! I should just hope so. . . . I'd like to see the trouble I couldn't get over."

The girl smiled, a splendid, sufficient smile that made Katherine suddenly aware of her own weakness.

They were close to the village. She could see the long stretch of the green, with its duck-pond and pump; the thatched houses grouped round it, brown and mossy and old; the red brick of a row of new cottages; the latticed windows of the old-fashioned inn.

On the other side of the green stood the little old church, in which slept the Flemings of long ago. One of them had been a crusader. Katherine had put an ivy wreath on his tomb before she had left home to take her place in the Labour war. She remembered the sentiment with a touch of pity for herself. She was coming back from her crusade uncrowned. She bore neither victory nor death. Then her pulse quickened, her cheeks flushed. She bent eagerly forward. Beyond the church she had caught sight of the ivied gables of Great Lowlands.

"Shall I put you down here?" asked her companion. "There's The Three Soldiers. This is my way to the stables. And mind you fall back on Laburnum Drive if you find you can't get in at Great Lowlands."

After a glance and a smile at the manly pose of the girl in the cart, and the capable air with which she held the reins, Katherine stepped smartly across the green.

There was a new spring in her walk. Her load had been lifted by the cheery strength of a friend. Life seemed less hopeless than it had been an hour ago.

She had not thought the village was so pretty. Now she noticed the sun-flecked lights and shadows on the green, the line of white ducks waddling to the pond, the waim tones in house and wall, the soft blurred effects of moss and lichen. After the strained face of London Plimpton's was like that of a rosy sleeping child. The garden gate of Great Lowlands stood open. Moved and excited, she walked in and passed under a row of lime-trees to the house.

The emptiness and dreariness of the garden went with her as she entered the house by the French window opening on the lawn. Her mother was on the sofa in the room. She stretched out a thin hand laden with rings.

"Oh, my child, you should not have come!"

The worn face sent a pang to Katherine's heart. She kissed it gently.

"But, mother, you sent for me."

"Yes, I did," Mrs. Fleming said fretfully. "But I never expected you to leave your work and come off in this impulsive manner! If you had arranged to come in two or three months it would have done."

"But you are ill, and the farm is being ruined," said Katherine, chilled at her reception.

"But will it help the farm to have another person to support? Remember that our income is limited, and you have been independent for years. Maik should have thought of this. You ought not to give me another burden. . . . And you don't look strong either, not equal to farm-work. My child, you have done a foolish thing to come here."

Mrs. Fleming picked up her lace handkerchief and sighed delicately as she looked at her daughter. She was a thin, elegant woman, who had once been pretty; but one saw only the fretfulness of her mouth.

Katherine gazed at her, struggling with pity for her

weakness, and anger at her words. So this was what her sacrifice meant? . . . She could have laughed at the irony of the thing.

"I will go to my room and take off my things," she said hoarsely.

"I don't suppose it is ready, Katherine. Jane is out, and Mary is ironing. I told them to leave the room till you came. You can go to mine."

With a stormy face Katherine went up to the bedroom that was called hers. She threw open the door and looked in at the unswept floor, the furniture swathed in sheets, the naked bed. There were no curtains at the window, but the ivy trailed a branch of bright green across it.

She flung open the casement and leaned out, her elbow on the sill propping her head, her heart bursting with passion and pain.

And this was all that her sacrifice meant—an added burden to her mother! Her thoughts were salt with tears. She did not notice the touch of the breeze on her forehead, the light fingers of the ivy on her hair. She was in the grip of that chilly welcome. Ah! how vain it was! She had given up everything, everything! and found! . . . what had she found?

Her blank eyes travelled across the snow of the apple-trees in the orchard, and beyond the green to the little grey church on the slope of the hill. They saw only the irony of life, its vanity, its vexation of spirit. All at once something soft and perfumed dashed against her cheek, and a bunch of rose petals fell on the window-sill.

She looked down into the yard, and met a broad smile from a man who, with legs planted apart, was in the act of aiming a handful of leaves at her.

"Hillo, Kit! So you've turned up again!" Tom called. "Well, come down and let's have a look at you. What are you grizzling about all alone up there?"

Katherine slowly withdrew from the window, and went down into the garden. Tom gave her a casual salute, but held her at arm's length afterwards, and studied her gloomy face.

"Well, I declare you don't look a bit pleased to see a fellow!" he said gaily. "What's up, Kit? Are you bad-tempered, or only hungry?"

"I believe I am both," she said, half-smiling at his twinkling eyes. She noticed that he had grown more manly, and she felt a gratification in calling this well-built, handsome fellow her brother. "I am as bad-tempered as I can be," she added, her mouth quivering to the smile.

"Of course! You have had no dinner; and the old lady has been giving you the dolefuls. Well, look here, I am hungry too. Just go into the arbour and wait."

Katherine walked slowly into the arbour, over which the traveller's joy rioted in early leaves; and in a short time Tom came back with a tray heaped with apple-pasties, bread and honey, a junket, and a jug of milk.

"None of your lady-like afternoon teas for me!" he said, setting down the tray. "Jane is a Devonshire lass, and knows how to make pasties and junket. They're better than bread and butter wafers, Kit. Try 'em."

In another minute Katherine was biting at a pasty, a mug of milk in her other hand. The first mouthful cheered her. She had not realised how faint and hungry she was. She took a long draught of milk, and sighed with pleasure when she put down the mug.

Tom watched her, pleased, his face round with the pasty he was eating.

"Good?" he mumbled.

"Awfully good," she answered.

They both laughed, then set themselves to the tray again, honey and junket and bread disappearing under their onset. Katherine began to understand that the joy of life is intimately connected with the fulness of the stomach.

The fresh air, the young leaves, the smell of the orchard, made a dainty setting for the country fare; and when she had finished, her face was rosy with content.

"This is better than tea at the Scribblers'," she said to herself; "only Celandine Ambrose ought to be here to make a rondel to the junket."

"Well, you look a little more fit, old girl," Tom chuckled. "And now perhaps you will tell me what the dickens you mean by turning up in this fashion?"

"I think you might have met the train," she said reproachfully.

"Couldn't; had to go on business of Peggy's."

"Who is Peggy?" Katherine asked.

"Oh, Peg is my girl, and a rattling good girl too. That was a rose she gave me I threw at you. . . . None of your fine-lady airs about her."

Katherine remembered the allusion in her mother's letter to Tom's infatuation, and she dropped the subject with a shiver of distaste.

"How is it things are in such a bad way here, Tom?"

"But they aren't!" he answered cheerfully. "At least, not worse than usual. The mother is always complaining for nothing. If you listen to her she will give you the blues and no mistake."

"Then things are not going to ruin? The crops have not failed?"

"Not a bit of it!" he laughed. "Of course you can't expect to make a silk purse out of a sow's ear, and you'll never get good crops out of this farm. . . . For one thing, it wants draining. . . . That old fool Collop is always telling me that!"

"Then why don't you drain it?" she said quickly.

He shrugged his shoulders. "Reason why! But what has brought you back so suddenly, Kit? Mark given you the sack?"

"I've come back to see if I can't make things better here."

"Well, you can't! Do you think you are going to work miracles? I tell you the place has beaten me. What with the weather, and the price of corn, and the new-fangled notions, farming is the very devil to pay. It's sheer waste of flesh and blood. The best thing you can do is to chuck the whole thing and go back to town. That's why I didn't send for your traps. You can take the next train back, and I'll drive you to the station. I'll be delighted to do it."

CHAPTER IX.

A RETURN TO NATURE.

KATHERINE slept the sleep that is weighted by a weary mind. When she woke in the morning she felt a strange zest in the day. Instead of the hoarse roar of Goodge Street there greeted her a delicate silence threaded by the song of a bird; a busy twittering, the tap of leaves against a lattice. She opened her eyes on chintz dotted with green, the hangings of her little white bed. Curtains and sheets smelt of rosemary and lavender, and Katherine started up with a delighted sniff.

She smiled as she saw her room. It was spring-time there also, a dainty green showing among the white. At the window snowy curtains framed the ivy leaves; the sun made daffodil splashes on the wall, and where it touched the carpet the butter-cups blossomed. She sprang out of bed, stretching her limbs luxuriously as she remembered she need not begin the day with a rush. Her bath stood ready, and the clear water pleased her. "To be clean is the first step towards happiness," she said as she plunged in.

Then she remembered that she had no cause to feel glad, to be stirred to any gay tumult. She faced failure. She had given up her work in London, and she was not wanted at Great Lowlands. She had offered up herself on the altar of a useless sacrifice.

Her brow clouded; but while she dressed it cleared

again. Who could be miserable on a day flooded with sunshine? Even her perplexities were simplified by the sounds of cheerful life outside. There seemed to be room in the world for her to-day. Away from the crowded life of London her limbs were free to live and move and have their being. There was space for breath, space even for the ideal calm she had once sought;—the voices outside were part of the silence from strife.

She could hear the fowls clucking, and someone speaking: "Come, my dears, come. Breakfast is ready; Mother's got your breakfasses ready. Chuck! chuck!"

Katherine put her head through the window. Under the apple-trees in the orchard she could see a little old woman in a figured print gown carrying a wooden bowl. At her heels flew and scrambled a brood of chickens, and the old woman laughed and chuckled as she stepped gingerly so as not to tread on them. "There, my darlings, there! Don't be too pushing, you yellow boy; give your sisters a chance, like a little gentleman."

The old woman had a little round face with a pretty pink on it; and she wore a pink sunbonnet over her white hair. Her gown was sprigged with rosebuds, and she made a charming picture under the apple-trees.

Katherine's face brightened as she saw her. "Dear old Martha, what a darling she is!—and as vain as ever!"

She hurried over her dressing, and ran downstairs, and out of doors, calling "Martha! Martha Collop! where are you hiding?"

"Here, missie, here;" and Martha came bustling round the fowl house, her face beaming. She put down her bowl and made a curtsey, then ran to Katherine and kissed her.

"I'm real glad to see missie back. You won't mind the old woman, duckie? I made my obedience, but I says to myself, 'Bother! I must have a kiss.' I does love to kiss a soft face; yes, I does."

"I think you are the only person who is glad to see me back, Martha."

"What does Miss Katherine say that for?" Martha asked reproachfully. "As soon as I knowed you was comed I took little Snowdrop,—that do be the white chicken as I were terrible fond of,—and I off with his head as quick as a swallow. He do be lovely plump, and will make missie a sweet toothful."

"Oh, Martha, stop!" Katherine cried, putting her hands over her ears. "How can you kill the creatures you love?"

"Ay, I were terrible fond of he, but I couldn't-a-bear to have en die hard. I just catched en in my hand, and he knowed I wouldn't hurt en; and before he had time to sneeze there was his head off. . . . Ay, he died very peaceable, did Snowdrop."

"How is Collop?" Katherine asked.

"Well, missie, Collop be but tottering. I tells en he ain't so young as he might be, but he don't believe me. He do be a foolish old carle, Collop," she added with the conscious look of a girl speaking of her sweetheart.

"I must go and see him," said Katherine. "And how are all your children, Martha?"

"They do be getting on wonderful, duckie. I was like to lose the grey pigeon in the winter through information in his crop. But I cut en and emptied en, and sewed en up again, and now he be setting on the purtiest eggs you ever seed."

7 *

"Oh, Martha, you are too funny with your children," Katherine laughed, moving away.

"Don't go, missie, don't go!" said Martha, eagerly. "I be right upset waiting on Mr. Tom. Fan had seven pups last night, and the poor lass can't rear en all; and I'm waiting on Mr. Tom to say how many must be drownded."

"Where is Mr. Tom?" Katherine asked.

"He be sweethearting, duckie. He do carry on, to be sure. Up with the sun and away he is, and the lass spoiling her clothes in the wet grass. . . . But there! a young man a-courting is neither to have nor to hold. And no blame neither, for what be a man worth if he ain't a-follering of nature?"

A merry twinkle set a light in Martha's eye. "And Collop do say," she added, "long courting makes short farming. And there's Fan and the babies pulling till she don't know which is herself and which puppy, poor lass!"

"Martha, does Collop think the farm is being neglected?" the girl asked slowly.

"There's small doubt o' that, duckie. . . . But what can you expect of a young man with all his juices in en? 'Miss Katherine, 't was her had ought to have farmed the land,' Collop says every day. And if you'd bide on, duckie, 't would surely be the saving of the place."

Katherine stood with troubled eyes. She felt quite equal to managing the farm and giving orders to the men; but how could she do this if her mother and Tom were not willing?

"What sort of girl is this Mr. Tom spends his time with, Martha?"

A roguish look knotted together the wrinkles on the old woman's forehead. She chuckled delightedly.

"Lor, missie, her is neither lad nor lass, nor man nor maid. Not but what her be personable. Breech her, and her would be woman; but being gowned, you sees the man in her. . . . And Mr. Tom is off with her, and poor Fan in her trouble. . . ."

"Seven pups, did you say, Martha?" . . . There was a sudden decision on Katherine's face. . . . "Well, get rid of three. Save the best. You can tell Mr Tom I gave the order. . . ."

"I'll go this very minute," said Martha, gleefully. "I tell Collop 't was Providence what's putten the pond nigh to Milkmaid Cottage for the young things to go peaceable out of this weary world."

Martha sighed happily as she hobbled away, and Katherine turned and went in to breakfast.

She had not finished when Martha knocked at the door and came in with an air of mysterious gaiety.

"Oh, duckie," she cried in a loud whisper, "I can't drowned en, not a single one on en. . . ." She clasped her hands in an ecstasy. . . . "The pups is all little boys, everyone o' the seven! . . . And I couldn't drowned a little boy,—no, not if 't was ever so . . ."

"And how is Fan to bring up seven pups?" Katherine asked.

"Oh, Fan," Martha said scornfully; "her is nob-but a woman, and it's woman's duty to bear children. . . . Fan 'll just have to do her duty by the seven."

Katherine remained in the breakfast room, thinking over the situation. Mrs. Fleming was still in bed; Tom had not come in.

The French window was wide open; a bed of narcissus

loaded the air with fragrance, and a light wind tossed the
smell into the room. A thrush sang madly, swaying on
the topmost branch of the fir-tree before the window.
Beyond the garden a field of struggling corn sloped up-
ward to the dead oak that marked the western boundary
of the farm.

Katherine's eyes clouded. The flower beds were rank
with weeds; the ground was strewn with dead needles
and cones; the corn in the field was blighted. Someone
was needed to snatch the place from ruin. She saw work
before her, and her fingers ached to begin it. Opposition
had always stirred her, and because she was not wanted
here she longed to stay.

She sprang up and ran into the garden. But the
luxuriance of the season had hidden defects and covered
up faults; and where they were glaring, as in the un-
tended lawn, the dandelions and daisies rollicking unabashed made her pardon them. The neglect in the
kitchen garden was more serious. Her eye caught the
ruined asparagus bed, the fruit-trees unprotected from
frost. The peaches on the south wall held straggling
branches towards her; an apricot had torn itself from its
fastenings and was trailing on the ground.

"What in the world have they been doing?" she
thought impatiently. "It is so much capital being thrown
away. . . . Well, it is high time I came to the rescue. . . ."

It was a relief to get beyond the walls into the rows
of strawberries that filled several acres of ground. This
crop, at least, was hopeful. . . . She lifted her eyes from
the buds lurking among the leaves, and saw an old man
coming towards her. It was Collop, a tall figure crowned
by a face gnarled and knotted like the trunk of an oak.
Katherine noticed that he seemed dry and withered like

a dead branch. Not a muscle of his face moved at the girl's smile.

"Morning, Miss Katherine," he said gravely. "Hope I sees you well this morning."

"Yes, thank you, Collop. How are you?"

He leaned one hand on his stick, and wiped his mouth before he spoke.

"Well, missie, I beant partickler well," he said slowly. "I've got too much on my mind, I have, for to feel comforrable like. You see, missie, 'tis here. . . . There's nobody to see to things but me, cos Master Tom,—well, he don't apply his mind like. No use having a mind if you don't apply it. You must apply the mind." . . . He shook his head and thought a moment, his eyes fixed on the distance. . . . "Now if you was a-going to stay at Great Lowlands, Miss Katherine, you and me, us could work the farm; because you see, us should apply our minds together. . . . Now, I say to Master Tom, I say to en, sez I: 'Master Tom, there's that old Suke.' . . . That old long Jersey, you see, missie. . . . 'She be past calving, and past milking too, nearly; what be the use o' keeping of she? Her ought to ha' been sold three year ago.'—'What's the use o' selling her?' sez he. 'Sha'n't get nothing for her. Sell that young heifer and calf,' sez he; 'her'll make some money.' . . . And so 'tis with most everything that be worth anything. 'Tis selling what's worth and keeping all the old truck that do be fit for nowt."

"Hm!" said Katherine. "That's bad farming, isn't it?"

"Bad farming, missie? Ay, it *be* bad farming. 'T is wuss than bad. It do be right down wickedness to keep cattle just to turn into coin for a man's own pleasure, and to take the very meat out of the beastes' mouths. What do'ee think, missie?" he said, digging his stick into the ground. . . . "Theer be the Home-close, the best meadow on the farm. . . . Ah, the old master, he used to say, 'Collop,' sez he, 'that meadow has turned out ten pounds' worth of hay an acre this year. . . .' Good crop that, Miss Katherine; and Master Tom what did he do this spring but cart away twenty tons of the best soil in that theer meadow:—draed it away, missie, and what for? Why to make a pleasure ground wi'en for to knock about balls in en wi' his swaitheart. . . . Ha!" said Collop, drawing in a long hissing breath, "if the old master had seen en, he'd ha' knocked en about, he would, like a ball! . . ."

"What's he done with the soil?" said Katherine.

"Why, put en in that old hole by the drive that used to be a quarry, where you used to play, Miss Katherine, when you was a girl. Didn't look well, he sed, coming up the drive to see that old hole. So he had en filled up; and a fine crop o' weeds he hath a-gotten there to be sure. . . ."

Collop jerked his head up and sniffed ironically. "Now if you would stay on a bit, missie, us two could get things a bit straighterer." He turned glassy eyes on Katherine, and drew himself up and waited her answer.

She stood silent, her face grave. Then she lifted her head with a quick little movement of decision. She would show that she was needed. She would prove that she could succeed where Tom had failed.

Collop did not need words to tell him how she had decided. He lifted the palm of his hand in a half-military salute and went on his way.

Katherine's eyes were bright as she passed into the meadows, where the grass was already laid up for cutting. It was thick and lush, and promised a heavy crop. Here

and there a buttercup peeped out, a golden sun paling
the dim moon of the last primrose in the hedge. She
gathered them, and said unconsciously to herself:—

> "'O Love, your fingers hold
> The golden key of the spring.'"

The thought added a deeper radiance to the flowers.
"Brighter than these," she whispered, as her mind reached
out over the blossoms towards another mind, to answering
thoughts, and comradeship, and love. But Franklin's
memory was under lock and key. She dared not open
the Pandora box in which he was hidden. It was Ambrose who filled her thoughts, she told herself, as she
passed along, looking like the spirit of the year in her
green frock, with the wistfulness in her eyes called there
by the tender pulsing life of the spring.

She strolled dreamily on, and, rounding a hedge,
came face to face with two people before she suspected
their presence.

They all stopped together, Tom half-bashful, his arm
dropped from the girl's waist.

"Hillo, Kit, you nearly knocked a fellow over!"

Katherine's eyes shot past him. She held out her
hand, smiling. So this was Tom's friend—no village lass,
but the girl who had driven her home the day before.

Miss Saunders took her hand with a frank laugh.

"So you are Kit!—what luck!"

"Hillo, do you know Peggy?" Tom cried amazed.

"I met Miss Saunders yesterday," Katherine said cor-
dially, delighted to find that Tom's choice was so much
to her own liking.

"Goodness, to think I didn't know you!" Peggy cried.
"Yet it must have been your likeness to Tom that attracted me."

"Of course it was!" said the beaming Tom. Encouraged by Katherine's mildness he slipped his arm round Peggy again. . . . "Kit, this is the rattling girl I was telling you about. . . . We are sweethearts, aren't we, my dear?"

"Rather!" said Miss Saunders, vigorously. "You are out very early, aren't you, Kit?"

"So are you!" said Katherine, laughing

"Oh, well, you see, being a busy woman, I have no time for sentiment unless I make time. And really it is awfully jolly to do one's love-making by sunrise:—

> "'Brushing with hasty steps the dews away
> To greet the sun upon the upland lawn,'

and all the rest of it, don't ye know."

The quotation pleased Katherine. She liked the thought of love in the fresh morning, and it was not haid to find excuses for Tom. What man could resist a walk through green fields with Peggy, when her eyes were tender and the mystery of dawn was round young love?

"I am afraid I shall not be able to say Tom is wasting his time," she said prettily.

"Kit, you are a brick!" Tom exclaimed. "And, I say, since you aren't going to cut up rough about Peggy, you might as well stay on here and keep the old lady quiet "

———

CHAPTER X.

PEGGY AT THE FAIR.

"WELL, it's confounded meddling on your part to interfere with my orders," said Tom, hotly.

His face was very red, he had burst into the breakfast-room in a rage, and he stood looking angrily at Katherine, who was at the table doing accounts.

"It was time someone did meddle," she returned quietly. Her steady eyes probed to his conscience; he shifted his ground uneasily.

"Look here, Kit," he said, changing his tone, "I'm not going to have you fooling round playing master. Jackson wouldn't give credit for the last fodder we had—curse his cheek!—and I told him I'd never give him another order. . . . And you go paying ready money for his rotten stuff."

"We must buy fodder, Tom," said Katherine. "The cows are half-starved. They give a quart of milk where they should give four. . . ."

"Well, that's not my fault. . . . Why don't you speak to Collop?"

"I did. He said we needn't expect milk while the cows are in the hill fields."

"Collop is an old fool!" said Tom, testily. "If I had listened to him I wouldn't have laid up all the meadows for hay this year. . And think what grand crops we should have missed!" He glanced triumphantly at Katherine.

"Meanwhile we lose on the cattle," she said, with an aggravating superiority in her voice. "There isn't enough pasture for the cows, let alone the sheep and the young bullocks."

"And I want to know who gave the men their orders to-day?" Tom ignored the reproach.

"I did," said Katherine. "They can't loaf about all the morning waiting till you come in."

Tom threw down his riding-whip on the table, and lifted his head masterfully.

"Hang it all, Kit! You are playing it rather high, you know. The farm ain't yours."

"It may be mine some day," she interrupted.

Tom remembered his father's will.

"Pooh! not likely," he said. "Anyhow, things can't go on like this. . . . Either you manage the place, or I do. . . . Which is it to be?"

He drew himself up and looked at Katherine, and as he looked the definiteness in his gaze wavered.

Her silence told him that his inches were no match for her will. Her pose, the concentration on her face, her questioning eyes pointed contrasts with his high-handed bluster. The weakness of things left undone unmanned him. For a moment he kept his attitude of indignant protest and gazed sternly at the girl. Then the absurdity of the thing struck him. He slapped his thigh and burst into a good-natured laugh.

"My word, Kit, it's a farce if ever there was one! To think of a shrimp like you challenging me on my own ground! Do they teach farming in newspaper offices? . . . Well, I'm sick of the farm. I don't mind if I let you try your hand at it for a bit."

"Thanks," said Katherine, loftily. "I mean to try."

She could not help a smile at his astonished face.

"You will see that I can do it," she said with decision. Then she rose and put her arm through his coaxingly.

"Meanwhile, Tom dear, do come and help me choose the sheep for Plimpton fair."

"Not I, my fine lady," he said teasingly. "If you manage the farm you manage it by yourself I have plenty on my hands."

"What are you going to do to-day?" she asked.

"Oh, I'm going to Grimple market. . . . And by the way it's time I was off."

He glanced at the clock, and took up his whip.

"I'll go too," said Katherine, eagerly. "I haven't been to market for ages."

It was a fine day. She had been at home a fortnight, and in all that time she had had no amusement. The sunshine beguiled her. She would like to swing through the country lanes on her pony. Tom's careless gaiety was, after all, a relief from the earnest discontent of the Labour leaders. It rested her strained nerves, and toned in with the joyous abandon of nature.

But Tom had made other arrangements for companionship.

"Tut, tut!" he mocked. "How would the grass grow and the potatoes sprout if you were not here to give them a leg up? No, Kit, my dear. If you're a farmer you can't amuse yourself. You must stay at home and do your duty by the land."

Katherine laughed amiably at his enjoyment of the sarcasm. "Well, I'll leave you to represent Great Lowlands at the market," she said good-humouredly. "To be sure, the eggs and butter that should be there will be absent."

She stood at the window watching him as he cantered

away down the drive, after making her a sweeping ironical bow. He looked his very best on horseback.

No wonder that Peggy admired the handsome fellow, Katherine thought with a sigh. Then she dismissed Tom from her mind and went with the old cowman to choose the sheep for Plimpton fair.

Where the road parted by the common, Peggy was waiting for Tom. He saw the pride with which she watched him coming, and it consoled him for Katherine's scorn. Peggy's open devotion restored his self-esteem. What did he care for a midge of a girl, when he could twist a fine woman like Peggy round his finger? Tush! let Katherine prove her superiority. He was quite willing to give her the chance. . . . Besides, now he could spend his time as he liked. No one could reproach him for neglecting his work when Katherine had taken it out of his hands. There was a fine carelessness, a triumphant gaiety in his manner that delighted Peggy as they rode to Grimple. She answered his mood in kind: they jumped the fences, and raced each other, and finally, flushed and laughing, they entered the town,—a pair of hearty young lovers with the spring in their blood.

They put up at the Wheat Sheaf, and then walked towards the market-place, the girl's face sobering, her eyes critical and alert for business. It was Grimple horse fair, and more than one young farmer stopped her for an opinion of the horse he had bought or wanted to buy.

Tom stood beside her, flaunting his intimacy with Miss Saunders. He was proud of her knowledge and smartness. They reflected credit on himself, who had taught her.

In the High Street a chestnut mare was showing her paces, and at the same time her vices. Peggy stopped.

She stuck her hands in the pockets of her riding-coat, and, head on one side, a cynical smile on her lips, watched the performance.

At last the mare unseated her rider, and came trotting easily down the street. Peggy went forward, caught the bridle, and patted the quivering animal into confidence. Then, the reins on one arm, and her habit hitched up on the other, she sauntered up to the dealer, who was swearing at finding business "off" for the moment.

"What do you want for her?" she asked casually.

"Five and fifty guineas, miss, and not a penny less."

Peggy liked the look of the mare now she was standing firm and square on her legs, but there was a fine irony in her voice. "You're surely not opening your mouth half wide enough for such a sweet buck-jumper.... Here, I'll give you thirty pounds for her, and take her faults in as a gift."

She had seen the powerful double bit, too high by an inch in the mouth, and the curb chain a couple of links too tight. "An easy Pelham, a slack curb, and a pair of light hands are all that she wants," she thought.

She stepped back a few paces, and let her eye run first over the mare's near side from between her ears to the tail, then in the same way looked at the off side.

"Hm!" she said, pursing up her lips.

She stooped and felt the legs with their tendons like iron rods, and finished up by opening the mouth.

"Rising five," she said to herself, "and the look in her face is mettle and courage, not temper..... I'll have a deal. . . ." She turned to the man. "Hm!" she said again, disparagingly. "If guineas will part you I'll spring the extra shillings and risk it."

"Not by a houseful!" replied the dealer.

"Well, you have the mare and I have the money," she said, turning away indifferently.

"Don't be in such a hurry," said the man. "The mare's shadow on the wall is worth all I'm asking you. But I'm no Quaker; you can take her or leave her at five-and-thirty."

"Done in pounds!" Peggy cried, "if you give me a sovereign back for luck."

"We'll split that," returned the dealer, "and the mare's yours." Peggy haggled no longer, but, swinging her habit round, found the opening in the skirt which led to a pocket tied round her waist. She drew out a roll of notes, and counting out seven offered them to the dealer, then opened her other palm for the luck-penny.

This the man solemnly and half-reluctantly jerked out, and then Peggy delivered up the notes

"Ever carried a lady?" she said carelessly.

"Well . . . not as I knows on." The man scratched his head deprecatingly;—but he had his money. "I doubt the last lady as had her would sooner mount a clothes-horse than that there mare," he added.

"Bring her round to the Wheat Sheaf," Peggy commanded. She looked her purchase up and down, then turned to Tom, her white teeth showing in a broad smile.

"What do you make of her? Ain't she a beauty?"

"She's a nasty temper," said Tom. "What'll you do with her?"

She laughed. "Sell her again for ten pounds more."

"I'd like to see you do it!"

"You'll see!" she returned.

At the Wheat Sheaf Peggy told the hostler to put her

saddle on the mare. She went out herself and saw that bit and curb were well set.

"You aren't going to mount that tricky business?" Tom cried.

She tossed her head. "I bet I am!"

"I'll not have it," said Tom, masterfully. "It's as much as your neck is worth. I forbid you to attempt it."

"Forbid your grandmother!" she said lightly, and leaped into the saddle. The mare reared, but Peggy sat her trimly. A minute after, with many a prance and curvet, they were making towards the crowd in the High Street.

Tom watched the progress, anger fighting with anxiety. It was the first time Peggy had defied him; but as he saw her skill in controlling the mare, vexation and anxiety gave way to pride. He loitered about, listening to the criticisms on her.

"My word, but the lass is a bold 'un! And she's gotten spirit. I wouldn't be paid to mount that tempersome baggage."

"You! You couldn't mount a bubbly-jock! . . . Peg Saunders 'll mount any brute living. . . . ."

"She's a fine smart maid . . . well set up, too."

"As fine a figure of a woman as ever God made! She'll take some breaking-in . . . the sort o' wife to suit me."

"Lord! I'd as lief wed a steam-plough. No breaking in there. He'll be a bold man as tries it. . . ."

The talk tickled Tom's sense of ownership. He stroked his moustache proudly. He was going to marry this spirited woman. He could master her as easily as she mastered the mare. . . . The smile in his eyes was dimmed by a sudden thought. She had taken her own

The Gods Arrive. 8

way just now in spite of him. Would the question of
wills between them always end in his defeat? . . . A fierce
wish to prove his mastery awoke in him. Peggy had
never seemed so desirable as now, when, seeing her
prowess, he was uncertain of her. It would be worth a
man's while to manage a woman who could manage a
horse like that. . . .

He waited about for her; and when he lifted her
down from the saddle the fire in his glance set her pulses
beating.

She turned from him to a man who had followed her
and was now examining the mare. He was one of her
customers. The consciousness on her face gave way to a
business-like alertness.

"Any business, Mr. Rogers?" she said, with a sudden
brilliant smile.

"Well," he said slowly, "I dunno as I'd made up my
mind."

"I ain't selling," said Peggy. She nodded to the
hostler. "Take her in. Give her a feed."

"Not so fast, not so fast, Miss Saunders. Fact is, I
like her looks . . . nice feet . . . good action . . ."

"Don't I know that?" Peggy laughed. "She'll foot it
nicely to Plimpton."

"That depends, that depends, young lady. You're
in such a hurry . . . now, then, what'll you take?"

"She's vicious," said Peggy, drily. "Has a pretty
trick of shying."

"All the more reason to sell when you can."

"Think I don't know blood when I see it?" She
moved away.

"I'll give you forty sovereigns; there now, that's an
offer . . ."

Peggy walked towards the inn-door. "Forty-five;" he followed at her ear. The handle of the door was in her hand. "Fifty! and here's the money. . . ."

"And there's the mare!" she turned unexpectedly on him.

They struck hands on the bargain.

Tom hurried after her into the inn-parlour. His pulses were beating faster than usual, spurred by the praises of the girl's spirit and cleverness. His eyes had not lost the abandon of the ride to Gimple; and, meeting them, the madness of the morning overtook Peggy again.

She laughed as she ran round to the other side of the table. "I've made sixteen sovs on the mare, Tom. Want 'em?"

"Bother your money . . . I want you," Tom answered.

CHAPTER XI.

THE ETHICS OF THE SITUATION.

"WELL, you *are* blue!" Peggy shouted to the melancholy figure in the boat. "Why are you so miserable, Kit?"

Katherine was sitting with one of Fan's puppies in the boat, which was drifting among the lily leaves and duckweed in the middle of the pond. Her face was hopeless, but it cleared at the sight of Peggy standing on the bank, a hand on each hip, her legs planted firmly apart.

"Will you come aboard?" Katherine called.

"That was my intention," said Peggy.

Katherine took the oars and pulled to the bank, and Peggy settled herself in the seat in the stern of the boat.

"You are a nice midsummer maiden," she said severely. "What in the world are you grizzling for? Anything wrong?"

"Everything!" Katherine cried passionately. "Everything!"

"That is to say, Tom isn't behaving," said Peggy, chewing a twig of willow with a wry face.

"It isn't only Tom," said Katherine. "It's mother, and the house, and the land, and the hay, and the cows. . . . The whole business is maddening!"

"Your liver is out of order," said Peggy, encouragingly. "The place is trim and tight;—the garden is a pretty dear, as Martha says."

"That is just it!" Katherine interrupted. "Whatever my pair of hands can do I may do; but the instant I need help or money I'm stopped short. The gardens are in order, and I want to set to work on the farm; but Tom won't help, and mother frets and says there's no money. Tom's mismanagement must have done away with what little there was. Farming doesn't pay now unless you put your brains into it."

"What's wrong with Tom's farming?" said Peggy, shortly. She did not like the subject, but she was eager to defend Tom.

"He cares for nothing as long as he has a good horse to ride, and makes a good show at the fairs, and has money to spend. Look at the cattle. . . . You know what the poor starved things look like. Last winter there wasn't enough for them to eat; and there were forty young bullocks he had to sell for a song in the very cheapest time. He'd have made double the price if he could have waited till spring. Now he has laid up all the meadows in hay, and left thirty acres of the worst pasture for ten cows, three hundred sheep, all the calves, and the horses. It's perfect madness!"

"Hm!" grunted Peggy. "Tom must have his reasons . . . ."

"Reasons!" Katherine cried bitterly. "With the men clamouring for corn for the horses, and the shepherd for cake for the sheep, and Collop worried about the cows . . ."

"Collop is a cheerful soul," laughed Peggy. "I don't wonder he makes the cows too miserable to give milk."

"It's not a laughing matter, Peggy. . . . I go to the fodder merchant, he can't give us any credit. I go to mother;—there's no money. I go to Tom. 'Sell the damned sheep,' he says. 'And how will you buy for next year?' I answer, and the cows are starving. It's a hopeless mess!"

"Well, cut the hay, and give it 'em," said Peggy.

"We have cut some, but think of the waste of it," said Katherine.

Peggy shrugged her shoulders. "Goodness! you *are* hipped."

"You would get hipped in my place," Katherine said furiously. "I am wasting my life. . . . If it were not for the pups and the boat I'd have nothing to make my days tolerable."

"You are lucky to have two things to make them bearable," said Peggy, drily. "I am grateful for one."

"Your profession?" said Katherine.

Peggy sat up straight. "Good gracious no! A profession is only a makeshift. Love is woman's real business. I can imagine devoting myself to horse-training, but only if Tom were in it; so it's probably really Tom that I should devote myself to."

"But are you doing even that?" said Katherine, severely.

Peggy flushed rosily, remembering the hours she spent with Tom.

"I think I do," she said, hanging her head, and attempting to look coy by the aid of a finger in her mouth.

"Goose!" said Katherine, catching her expression. "I didn't mean that," contemptuously; "that isn't devoting yourself to Tom,—that's only fooling with him. Are you making him a stronger man? Is he doing better work because of you?"

The two faced each other, Katherine looking straight at Peggy with firm lines gathering round her mouth. She had long wanted this talk with Peggy.

Peggy seemed to shrink and grow small. She tried to wriggle out of her position.

"Aren't you managing the farm?" she said suggestively.

"Yes, I am; but why? Because Tom neglected it for you." There was silence for a while. A boat is an awkward thing to quarrel in, and Katherine held the oars. Suddenly Peggy's eyes fell.

"I'm afraid you're right, Kit," she said humbly; "but you know I have no influence with him."

"No influence?" repeated Katherine, scornfully. . . . She stopped. What would she gain by hectoring Peggy? .. She went on more gently: "You must have some influence, Peggy, good or bad. Everyone has. . . ."

"Well, perhaps mine's bad according to your reckoning," said Peggy, breezily. "But you know, Kit, I'm not sure that mine is a worse way than yours. . . . Anyhow it's a less melancholy one; and it's better to make two people happy than one miserable. You like going in harness. I'd rather be an untamed colt and follow my own free will and fancy."

Katherine shook her head. Her own feelings had been too long under the mastery of her will for her to be much in sympathy with Peggy. Deep down in her heart was the buried thought of Franklin, stirring now and then and forcing a way up to her consciousness. It framed her answer now.

"When one loves a man one wants to be an influence in his life, not a doll for him to play with," she said gravely.

Peggy shrugged her shoulders. "Bless you! we are as different as we can be. I'm a gay butterfly, happy in the sun, and miserable out of it. Just now I'm quite content to sun myself in Tom's smiles."

She nodded and laughed at Katherine's sober face.

"You make a mistake in giving him everything he wants, and demanding nothing, Peggy. By and by when he meets someone else he will throw you off like an old glove. . . ."

Peggy snapped her fingers—"Hear! O Cassandra!"

"I'm no prophet," said Katherine, quietly; "but everyone knows that the future will grow out of the present. Tom has no stability. He is horribly reckless. As soon as he gets a thing he doesn't care for it. Because of him I am wasting my life here, and I see no way out."

"There is always a way out," said Peggy.

"How?" Katherine asked.

"The white gate."

Katherine stared at her. "You mean? . . ."

Peggy nodded.

"That's the traitor's gate," said Katherine, shortly. "I'd never go out by it."

"One never knows," said Peggy, knitting her eyebrows together. Her face was suddenly clouded. Katherine gazed at her surprised.

"Is that your butterfly mood?" she asked. "Look here, Peggy; when I came down here last month I felt like that; and it was you who helped me out of it. You seemed so free and healthy, and you feasted on life. I never saw anyone more simply glad. . . . And all the time you have had this skeleton of a thought at the feast. . . ."

"It was you who took my skeleton out of his cupboard, Kit. But it's well to know your resources," said Peggy, heartily. "If life gets the bit in his teeth and runs away with you, it's well to put your hand on the curb. When your horse won't move, you like to know your spur is on. . . . Hand me over that puppy, like a good soul."

"Certainly not, he's asleep. It's a shame to disturb him."

"What a mixture you are!" Peggy exclaimed. "You are hard enough on your kind, but tenderness itself with young things. Martha says you are a born mother. . . ."

"Martha thinks to bear children is the whole duty of woman." Katherine smiled. "She never learned the shorter catechism of the modern woman."

"She is a pagan," said Peggy, briskly, "and I love her for it. . . . Kit, I see Tom eating strawberries. I must go and help him."

"Help him! Go and stop him!" Katherine cried.

"Mark and Tonina are coming over this afternoon. We must have strawberries for them."

"Hm! What is Tonina like?" Peggy questioned.

"A strawberry," Katherine answered. "Red and round and sweet, with little hard seeds of obstinacy in her."

"Why did they come to Grimple for the honeymoon?"

"Mark had to go on business;—they are starting a Labour Bureau there. I don't think Tonina is enjoying it. She says there isn't a decent inn in the place."

"There's the Wheat Sheaf," said Peggy, quickly. "A dear old place with large rambling rooms . . ."

She stopped suddenly and awkwardly, but was reassured by the other's unconsciousness.

"I know," said Katherine. "Tom put up there the night he stayed over the horse fair."

Katherine was pulling to shore; Peggy stood in the boat ready to get out, her face red and eager, her feet impatient.

"Don't pull in," she said. "I'll jump as soon as we are near enough."

Katherine disdainfully noticed her excitement. What a poor thing was a woman's heart when a man like Tom could call that rosy consciousness to Peggy's face! . . .

"You can't jump," she said. "The pond is deep at this end."

"Pooh!" said Peggy. "Besides, I can swim."

She stepped on the seat as she spoke.

"Don't!" Katherine screamed "You overbalance . . ."

Another instant, and the two girls were under the water. They rose together and Peggy seized Katherine's sleeve. Then with a sweep of her disengaged arm she caught the rudder of the boat and held on to it.

"You must swim ashore, Kit."

"I can't!" Katherine gasped.   "My skirts . . ."

"All right: I'll manage. . . ."

"The puppy! the puppy!" Katherine screamed, as the dog rose close to them and sank.

One instant Peggy thought of the network of roots, and the difficulty of the dive; then "Hold on to the boat," she cried, and loosing Katherine disappeared after the pup.

Katherine's teeth were chattering.   It seemed a long, long minute before Peggy rose.   She shook the water from her hair and floated alongside the boat.

"Take the precious pup, Kit, and I'll get you both to land."

But Martha Collop had seen the accident from Milkmaid Cottage, and was running down to the pond, Fan at her heels.   At the sight of the puppy Fan gave a yelp, pushed into the water, seized the pup, and swam to shore.

"Thanks be to goodness the baby is safe!" Martha screamed.   "But oh! my good fortunes, you'll take your deaths the pair on you . . . not to speak o' my rheumatiz . . . and who's to fetch you out?"

But in a few strokes Peggy brought Katherine to the bank, where the two stood, shivering and laughing, while Fan licked the puppy and comforted it.

"Ah, the pretty pet!" said Martha, "a sup of his mammy, that will hearten he. . . . And you're both very wild young misses, and deserve what you've gotten, yes, you does. . . . Come right into the kitchen.   I were making Collop a sup o' onion gruel, and Fan shows as the way to warm the outside is to warm the inside.   So you'll both on you just drink it."

Katherine shuddered at the name of onion gruel, but Peggy shouted with laughter. The June day was hot; a blazing sun struck through their wet clothes, warming them. They could afford to laugh at Martha's threats.

"Ah, you may laugh, missie," said Martha, reproachfully. "'T would ha' been no matter for laughing if the baby were drownded."

Peggy's face sobered, but it cleared again, even before Katherine spoke.

"It was Miss Saunders who saved the pup, Martha. She really risked her life for it."

"And quite right," said Martha. "I don't know what Fan would ha' said if her had lost en. Her thinks a sight o' that pup, being the last one borned. . . . But go right into the wash'us, duckies, the couple on you; and take off your things where you won't spoil no floors. I'll fetch you my Sunday gown, Miss Katherine; but a pair o' Collop's breeks will be more the cut o' missie there."

Martha chuckled gleefully as she hobbled off.

Seeing the two girls that afternoon no one would have recognised the bedraggled figures of the morning.

To impress Mark and his wife Peggy had put on her most dashing tweed with brass buttons. Katherine's soft delaine contrasted with Tonina's black and yellow stripes

Tonina was suffering from an interview with Mrs. Fleming; but in the open air her spirits came back. Katherine and Tom made much of her; and the delightful orchard, the rose garden, the strawberries, atoned for her depressing welcome. Mrs. Fleming's most elegant attitude on the sofa, her daintiest tea-gown, and tearful pathos had adorned Tonina's reception.

Mark was proud to show Tonina his home. He had

never seen Great Lowlands in such excellent order, and
it did not occur to him that it was Katherine's work.

"Kit ought to thank me for sending her down here,"
he said to himself. "I wouldn't mind having such a
comfortable berth myself. It's done her no end of good.
She's a different girl, softer and gentler too. . . ."

He glanced critically at her, a girlish figure beside
Peggy.

There was a look on her face it had not worn in
Goodge Street. Mark had brought Franklin over from
Grimple, and the first sight of him had transformed Katherine. She had greeted him quietly and coldly, but her
heart had wakened at his touch, and the life of a blossoming springtime was on her face. She knew that whatever she might profess to believe, her love for Franklin was
not dead.

He had come to Great Lowlands to get away from
Labour questions; but when he saw Katherine he wondered if he had thought of meeting her. . . . He would
have liked to ask her about her life, but she gave him no
opportunity.

She left him to Mark while she fluttered about, chat-
ting to Tonina, laughing with Peggy, setting tea in the
orchard.

His eyes followed her. He found Mark's conversation a tiresome intrusion on his thoughts He was wondering if this soft-gowned, soft-eyed girl was the passionate
Katherine of his remembrance.

"She is finding her real self; she is developing," he
thought as he watched her.

By and by Mark went into the house to talk to his
mother; and Franklin, with a certain irritation, found himself handed over to Peggy. Her independence and slang

set him musing if he had ever thought of Katherine as mannish, or modern, or unwomanly. He looked again at Katherine, who was beside Tonina, and his eyes lighted up pleasantly as they rested on the slim, girlish figure. How simple and dainty she was contrasted with Tonina's gorgeous colouring! . . .

Tom had fallen under Tonina's fascinations. She liked the admiration in his blue eyes; and, in her desire to make friends with Mark's people, she set herself to charm the handsome brother. Her flattery was new, and subtler than Peggy's honest admiration. Tom loitered beside her, neglecting Peggy, who affected to be engrossed by Franklin.

Tea was spread near the blossoming rhododendrons in the orchard, where the grass was newly mown. There was a smell of new scones, and cream stood thick in glass jugs. The china was old and quaint, set in a tracery of golden bars, that quivered with the trembling of the leaves.

Tonina saw it all with delight, and trilled out gaily:—

"Under the greenwood tree
Who loves to lie with me,
And tune his merry note
Unto the blackbird's throat,
   Come hither, come hither, come hither!
Here shall he see
No enemy
But winter and rough weather."

Tom gazed admiringly at her. She looked with her red cheeks and dark skin and flashing eyes like some brilliant flower among the grey apple-boughs. They gathered round her at her song, but Mark drew her down beside him on the grass.

"But I want to sing," Tonina pouted, half rebelling.

"But I want tea," Mark answered, "and it's getting cold."

"Oh, but this man is *bête!*" Tonina laughed, with a little shrug. "He has not the soul of the artist; he cares but for his dinner. . . . A strawberry,—it is more to him than the divinest sonata. . . ."

Mark stopped her grumbling by a strawberry between her red lips. "At this moment strawberries and cream are divinest realities," he said. "Come, Kit, you wouldn't change places with us now, would you? This is better than Goodge Street, eh?"

Franklin twisted round sharply to Katherine. He wished to hear her answer. He saw her sudden flush, the old bitterness hardening her mouth.

"It is not always afternoon at Great Lowlands," she said.

Franklin bent towards her. "Would you choose to go back to town and leave all this, Miss Katherine?"

"Would I choose?" she answered; and the cry of pain in her voice startled him. . . . He wondered if he had imagined it when the next instant she turned smiling to Peggy.

"What do you say, Peggy—town or country?"

"My goodness! How can any person with eyes and a nose ask a question like that?" said Peggy.

"But I think that Katherine is right," Tonina broke in. "The country, oh, it is very dull. . . . I am bored at Grimple. . . . I would I had run away to London again."

Katherine looked quickly at Tonina. There was a pout on her lips, and a longing in her eyes that had not been there in the old days. Mark kept his face bent on his plate, and Franklin broke the awkward silence.

"It is my fault that you are bored, Mrs. Fleming. I take up Mark's time, and you are left too much alone."

"Ah, no!" said Tonina, lifting her big eyes pathetically. "It is not then that I am bored. For no! I have my violin. . . . It is the stupid Mark who is jealous of my violin-love. . . ."

"I should think so, indeed," Tom exclaimed. "A man would be jealous of a fiddlestick if it took you away from him. . . ."

Katherine led the talk away from the subject, and when they had finished tea she rose.

"You will let me run away now? The cowman is ill, and I want to see to the cows."

A little later they saw her going through the meadow, driving before her the udder-laden cows. She had changed her delaine for a print petticoat. She carried a stick and a pail, and her hair blew loosely in the wind.

Franklin sprang to his feet.

"Did you ever see the like?" said Tom. "That's one of Kit's fads, to milk the cows like any farm lass . . . ."

"There's no need for her to do that sort of work," said Mark, angrily biting at his moustache. His face was darker than usual.

Tom shrugged his shoulders. "Collop is ill, and she says the boy doesn't milk properly. She is a regular missus, is Kit, and makes everybody about the place sit up. She's too masterful for me."

"She is a brick," said Peggy, suddenly. "A right-down sensible girl. She is worth a round dozen of ordinary women."

Franklin glanced kindly at Peggy, whose face had flushed in her vindication of Katherine. Then his eyes strayed to the figure driving the cows in the distance.

By and by he strolled off towards the farmyard. It was not difficult to find the cow-sheds. He stopped by the window and looked in. Katherine sat on a stool milking, her head pressed against Suke's lean side, her sleeve rolled up, showing the dimple at her elbow. The milk was frothing into the pail in a steady flow, and Franklin noticed that her fingers had grown plump. Her face in profile had lost its sharpness. He saw her lips move, and heard the words:—

> "Though I do my best, I shall scarce succeed,
> But what if I fail of my purpose here?"

She was silent, then she began again in a more assured tone:—

> "Let a man contend to the uttermost
> For his life's set prize, be it what it will . . ."

With face twitching, Franklin drew back from the window. It touched him whimsically to hear Browning quoted to the cows. The scene jarred on him, showing him a glimpse of the sentimental enthusiast. It implied so much more true socialism and New Religion than Katherine had ever possessed that it branded insincerity on the whole of her farm life. . . . In a little while the frown cleared from his eyes. Almost against his will he went into the shed.

She looked up, but there was no light of welcome in her eyes.

"Don't come too near, please. Suke has a trick of kicking. And I am no longer in society dress."

"It is all very pretty and pastoral," he began, then stopped. "No, it isn't," he said bluntly. "It's affected and exaggerated. . . . Miss Katherine, can't you, even here in the simplicity of nature, do without a . . . a pose?"

She looked up sharply. "You men are so consistent! When I wore a pretty frock Mark told me I could not be a working-woman. Now I wear the dress of my work and you call it a pose!"

"It's not gowns, it's the spirit in which you work!" he said impatiently.

She looked steadily at him. . . . "Yes?"

He saw the dangerous light in her eyes, the proud set of her head. A sudden cowardice seized him. No, he could not find fault with her. His expression softened. . . . His eyes stayed with hers. . . . There was a deep, full silence. Then it seemed that Katherine's glance had fled trembling from that long contact with his; and he was left alone burning with strange fire.

"Would you . . . would you like some milk?" she faltered.

"I . . . think . . . no . . . I can't take it. . . ." He scarcely knew what he was saying. . . . "Have you nearly finished? Can I speak to you?"

"We can talk here," said Katherine, hurriedly. "How is the Labour question progressing? I sha'n't feel that I am. . . . wasting time . . . if we talk . . . while I work. . . ."

"Don't you think it's . . . unusual . . . to touch on that subject with a milkmaid?" he smiled, recovering himself.

"I think it is," she answered coolly. "And don't you think there is something wrong with a question that is not to be discussed with the class it affects most?" . . .

Her eyes darkened with thought; her fingers paused on the cow's udder. . . . "The Labour question seems to affect the labourer less than it affects the Labour leader," she added.

The Gods Arrive.   9

"Yes?"

"Oh, don't you see?" she cried eagerly. "Look at the people round here; they know nothing of questions. They eat and they sleep, and work and are healthy. The problem of existence doesn't trouble them . . . it solves itself."

"Then you have lost sympathy with my work?"

She hung her head, but he had seen the colour flood her cheeks.

"It is not that," she said shyly. "But all these questions are like the customs civilisation forces on us. They only cramp and distress us. Why don't we leave ourselves to nature? Earth would support her children if we lived simply and naturally."

"The life here satisfies you?" he asked.

"Satisfies me?" she said bitterly. "I work like any farm drudge, and for what? . . . I get no thanks. . . . Tom and mother oppose me on every point, and you think . . ."

"I think you are doing good work," he interrupted hurriedly; "better work than if you were—for instance— writing an inadequate treatise on the Labour Movement. . . ."

She started up passionately, and knocked over the milking stool.

"You don't understand! You never do understand me!" she cried. "You have no faith in me. You think I am good for nothing but this . . . though at Newnham . . ."

Her voice broke, but her eyes flashed eloquently.

His silence piqued her into consciousness of her short petticoat and her bare arms. The anger died from her face, and a reluctant smile answered the gleam in his eyes.

"Oh, I know there is humour in the situation," she said, half-laughing, half-angry. "It is funny enough when I think of it. Pray laugh, if you want to."

His face lighted up.

"I don't want to laugh, Miss Katherine. I want to shake hands and congratulate you on possessing a sense of humour."

She laughed a little as she put her hand into the one he held out.

"It is harder than yours," she said bashfully. "I am a labourer now. . . ."

"Yes," he said, "you are working. I am only thinking of working. . . . I want you to let me help you. . . ."

She drew away her hand suddenly from his lingering hold.

"You can carry that pail to the house," she said, drily. "You will see one of the maids there."

She pointed to the pail, but he looked hesitatingly at her.

"And are you coming too?"

"No," she said brusquely. "I am going to feed the pigs."

Franklin took up the pail and walked away without another word. The girl piqued him. He was baffled by her contradictoriness. This brusque manner was cold water on the flames lighted a few minutes before. "To feed the pigs" jarred again on his trust in her. Was it possible that the girl could be sincere when she seized every opportunity of assuming an alien character? What did she mean by all this show of humility, this doing of the lowliest work of the farm? Tush! she had no sense of proportion; she overdid her part. . . .

By the time he reached the house he had worked

himself up into the old condition of irritation against
Katherine, and it mastered his wish to talk to her about
his plans.

CHAPTER XII.

GODS OR MORTALS?

WITHOUT knocking, Tonina came bursting through the
French window.   Inside the room she stopped, laughing
at Katherine's astonishment.

"Tonina?"

"And who else?" Tonina cried gaily, kissing her.
She threw hat and gloves on the sofa and sat down.

"Pouf! it is warm!"

"Tonina, what has happened?" Katherine asked
anxiously.

The letters from Ridgmont Gardens had lately hinted
of difficulties between Mark and his wife.

"I've run away," said Tonina, taking a malicious
pleasure in Katherine's alarm.   "I would amuse myself.
That is not possible when one is married."

Katherine's face cleared at sight of the wicked eyes
a-sparkle.

"How will you amuse yourself at Great Lowlands?"
she asked, smiling.   "And how will Mark amuse himself
without you?"

"Pouf!" said Tonina again, sweeping Mark away with
a wave of her hand.   "When Mark is alone he bores
himself; when I am with him he bores me."

"Haven't you been well, Tonina?"

Katherine studied the face, thinner and more care-
worn than on Tonina's first visit to the farm a year

before. Tonina's gay manner dropped off her like a mask. She sank back on the cushions.

"I am tired, little Katherine," she said plaintively. "And I am hungry for the sun and the light. And there is no more music in me. . . . And I remembered the summer, and the merry life under the apple-trees; and I said to Mark, 'I will go to little Katherine. . . .'"

"Tonina, that was lovely of you!" Katherine lifted the drooping face and kissed it heartily. "I am so glad you thought of coming. You must be in the sun all day. You shall help me with the hay and in the gardens, and you will soon grow strong again. . . ."

"The good God forbid!" Tonina laughed. "Figure me with the hands all red and the face all brown! . . . Ah, no! But we will eat strawberries together, and pick the roses, and lie under the trees, and so will we make holiday."

Katherine threw a dismayed thought to her work. How could she spare time from the farm to make holiday with Tonina?

"But, Tonina, I can't idle all day. You must work with me or amuse yourself without me. . . ."

Tonina pouted. "Oh, but that is quite impossible. If then you do not amuse me, who will?"

Before Katherine could answer they heard a gate fall back noisily, and a sound of hoofs ringing on the road.

"There is Tom!" Katherine said. "He has been trying one of Peggy's horses. He says he wants to buy it; but it will end by her giving it him. But it's a lovely creature . . ."

Tonina darted to the window, and clapped her hands at the sight of Tom, mounted superbly, trotting down the drive.

"Ah! but he is Phœbus Apollo, this gay Tom!" she cried. "I would Mark looked like that . . . Tom must teach me to ride also."

"I'll be thankful if you can get him to do as much," said Katherine, drily. "I never saw such an idle fellow."

"So the better for me," Tonina cried gleefully. "So he shall amuse me. Let us go to meet this idle monster."

She sprang out of the window and ran down the drive. Her red frock caught up, a many-frilled petticoat falling about her like the petals of a scarlet rose, made her a sudden blossom under the green linden branches.

Tom reined up before the brilliant little creature that danced like a will-o'-the-wisp in his path. He leaped from the saddle, smiling his brightest welcome. Tonina caught his hand in both hers and shot radiant eyes at him.

"Set me on this splendid horse, you handsome Tom. I too would look divine."

Tom reddened and laughed bashfully as he lifted her to the saddle and held her there while Katherine led Rocket along the drive.

In three days Tonina had made her own place in the house. She talked to Mrs. Fleming, fascinated Tom, and did not interfere with Katherine.

Out of doors she wanted no society but Tom's. He taught her to ride, to drive, to row. When they were not engaged with these serious occupations they were playing hide-and-seek in the hay, or tennis in the old quarry. Tonina's violin lay dumb in its case.

Peggy was breaking in a young horse, and did not join the idle pair, who made holiday for a long fortnight.

Then one evening Tonina took her violin, and played for hours. . . . The next morning she left the farm as suddenly as she had arrived. She had found her art again.

She stood at the carriage window tossing kisses to Katherine, her old bright self. But Tom watched her from the platform with a new look on his face.

. . . . .

That afternoon Katherine was weeding a bed of onions when a shadow fell on her work. It was Peggy, who had come up unobserved.

"Hillo, Kit! So Tonina's gone at last?"

"Why didn't you come to say good-bye?" Katherine asked.

"Afraid of betraying my grief at losing her," said Peggy. "Has Tom recovered from his yet?"

"Tom? I haven't seen Tom," said Katherine, straightening herself. "What do you mean, Peggy?"

"You blind bat! Haven't you noticed his infatuation?"

"Don't be absurd, Peggy," said Katherine, impatiently. "It is not like you to talk in this way."

Peggy laughed lightly. "Well, we'll not quarrel over Tom. Tonina's gone, and it's all right."

"It would have been all right, however long she had stayed," said Katherine, doggedly.

Peggy laughed again. "Let's forget Tonina. . . . Did you see that your friend Franklin had been distinguishing himself? He opposed all the Labour people in the coal strike; and in spite of them he has made terms with the masters and got a victory for the men."

"How splendid!" Katherine exclaimed, flushing.

The thing was with her for the rest of the day. It

woke the slumbering thought of Franklin, but she was too busy to dwell on her pride in him.

At last night came, and the house was still. She climbed to her room, and throwing open her lattice, she drank in the peace of the moonlit night. There was peace in her heart too.

Success had come that summer with the fruit. The garden was paying well. Strawberries and new potatoes were bringing in already a harvest of silver.

Mrs. Fleming wept at the indignity of selling "like common gardeners," and Tom mocked; but Katherine went her way, being helped by Collop and Martha.

It was easy enough to have her way. Mrs. Fleming, seeing that she was not consulted in house or farm, spent her days on the sofa, reading novels; and during the last fortnight Katherine might have sold all their stock and Tom would not have known it.

Tired as she was, Katherine felt a glow of pleasure in her work. It was pleasant to know the men said Miss Fleming was best man at Great Lowlands, and was saving the farm. If the thought of her ruined career came to her she put it aside. Life was not over. When the farm was saved she would return to London, write her book, and become a leader in the Labour movement. It was right that she should return. Tonina had told her that Mark had given up the cause, and taken a post as editor of a society paper. It paid better than public questions, and the flat in Ridgmont Gardens was expensive.

Katherine's lips curled as she thought of Mark. Tonina's talk of him showed that he had grown mercenary and selfish. Well, she would return to help the people's cause. Meanwhile she was not wasting time. On the farm and in the village she saw the Labour question from the inside, and she felt she had a surer grip of the subject.

She had more grip of herself too. A year of out-door life had settled her nerves, her ideas were no longer hysterical; she had more balance. She had found that the educated mind told on the farm as well as in journalism.

She had gained other knowledge as well. She had learned the secrets of sky and cloud; of the warm red earth and its burden of green, and the knowledge was all the fairer for the Greek idea in which she could enfold it.

The breezes had more life when she summoned them to the Tower of the Winds and saw the winged procession floating round the capital. Every tree she knew held its Dryad, every stream its Naiad. In the torn furrows of earth she had glimpses of life that "made her less forlorn;" and in every field she saw Demeter with the wistful Persephone beside her.

"It is a good life," she said to herself, as she looked through the grey lichened trunks, and saw on the grass the trembling moonlight bars like the score of some wizard melody. "It is a good life; but the gods don't arrive; not Jove and not Eros."

Her thoughts turned wistfully to Franklin. He had kept silence all these months, and had never returned to the farm. And yet she had been conscious of a change in him the last time she had seen him. There had certainly been meaning in that glance. . . .

She pulled herself together. Had she not resented his persistent misunderstanding of her? Had she not set aside the thought of him all these months? . . .

But she was proud of him to-day, of his independence and truth. He was a strong man, not a pretty boy like Celandine Ambrose. He was blunt, even rough in manner, but his grave face held possibilities of tenderness. His eyes could be wonderfully kind. . . .

She stopped herself again. . . . After all, Franklin was nothing to her. . . . And why should she dream of love? Mark had loved, yet he had grown selfish. Peggy loved, and it made her unkind and suspicious. Martha loved, and she had to bear the burden of Collop's failing health. "Oh, what a plague is love!" Katherine sighed. "Why should any woman wait for it as the gift of the gods?" And yet . . . Ah! it was a good gift, with all its pain and disillusion and agony. . . . Peggy had had the gladness of the merry dawn in the corn-fields; and Martha helping her old man down the valley was tasting the sacrament of love.

Tears gathered in Katherine's eyes. "Neither death nor life, nor things present nor things to come, will bring us anything better than love!" she cried passionately. . . . "And I would give up everything for his love. . . . He doesn't know how empty his life is. . . . And he will grow old and need a woman's love. . . . If he only knew how I love him! . . ."

She looked into the shadows, and her face showed sharp and strained in the moonlight.

Suddenly her eyes sprang between the branches below. Something whiter than the light was moving there.

She leaned forward, holding her breath, and her hands tightened on each other. . . . Dim and cold and ghostly two figures threaded the light and shade of the orchard. The bare, beautiful forms were surely more than mortal. The wind carried their voices through the orchard in soft whisperings.

Katherine scarcely breathed. "The god's arrive," she thought; "Jove himself and Eros. . . ."

She pinched her arm to prove that she was awake. Then a cloud darkened the moon, and when she could see again, the orchard was empty and silent but for the quivering music bars on the grass.

She turned dazed into the room. Who could be in the orchard at that hour? Tom had long ago gone to bed, and the men left the farm at sundown. Besides, the naked figures had been slight and boyish. . . . Who could it have been if not unearthly visitants?

Like a pleased child Katherine clapped her hands and laughed aloud.

She had seen—

> "White presences upon the hills,
> And heard the voices of the immortal gods."

PART II.

CHAPTER I.

OH, WHAT A PLAGUE IS LOVE!

"WE shall soon have a frost," said Katherine, blowing on her fingers, red and tingling with cold. "Peggy, don't you love these autumn days?"

It was Sunday afternoon. The two girls were sitting in the arbour in the orchard. The smell of the traveller's joy a-blossom mixed with whiffs from the bruised apples lying on the grass. Overhead the fruit hung, clustering redly. Peggy's eyes strayed between the boughs to the green of young pines bounding the yellow fields.

Her face had grown thin lately, but there was the old sturdy ring in her voice when she answered,—

"Can't say I do. There's something depressing about harvesting."

"Depressing!" Katherine echoed. "It's the triumph of the year. There's not a note of sadness in it."

"That's all nonsense," said Peggy. "It's sad; it's horribly sad. You see the awful inevitableness of nature, —the tremendous power drawing like from like. . . . You feel the doom of consequences. You know you have to reap your crops . . . And if you think about it at all it drives you mad."

Katherine turned amazed eyes on Peggy.

"Fact, Kit," she nodded, a smile twisting her lips. "Saul among the prophets, and Peg Saunders among the preachers."

"I don't see how you can joke about it," said Katherine.

"Gracious! I'm not joking," said Peggy; "but a light seat will carry you better over the fence. Laugh and grow wise is a good old saw. . . . No, Kit, I don't like harvest fields; I prefer pine-trees. . . ."

"Aren't my pines coming on splendidly?" Katherine exclaimed. "I'm so proud of my plantation."

"What's the good of planting trees? You'll be dead before they're grown."

"I plant for the immortal gods," said Katherine, proudly.

Peggy laughed at the classic answer. "You'd have done better to see to the human trees round you," she said, suddenly grave. . . . "Tom, for instance."

"What has he been doing?"

"He won't let me give him Rocket, as fine a piece of horseflesh as ever you saw. . . . And I know he can't buy him."

"I'm glad he has enough self-respect to refuse the present," said Katherine.

"It ain't self-respect. . . . By that same token he has refused me," said Peggy, brusquely.

"What do you mean, Peggy?"

"What I say," Peggy answered. "Tom's off with the old love, and on with the new."

"Tom has jilted you?" Katherine cried.

Peggy knotted her fingers together, and her eyes looked straight before her.

"The coward! the base coward!" Katherine exclaimed. "I'm ashamed to own him."

"It's not Tom's fault," said Peggy, stonily. "It's the natural end to a butterfly love. If you catch your butterfly, you bruise its wings, and it's not worth keeping. . . . You told me it couldn't last; he would find some-one else. Well, he has found someone else. . . ."

"But who is there?" Katherine asked bewildered. "There is no one here. . . ."

"There is Tonina. . . ."

"Absurd!" said Katherine, frowning. "Tom never sees Tonina."

Peggy laughed a bitter, mirthless laugh.

"It is you who never see Tom. The thing has been going on these three months, ever since she was here in June. Tom has gone to town every week, and you were only relieved that he was out of your way. It's your fault if he is ruined. . . ."

"My fault! But I never interfere with Tom."

"That is just it," Peggy answered. "You never inter-fere with Tom. You leave him free to go to the devil if he will. . . . You came and took his one duty—the farm —from him. . . . Why didn't you teach him to manage it, to see his duty to the land and the crops and the cattle and the men? But no! you turned him adrift with nothing to do. . . . Then you came and told me what I ought to do. . . . That was right enough. It was true what you said. It has come true, you see. . . ."

Katherine listened to Peggy's hopeless tones, her face changing from red to white, from white to red.

When Peggy was silent she lifted her head haughtily.

"Every just person knows I have sacrificed everything for the farm. I've done all I could for Tom. It's not my fault that he is despicable."

"Yes, yes, you have done all you can," Peggy interrupted.

"One can never do much for a person one despises. . . . You need trust and love. You never trusted Tom's manhood,—just as I never loved him in the right way. And now it is too late."

The humble, broken words went to Katherine's heart. She took Peggy's hand.

"No, it is not too late. We will try together, Peggy. No one has come between you and Tom. . . ."

"If you could have seen anything beyond your own good you would have seen otherwise long ago," said Peggy, curtly.

She got up from her seat and walked off, whistling gaily.

But Katherine had seen her pitiful eyes.

"Oh, what a plague is love!" Katherine thought as she watched her.

She sat still, pondering on what Peggy had said, resentful of her accusation. . . . But of course there was nothing in it. Peggy took a warped view of the situation, and did not understand her difficulties with Tom. . . . As to his coldness, there was nothing in that either,—a little pique at his refusal of the horse. The story of Tonina she dismissed with a shrug. Peggy had always had an unreasoning dislike to Tonina. Tom would never break faith with Peggy. He was a lazy fellow, but lovable; and he had a good heart. During his mother's long illness he had carried her downstairs every day, and wheeled her about the garden for hours. Katherine remembered her home-coming, and the lunch he had given her in this very arbour. He had been simple and kind and affectionate then. Fifteen months could not have made him base and a coward. . . . She had only to speak to him, and he would make up this little lovers' quarrel.

As to this story of visits to Tonina,—that was ridiculous! . . .

She gave herself a little determined shake. She would
see Tom and set things right at once

On her way to the house one of the maids met her.
"If you please, miss, Collop's dying; and Martha says will
you go to the cottage as soon as you can."

Without a word Katherine turned towards Milkmaid
Cottage.   All the eager decision and quick method had
passed from her face.

"Poor Martha! poor old Martha!" she said pitifully.

She pitied herself too.   If Collop died, who would
help her with the farm?   It was he who had told her
the right thing to do,—when to cut the hay, when to hoe
the turnips, when the corn was ripe; what bullocks to
sell, how many sheep to keep,—all the daily order and
sequence which belong to the farm life, which looks so
astonishingly simple, and is in reality so bewilderingly
complex.

Her success had been due to him, and no one had
suspected that he was the god behind the machine.

She passed the pond, and noticed the dip of boughs
in the water, the ripples made by the wind, the swing of
the plants in the tiny waves.   The forget-me-nots made
her think of Sarah's book-mark with its blue flowers and
hearts and love-knots.

The boat was moored under the trees; it rose and
fell softly with the moving water.   Her thoughts went
back to the summer morning long ago when she had
lectured Peggy in the boat; and now it was Peggy who
accused her. . . .

She opened the garden gate and passed up to the
cottage between the rows of hollyhock and sunflowers that

Martha loved. A great green cushion spiked with purple lavender pins stood beside the door; and under the bush Fan was asleep with a two months' puppy. Fan opened her eyes, and wagged a lazy tail in welcome. The house was very still. Katherine looked through the kitchen window, and she shuddered at the sight of a crouching figure by the fire. It was Susan Parkin, the professional "layer-out" of Plimpton. . . . Then Collop was dead. . . .

She stepped on tiptoe into the kitchen.

"When did it happen?" she whispered.

The woman lifted her head. "He ain't gone yet, drat en! He takes a tarrible long time a-dying; and I durstn't leave he though there's another waiting as may go any minute."

"Why do you stay?"

The woman seemed to be measuring the girl's chances of life. "I'm bound to stay," she answered. "Martha Collop is that contrary, her says as her will lay out Collop hersen, and nobody sha'n't touch the corp. . . . It be taking the very bread out of a pore woman's mouth, and I be setting here to stop en. I ha' the ironing board ready and the towels and bandagings; and the minute the breath do be out of en I'll nip up and get he laid out before Martha's done her grieving; which be nat'ral to a widder left respectable and no family."

Katherine went to the door and flung it wide.

"Go out of the house this minute!" she said, her cheeks white with anger. "Do you hear me? . . . Go!"

She stamped her foot; and Susan Parkin hobbled to the door, giving her a sideways, resentful glance.

"Hoity toity! and you're a young miss to be ordering in and ordering out," she grumbled. "And you'll be ordering me in to the great house before long. . . . I allus

The Gods Arrive.

knows en. . . . I do smell death in en months before; and so I telled Martha the beginning o' the week before last. Says I, 'Martha,' I says, 'wash your 'usband and make en comforrable, for I smells death in en.' And her that's to be young Mis. Tom her do be marked for death. . . . ay, I smells death in en. . . ."

Katherine savagely pushed the woman into the garden and locked the door. Sick with loathing she stumbled up to Collop's room. Hearing nothing, she pushed open the door and went in.

Collop had his eyes towards the window that framed a picture of leaves trembling against clouds white as the pillows on which he lay. A light wind wafted about the smell of herbs—thyme and mint and lads' love—that were under his fingers on the counterpane. Martha held his other hand. Her sprigged pink gown was the only colour in the room.

Katherine stooped and kissed her, in silence.

"He be past feeling or hearing, missie," Martha whispered. "He'll go peaceful, looking out on that friar's balsam he allus had a fancy for. I moved the curtains a-purpose."

"How beautiful everything is, Martha. You have made it all so clean."

Martha's lips trembled, but she looked round her proudly.

"He's been a rare man for things decent, my old man; never could a-bear dirt. . . . It do be hard lines to think on en going from dust to dust. . . . This arternoon I seed his time were come, and I up and puts on a clean print that Collop should see me as fair at the last as on the day we courted . . . I doubt they won't know to make him comforrable where he be going to. . .

Parson told he o' the angels and the music and the harps. . . . But Collop never could a-bear they German bands. He'd sooner hear the old woman's tongue than the finest music. . . . Missie, you're tarrible book-learned. You can put things better than such as we. I'd take it kindly if you told me Collop and me will live together again, please God."

Katherine was silent; a lump rose in her throat. Book-learning had given her no consolation for Martha. Philosophy could not satisfy the heart standing at the parting of the ways.

"My old man, he thought a sight o' you, duckie," said Martha. "Whenever as anything worrited he, 'Now, if Miss Katherine was here, her would ret it right quick as you're thinking,' he'd say. And that do be a great question: to know if me and Collop will live together again."

Her eyes questioned hungrily. Katherine groped among her memories for some truth on which the poor soul could stay her heart. In her mind was a confusion of premises and data; but there was no logical sequence to the premise of life but death. And, after all, was that a logical sequence? . . .

She remembered some lines from a Persian poet:—

> "A house, though a million winters old,
> A house of earth comes down at last;
> Then quarry thy stones from the crystal All
> And build the dome that shall not fall."

But what was there here of heart's comfort for the dying and the living?

Katherine was dumb. Her tears rolled down and fell on Martha's hand. Martha's fingers tightened on

Collop's. Her eyes left the girl's face and travelled to the dying man's, and stayed there hopelessly. . . .

Through the window came the sound of church bells ringing for evensong. . . .

The old woman got up slowly from her seat, and kissed the cold hand she laid down.

"It be time the fowlses had their suppers," she said. "I'll see to them if missie will stay with my old man."

"I'll go and feed them!" Katherine sprang up eagerly.

Martha shook her head.

"They knows me, and I wouldn't have 'em think I neglected 'em, no, that I wouldn't. And the old white hen be setting on duckses eggs, and I must see if any be comed out."

She went downstairs, and Katherine heard her calling, but there was no cheery note in her voice to-day. "Come, my dearies, come! Mother's got your suppers: come, dearies. Chuck! chuck! Quick, duckies, quick! Mother wants to get back to father."

When she returned she brought some tea, which Katherine drank, choking. She was so sorry for Martha, and she couldn't even comfort her.

There was nothing to be done for Collop. Katherine sat on, fascinated by the picture of the dying man and his wife.

While she watched a change came over Martha. Her face became full and rosy and young. Katherine shivered, seeing that strange youth. "Martha will die when Collop dies," she thought. She knelt down beside her and touched her hand.

"Martha, what are you thinking about?"

"I do be thinking o' the time we was courting, duckie."

"Tell me about it," said the girl, softly.

A happy light was on the old face. Martha spoke like one in a dream.

"I was a bit of a girl, sixteen past; and I were dairy-maid on a farm at a shilling a week, so you may know as I was young. And Collop were working on the turn-pike a-pulling down of some old housen, and he used to whistle at me going by to my work. . . . Well, gals was not so forward then—no, I am sure they was not! and I thought nothing on en till one day I met he alone. . . . And I got all in a flutter, and that shy I could only hang my head and stand making knots in my apron. And Collop said we'd take a walk the next Sunday to-gether. And I said, 'Oh, go along! I'm sure we won't then;' but I meant going all the same. And so we went on the Sunday. The sun shone lovely, and we went through the meddars, and him pelting me with big ox-eye daisies. . . . That was love toys. . . ."

She stopped. Her eyes were far away. Katherine pressed her hand. "And after that, Martha?"

"There was nothing said of love, dearie. And the very next week they moved en to another part. . . ."

"And then, dear?"

"I didn't see en for six year, nor thought about en neither. . . . And no more he did o' me, and maybe went a-courting to another sweetheart. . . . But one day my brother Harry comed in, and says he, 'Martha, there was a man to-day asking for you.'—'Oh, bother!' I says, 'go along with your tales. I don't believe you.'—'It's gospel truth,' says he, 'and he gived me sixpence, and there 'tis.' True enough, Harry had gotten a whole sixpence. . . . And the next week I went to be cook and dairymaid at Grimple. . . ."

"But, Martha, that was not all? . . ." Katherine softly broke the long silence.

"No, that it wasn't. One Sunday I were going to church. 'T was Foresters' day, and the clubs was marching wi' their bands. Me and some other gals was a-marching along beside 'em when I felt a knock between my shoulders, and when I turned there were Collop! . . . He was growed, and had a stubby beard, and carried a bow-arrow in his hand; and he wore a green sash over his smock as made he look a personable man. And 't was the bow-arrow he'd knocked me with. . . . 'Well,' says he. 'Well?' says I. 'Will you have a walk after church?' says he. 'Oh, go along!' says I; 'there's another young man after me.'—'He won't have you, then, for I will have you,' says he. With that I looked at en, thinking, 'Bother! I likes you!' But I only tossed my head at en to pretend as how I thought nothing of en. . . . But I went to church and sat in the gallery, and kept my eyes on en all through the sermon. . . ."

Martha's eyes were smiling now.

"Well, Martha, well?" Katherine said eagerly.

"Ay, duckie, 'twas well indeed. The very next Sunday, 'Sweetlips,' says he, 'I'm a-going to take you to my mother. I telled her I was courting, and you're to have your tea with my mother.' Well, missie, I was that shy. . . . But I went with Collop, as they was expecting of me, and I was just taken aback with the clean house." She went on quickly in pleased remembrance. "They was poor folkses, but they had a bit o' ground, and a pig or two, and everything was just as clean,—Collop's mother being a religious woman, with the minister visiting en constant. . . . The tea were set in the arbour lovely; and all round 'em there was cherry-trees and merry-trees, and gooseberries and strawberries and currants. And there was a beautiful cloth on the table as clean as a mouse. . . . 'Humph,' I says to myself, 'there's a deal o' cleanliness with very little grub.' For though the loaf was big as a cottage, the butter was the size of a walnut . . . But there was grace said, both before and after,— she allus had en that way, poor dear!—and when us was well through with the loaf her fetched out a piece o' meat and offered en. . . . Well, I could ha' laughed at such ways; and did, going home with Collop. And every now and again he'd put a cherry or a merry in my mouth. . . . But that was only love toys. . . ."

Martha was a long time silent. "Go on, dear," Katherine whispered.

"Six months after that we was married, duckie. I wore a slate-coloured alpaca, flowered, with a cape to match, and a white straw bonnet that costed three and sixpence, with white ribbons at fourteen pence the yard, and orange blossoms inside; so you may know 'twas good. And Collop was as fine as a bird, wearing black pants and a white linen smock with tippets. It was worked lovely, and split at the sides for the pockets. . . ."

"And was that all?" Katherine asked.

"That was nothing at all, missie. I hadn't been a-married long before I found out that Collop were nobbut a man. But from that day to this us haven't had ne'er a wrong word between us; no, not even when there were money-talk between us. . . . But I never was one to keep my old man short; he allus had a shilling in his pocket. He knowed he durstn't spend it, but it quietened en. . . . No, never no words between we there was, though we ha' been married forty year."

"You have been very happy," said Katherine.

"Ay, as happy as a pair o' linnets. . . . Oftens when I puts on a clean print I durstn't go into the kitchen if Collop were there.   I knowed 'twould be 'Gie us a kiss, sweetlips.'   He be so soft, be Collop, when I'm dressed up a bit . . . only to-day he ha'n't took no notice. . . ."

Martha woke from her dream, and fixed her eyes wistfully on the old man's face. . . . Then the smile faded, and lines and wrinkles chased the youth from her face.   Trembling, she rose and drew the lids over Collop's eyes.

"He be gone very quiet, as quiet as a worm, thank God," she said hoarsely.   "And that be the last of my old man till the burying on Wednesday. . . ."

She stood looking at the dead.   Katherine dared not move lest she should break the silence that had fallen in the room.   Martha stooped and stroked Collop's limbs; and twilight laid its shadows about the living and the dead.

Stepping very softly Katherine went downstairs.   The fire was out in the kitchen, and the empty grate smote her coldly.   She went into the garden and brought in Fan's puppy.   She lighted a candle, and by the deserted hearth she lived over again the terror and the pity of the scene upstairs.

She had never faced the question of death before. She had never looked into blank eyes, and felt the shock which loosens one's hold of both worlds.   Her heart cried out for some sure resting-place. . . .

The puppy in her arms looked up and licked the tears running down her cheeks.   She could hear Martha upstairs moving about, doing the last service for her old man.   How pitiful it was, she thought, the end of this forty years' love. . . . But was it the end? Would love meet love again? There was no escape from it; she was back again at the great question. She had no answer for it; but it had roused another:—

"Of love that never finds its earthly close, what sequel?" Martha had tasted life's best. What of the heart to which love only came in mockery?

A shadow passed the window, then came back, and rested on the uncurtained window.

The candle showed the girl sitting with grief-stricken eyes, the puppy, heavy with sleep, pressed against her face.

Franklin had never seen Katherine look so humble and sad and gentle. An unwonted tenderness stirred in him. He knocked and came into the kitchen.

Katherine started up, and the colour flooded her face. She reached out her hand, and her fingers clung to his, sending the blood through his veins in a tumult.

"I wanted to see you," he said quietly. "They told me you were here. . . . What a jolly little chap. . . . What do they call you, sir, eh?" He played an instant with the dog, pulling his ears and teasing him. "Can you spare me a minute, Miss Katherine?"

She drew Collop's arm-chair forward for Franklin, and sat down herself in the seat opposite.

"Poor old Collop is dead," she said, as if to explain her agitation, "and—and you surprised me. . . ."

"You are suffering," he said anxiously.

"It is not that," she answered gently. "But things are so hard. One strives and strives and strives, and it is all failure. Life is lonely, and death is lonely. . . And we are helpless before it all. Nothing serves. . . . We

cry out for eternity—and we can't even tell if there is an
eternity."

"The kingdom of God is within you," said Franklin,
shyly.   "Isn't that enough? . . ."

She did not answer.

"We are having a meeting at Grimple on Wednesday," he said, suddenly changing his tone.   "Pilchard is
standing for South Hampshire. Will you come and speak
for us?"

She lifted her head sharply, and he saw the life
flash back to face and eyes.   Her dejection was banished
by the ambition that braced the lines of her figure.

"To speak again!" she cried, with a long, slow
breath of delight.

"Yes; you could manage it easily.   You will come
then? Wednesday, three o'clock. . . ."

Katherine's face changed.

"I can't go," she said drearily.   "I must stay with
Martha.   It is Collop's funeral. . . ."

The shadow was on his face too when he spoke.

"I am very sorry; but of course you can't leave
the poor old lady. . . .   Well, never mind," he
said more cheerfully.   "We shall do very well without
you. . . ."

"Yes, you can do without me," she said bitterly.   "It
is always the same thing.   I am not wanted,—not here
nor in the Movement."

"You are certainly needed here," he said.   "Movements can do without us; we are not necessary to any
cause.   They will run their course without us.   We are
only necessary—men and women are only necessary to
. . . to each other. . . ."

He drew out his watch. "My time is up. I must fly. . . ."

He took her hand a minute. "There was something . . .But I will see you again. I must see you again soon."

Katherine sat still in her chair in a tumult of feeling from which Martha called her.

"Missie, will you come and help me to lay out my old man?"

And while Katherine's hands moved about the dead man, her thoughts were circling round Franklin and a living love.

CHAPTER II.

WOMAN'S INDEPENDENCE.

IT was late on Monday night. Katherine was lying on the sofa in the parlour, worn out after her work and the emotions of the day before. She was sitting up for Tom. She must have the talk with him that Collop's death had deferred.

Her thoughts wandered to Franklin's unexpected appearance at the cottage, and she forgot her weariness. . . .

Franklin had wished her to speak at Grimple! "I always knew he would change his opinion of me," she thought proudly.

But pride gave way to a softer feeling that poured through her like a flood of sunlight. "I wasn't mistaken," she whispered shyly, "I know he cares for me. . . ."

A sudden warmth set the blood galloping in her veins. She remembered his words, "Men and women are only necessary to each other." Had he begun to find that out? . . . Her heart laughed aloud in its gladness. . . . She tried to recall his features, and failed. Were his eyes blue or grey? . . . She only remembered their kindness. . . . She dwelt on the moment when he had held her hand. She had felt a curious sense of having lost her hand in his. There had been only one hand in that clasp. How strong yet how tender it had been! . . . And he was wise and strong and restful. If

he took life more seriously than most men she liked him
the better for it. That undertone of earnestness gave
stability. . . . Ah! how fine he was! And how she loved
him! How could she ever have thought her love was
dead? . . .

She got up from the sofa, lifting her arms with a fierce
longing to draw his face to hers, to feel her love resting
against his love.

Her bosom swelled; she seemed to grow taller and
fairer in the exaltation of feeling. She loved him! She
loved him! And he loved her, and would make her
worthy of him. . . . Ah! she was not worthy.

Her arms dropped; she withered and grew small.
. . . What would she give him for all he would give
her? Intellect? What was intellect worth when it could
not solve the problem of death? Success? But her success on the farm had been due to Collop. Energy?
Perseverance? But they were the tools of ambition.
Love? Yes, she loved him, but would her love last?

She had loved Mark in the old days when he had
helped her and given her independence. She had said
she could never be happy away from him; yet he had
passed out of her life, and she did not even miss him.
. . . She shivered. Peggy had said she could see nothing
beyond her own good. Was it true? Was her love merely
selfish?

She probed her love for Franklin, then with a sobbing triumph she lifted her head. Here at least she was
safe. She loved him for nothing that he could give her,
not position, not power, not the life that attracted her.
He was a poor man wearing shabby clothes. He was not
good-looking even. She loved him only for himself. If
he stood penniless, a beggar in rags, she would be proud

to marry him. If by dying she could serve him, death would be sweet. . . .

She breathed fast; her eyes smiled. "Greater love hath no man than this," she whispered. . . . But was that the supreme renunciation? She could give her life for Franklin; could she give up her love for him?

The triumph was over. . . . Her face grew blank. She crouched down beside the sofa, and her arms tightened across her bosom as if to strain to her the love she could not renounce.

"Hillo, Kit! What in the world are you doing down there on the floor?"

It was Tom. He came into the room, sat down, and began kicking off his shoes.

"Hang the beastly things! They've driven me mad all day."

Katherine came round to his side and looked down at the shoes.

"What is wrong with them?" Her manner was quite commonplace.

"Too beastly tight," he grumbled. "Enough to make a fellow swear. Get me something to drink, will you, Kit?"

"Supper is in the breakfast room, Tom."

Katherine's eyes passed from the fashionable shoes on the floor to the lemons-coloured kid gloves on the table. She studied Tom curiously. He wore the high collar and white tie of the masher. A coat of smart cut made the most of his excellent figure. He seemed unusually well set up about the legs. What did it mean? For whom did he dress like this? Was Peggy's story true? Had Tonina wakened the vanity that sleeps in every man, even in the most good-looking? Katherine brought Tom's slippers with a grave face. She watched him at his meal. He ate nothing; and when he had emptied the jug of home-brewed he stretched himself, yawning.

"Well, I'm off to bed. What are you so glum for, Kit? Anything up?"

"Yes," said Katherine. "I wanted to ask you about it."

"Humph! You don't often want to ask me about anything."

"I know," she said eagerly. "But now Collop is dead I want a man to advise me about things, and you must help me, Tom dear."

He looked amiably at her, and sprawled complacently in the chair he had pushed from the table. It might have occurred to Katherine that flattery was the road to his heart.

"Well, fire away, old girl. I suppose it's the new cowman you want to talk about. It's a new thing for you to want a fellow's advice. . . . Coming round to the ordinary woman, eh?"

"Yes," said Katherine. "I think, Tom, I want to be an ordinary woman. I want a man's love and strength. . . . It's better to have these than the most brilliant profession."

"Course it is," said Tom with superiority. "Didn't I always tell Peggy that. . . ."

He stopped, hitched up his collar, and excused his red face with, "This confounded necktie!"

"Peggy has been here to-day, Tom. I'm anxious about her. She is in trouble. . . ."

"What's that got to do with me?" said Tom, boldly.

He walked to the mantelpiece and stood with his back to Katherine, kicking the coal, and whistling.

"Tom, do listen!" she said entreatingly. "Isn't it your fault? Are you treating her well?"

He turned round sharply. "What has she told you?"

"She said you had given her up."

"And so I have." He laughed uneasily. "Peggy is not the sort for me. I want more spirit. Mark is a lucky dog. Tonina's a rattler if you like. . . . No getting round her."

"Peggy has spirit enough," said Katherine, warmly. "Her only fault is in loving you so much. Tom, it will break her heart if you throw her off."

"Not it!" he shuffled uneasily. "It's nothing to her. That sort of girl doesn't break her heart. . . . Well, if that's all you've got to say, Kit, I'm off." He yawned again.

"Oh, Tom, don't go! You haven't told me how Tonina is. And did the flat look nice?"

Tom fell into the trap.

"Ripping!" he said. "And Tonina was as larkish as ever. Mark didn't come home, so we had it to ourselves. Tonina knows how to amuse a fellow."

He twirled the end of his moustache and looked out of the corner of his eye as if he could have said more if he had wished.

"Tell me all about it," said Katherine.

"Not I! I'm dead tired. I'm off to bed. Ask me to-morrow."

Katherine sat over the fire thinking. Then Peggy was right; Tom's visits to town were visits to Tonina. . . .

In a while the trouble cleared from her eyes. He had answered her questions easily and naturally; there was nothing to conceal. His friendship with Tonina had been honest enough in the summer. They had amused themselves like two children; and Tonina was not the sort of woman to have a flirtation with a simple country farmer. Still, for Peggy's sake, his visits to her must stop. . . .

Katherine made up her mind to go to town and see Tonina after Collop's funeral. . . . She would take her some fruit; flowers, too, asters and sweet peas and Michaelmas daisies. Tonina loved forget-me-nots, but they were over.

Back again to her mind came the thought of Sarah's book-marker with the forget-me-nots, and "Remember Me when this you See."

Katherine wondered how Sarah was getting on, and the milkman Jim who had criticised her work.

"He was quite right," she thought humbly. "It would have been better to have made two sweethearts happy together."

She looked back with amazement at the girl who had refused to help Sarah's holiday. Could she ever have been so selfish? It would be impossible to act like that now. It would please her to help two lovers to be happy together. . . . And why shouldn't she help these two? She must find a new cowman. Jim might do for the post, and Sarah had been laundry maid at a farm. They might marry and come to Great Lowlands. . . .

The idea seized Katherine's imagination. She would go to Goodge Street and have a talk with Sarah. She grew excited over the plan that would atone for that regretted selfishness. . . .

Tuesday and Wednesday were busy days, divided from Thursday by a veil of emotion when she stood be-

side Martha at Collop's grave. She had no hope to give,
but she followed the rector's voice with wistful longing:
"'It is sown in dishonour, it is raised in glory. It is sown
a natural body, it is raised a spiritual body.'"

She slept at Milkmaid Cottage that night, and waking
in the grey dawn she felt the desolation of the house that
is empty of human presence. She sprang from the bed
with a cry for Martha. The silence was a frame in which
she saw the strange youth of Martha's face the day Collop
had died. . . . She hurried on her clothes, and searched
the rooms, afraid of finding the old woman dead.

The cottage was empty. Her terror growing, she went
round the pond and among the trees, calling, "Martha,
Martha, where are you, Martha?"

"Here, missie, here!" The old woman forced a way
through the underwood and came out into the open.

Katherine was pale; she ran to meet her, eye and
voice reproachful.

"Oh, Martha, how you frightened me! Why are you
out so soon, before five o'clock?"

There was nothing of the depressed mourner about
Martha. A roguish twinkle was in her eye; her sunbonnet
was newly starched and frilled; she wore a clean print
gown tucked high above the wet grass, and she carried
a basket of nettles drenched in dew. At Katherine's
question her face puckered up merrily.

"Hush, duckie," she said, in a mysterious whisper.
"I be gathering nettles for Susan Parkin's boys, saucy
warmints! Her do bring 'em o' Saturday nights to the
pump in the yard; and her washes 'em in the trough;
and they runs about naked, which it wouldn't be decent,
only boys *is* so pretty. And they gets in the orchard and
treats the rosydondrons shameful, pulling 'em about tar-

rible . . . I seed 'em Saturday, and I'd ha' nettled 'em on their bare bodies only for Collop lying a-dying. But I thinks to myself, 'Wait till my old man be safe underground, and you shall feel nettle-bite, you mischievous young vagabonds.' I thought on 'em yesterday, when I did see 'em at Collop's burying—yes!"

Martha sighed contentedly as she finished.

"But, Martha, nettles sting dreadfully," Katherine laughed, tickled at the contrast between her idea of Martha dead of a broken heart and the Martha before her.

"Ay, they do hurt tarrible sore," said Martha; "and it do go to my heart to sting they boys' bodies, boys is so prutty. But Susan Parkin have tormented me tarrible, waiting on Collop dying. . . . Ay, he gived her the slip, did Collop," she chuckled. "He wouldn't have laid easy if he had knowed he would make a corp for Susan Parkin."

She hobbled along gaily beside Katherine. The girl was silent. This, then, was the explanation of the white presences she had seen last summer. Would all her visions end in such prosaic fashion? Would the gods arrive to show themselves mischievous vagabonds tearing down the "rosydondron" bushes?

Peggy drove her to the station, her jaunty air flaunting itself unnecessarily, as it seemed to Katherine

She held the reins tightly, and managed Sambo with all her old spirit; but her gaiety was forced. Katherine's story of Martha and the nettles lost its humour in her hard laugh. She mocked cynically at the errand to Tonina, to Katherine's disgust.

"Look here, Peggy, why do you go on like this?

Where is your pride? What's the use of education if it
doesn't teach women to control their emotions?"

"Education be blowed!" Peggy said, sitting up sharply.
"You may educate a woman till she is brain from head
to foot, and a single glance from a man's eye will make
her forget everything but that she is a woman. . . . Oh,
you may stare! Wait till your womanhood gets hold of
you. Fight sex as you will, there comes a moment when
it conquers you. . . ."

"Nonsense!" said Katherine, vigorously. "Women are
growing independent of sex."

"A woman will never be independent of nature," said
Peggy. "Hold up, horse! what are you doing?" She laid
the whip smartly across Sambo's back.

"It's the same gate at which he shied before," said
Katherine, holding on to the cart as it swerved.

"That's the white gate." Peggy's sidelong glance was
full of meaning.

Katherine remembered the talk in the boat.

"Peggy!"

Peggy returned her look, shrugging her shoulders.

"Why not?"

"You are not a coward!" said Katherine, mastering a
sick fear that had taken hold of her at the expression on
Peggy's face.

Peggy laughed. "A coward? Not I; cowards fear
death. . . . Katherine, suppose it is *life* that I fear?" . . .

Katherine's heart seemed to stop beating.

"Oh, Peggy!" she said hoarsely.

"Yes," said Peggy, affecting carelessness. "I thought
Tom loved me. . . . It seems I was mistaken. He only
loved himself."

She whipped Sambo forward.

Katherine said nothing. After all, Tom was her brother. Then she touched Peggy's arm.

"Poor old Peggy! I am so sorry, dear."

Peggy's lips trembled.

"Kit, you're a brick!" She hummed softly to herself:—

"Come out, 'tis now September!"

"Peggy," Katherine interrupted, "it will all come right. It must. Tom may be selfish, but he is not dishonourable."

"That is where it is hopeless," said Peggy. "You can move dishonour; but the selfish man is never moved. . . . No, Kit; you can't make a saddle out of a bearing rein."

They were at the station, in which the train stood waiting. Katherine jumped hurriedly from the cart, and looked up to Peggy with a resolute purpose in her eyes.

"It's all right, Peggy. I will manage Tom. Don't worry; everything will come right."

She ran for her ticket and sprang into the carriage. The train puffed noisily out of the station.

CHAPTER III.

KATHERINE CLAIMS HER FRIEND.

KATHERINE was going back to London, which she had left with such bitter regret; but she felt no pleasure in revisiting the glimpses of her triumphs. Contrasting the old life with the strong human interests of Great Lowlands, the tragedies of love and death, she saw that in town she had not tasted life; she had only known its influence upon herself. At Plimpton she had been forced to play a part in the lives of others.

The train came into the region of roofs and chimney-pots. She wondered at the wretched aspect of the things she saw. The sun blazed on the dirt and poverty, on the jerry-built houses, the sordidness of slumdom. The air was thick with struggle. She longed for the clean breath of the fields.

She took a 'bus at the station, and gazed down at the crowd on Waterloo Bridge. It flowed, a swollen tide, over the arches, matching the turbid flow of the river under the arches The human stream moved on, as merciless, as ruthless as the water below. Here and there she saw a white face borne down by the stream, one of those that disappear in the living flood, over which the darkness closes.

In the Strand she peered eagerly about her, seeking the fascination that had once held her. But she saw only the strain of life, the fever and unrest of the faces hurrying by.

The flowers were absent to-day except at Charing Cross station, where the flower girls held out their wired roses. . . . At Great Lowlands honeysuckle wreathed all the hedges, and in every ditch meadow-sweet heaped the snows of autumn.

She walked along St. Martin's Lane, her eyes pitiful for the struggle she saw. How hard these faces were, how hopeless! She studied them with a new comprehension of the lives bearing the burden and heat of the day. These were no longer the "people," the "masses;" but men and women who lived and sinned and loved and suffered, battened down in brick and mortar like rats in sewers till death carried them out to liberty.

Katherine's heart swelled with longing to help them. She realised that she had not known the first elements of sympathy in the days when she had taken up the people's cause.

She went first to Goodge Street to find Sarah, stirred by the thought of seeing the house where she had lived and known her brief successes. But the dark little hall, with its shabby linoleum, its crooked umbrella stand, and dingy brushes, gave her a shock. Had everything been musty and dusty like this in the old days? It would be a great thing to take two people out of the life of the city into the broad free life of the country. . . . At Katherine's proposal, Sarah's eyes glimpsed Paradise.

It was pleasant to go from this first success to the second waiting her in Ridgmont Gardens.

Thursday was Tonina's At Home day, and she was playing to her visitors when Katherine arrived. The room was dark, the air heavy with the scent of yellow roses heaped in blue bowls on every table.

The girl smiled at Tonina, slipped into a chair, and looked round her.

The softness and luxury, the silk-shaded lamps, the half-tones, belonged to another world than that in which Mark and she had lived. Katherine's lips curled. No wonder that in such surroundings Mark had grown effeminate and selfish. . . . And Tonina would not help him into a more robust life. Katherine frowned at the beautiful woman in her clinging yellow draperies.

Celandine Ambrose was there; and Franklin, whose presence struck a harsh note in the harmony of the room. His face was tired, his clothes contrasted oddly with the smartness of the other men. Ambrose, curled and perfumed, seemed to belong to the upholstery of the place.

Katherine turned from him to Franklin, proud at the contrast between the two. Franklin, she said to herself, was the only man in the room. The others belonged mostly to the profession of amateurism. She smiled forgivingly, noting the arts that went to their expression.

By and by the music made way for conversation. The talk was full of catch phrases; it discussed the last new novel, the problem play, the smartest private view. Katherine listened impatiently. Not so long ago she had called this living; to make one in groups like this, success. . . . Her thoughts flew to Martha and Collop, to their simple love, their simpler life that was at the heart of nature. Love and life and death seemed to be things remote from the people here. The society crust could not bear the weight of realities.

Ambrose moved languidly to her side. The spark of eagerness in his eyes was blown out by her breezy greeting.

"How terribly robust you look!" he sighed.

Katherine laughed. "That is terrible, indeed."

"Yes," he said regretfully. "You have lost your exquisite delicacy, and . . . really . . . you are less . . ."

"Attenuated," Katherine said, as he paused for a word. "I think that must be it."

He looked sadly at her. That healthy complexion was positively coarse; and a double chin lurked in the roundedness of her face.

"You never came to Great Lowlands," she said mischievously.

"No, but another summer . . . among the roses," . . . he murmured.

"Who is that distressing person beaming on you, Miss Fleming? We have all been laughing at him. Somebody called him John the Baptist,—his clothes, you know. . . ."

"That is my friend, Mr. Franklin," said Katherine, in a clear high voice. "If he is like John the Baptist it is because he is not indebted to his tailor for his clothes. . . ."

Ambrose lifted his glass-covered left eye and fixed it on Franklin.

"'Pon my soul, an original person!"

Some people, Franklin among them, were moving. With a curt apology Katherine rose too.

Two spots of colour burnt on her cheeks, her eyes shone. She was going to claim her friend before those who had laughed at him. The men looking on grinned as they saw the meeting between the shabby man and the pretty girl. A soft shy light was in her eyes; her lips were parted. The expression on her face was beautiful. They saw her hand linger in his.

Franklin brightened as he spoke to her.

"I am sorry now that I am leaving so soon; but I have a good deal to see to before six; I am going back to Grimple."

"I go down by the six train, too," she said quickly.

"Good; I'll look out for you then."

He smiled again as he went out. His eyes had kindled at the warmth of her glance.

Katherine outstayed the other guests.

"I want a talk with you, Tonina," she said when they were alone. "I've come up on purpose to speak to you about Tom."

Tonina flashed a brilliant smile at her.

"Ah, *mon ami* Tom! He is the great bear and I tame him."

She settled herself among the cushions on the sofa, then took up a fluffy cat from the rug and began tickling and teasing it.

"Tonina, do be serious!" Katherine cried. "What does Tom do when he comes here?"

Tonina pursed up her dainty lips.

"He listens divinely. He sits with the eyes open, listening while I play and play and play."

"And when you have finished playing?"

"Ah, then he no more amuses me; and I send my stupid bear from me."

"I knew that was all!" Katherine cried triumphantly. "Of course that was all! But, Tonina, you mustn't let him come any more. It is spoiling him. He doesn't want to marry Peggy."

"Ah! so the better for Peggy," Tonina laughed softly.

"You forget she loves him," said Katherine, her face grave.

"Pouf!" said Tonina, expressively. "I, too, loved Mark; and now, . . . ah, yes, love does not last. . . ."

"You are wrong, Tonina, love lasts. It isn't love that you feel if in one month or in one year it is dead. Tonina," she went on earnestly, "it means everything to Peggy to marry Tom. You can influence him. . . . I want you to help me. . . ."

Tonina lifted herself from the cushions, smiling provokingly.

"And who has taught you that love lasts, little Katherine? Your friend who bores me with his talk of you?"

"Celandine Ambrose?" Katherine smiled.

"Ah, no, he is an angel! . . . No, it is our dull friend, Franklin, who is so in love with you. He has no eyes for me. He comes here but to talk of Mark's sister. . . ."

Katherine's eyes flashed with a great light. "He loves me! I wasn't wrong. Even Tonina sees it. . . ."

Her heart sprang forward to the journey that would set a crown upon the day. . . . Then the light faded from her eyes. She had only time for Peggy.

But Tonina would not be serious. She laughed and cooed and purred at all Katherine told her of the change in Tom; and she screamed with delight at the story of the fashionable shoes.

"He had pinched the feet for me; and I thought only how great they were!" she laughed, wiping her eyes.

Then she pushed back the hair from her forehead, and was suddenly grave.

"And what is it that I must do to this monster Tom?"

"You must forbid him to come here again," said Katherine; "and you must make him promise to marry Peggy."

Tonina pouted, but agreed, and Katherine sprang up gaily.

A great load was off her mind. Joy ran ahead to the meeting with Franklin.

"Where is Mark?" she asked, as she said good-bye to Tonina.

Tonina gave a little shrug. "I never see him. . . ."

"But he lives here?" said Katherine, flushing.

"He sleeps here," Tonina answered, "and he eats here; but live? . . Pouf! Mark does not live. He has the soul of a rat and no more. The stupid Tom has more soul. Tom is glad to hear my violin, but Mark . . ." She spread her hands.

Katherine looked at her with frightened eyes.

"Tonina, aren't you happy, then?"

Tonina flashed at her a curious baffling smile.

"Who can tell? We never know happiness till it has left us."

Katherine had barely time to get to Waterloo. She had to hurry away.

She ran on to the platform at six o'clock, passed the barrier, and came up to the train as the signal to start was given. Franklin stood beside an open door; he handed her into the carriage, and sprang in himself.

"I had just made up my mind to be disappointed," he said.

He straightened his *pince-nez,* and did not notice her flush, the sudden smile

"I had a run for the train," she panted.

They were alone in the carriage. He took the corner opposite to hers, and laid down his newspaper, smiling at her.

Katherine was all at once shy; a recollection of Tonina's words overpowered her.

Franklin seemed preoccupied.

"How did your meeting go off?" Katherine asked at last.

He shook his head gloomily: "A wretched fiasco. Pilchard is the last man for the place. I wish you could have been there to help."

She bent forward eagerly; her eyes seemed to dart at him.

"You are beginning to think I am of use," she cried.

Words and manner annoyed him, recalling the past. He bent his head gravely, and was silent. His eyes strayed to his *Westminster Gazette;* and so they travelled on.

But Katherine could not remain silent. She longed to hear his voice.

"They tell me you have been asked to stand for Hull," she said.

Franklin roused himself.

"I? Yes, I had thought of it; . . . but since then . . . The fact is I am leaving England. . . ."

"Leaving England!" she echoed.

Her tone startled him. He glanced curiously at her blank face. For some reason or other he hesitated to speak.

"Yes . . . the West Indies. I intended to tell you on Sunday."

"And I took up the time with my hateful moods!" she cried passionately. "Oh, if I had only known. But it is not too late? . . . You have not decided? . . . You are not going? . . ."

He lifted his brows. She exaggerated her regret, as she overdid everything. . . . He frowned down his disapproval.

"I've almost made up my mind to go. . ."

His quiet tones whipped Katherine's feeling into excitement. She could not think calmly. . . . She seemed to be losing him again just when she had found him.

"To go!" she exclaimed. "Oh, you can't mean it! You are not going away just when you . . . when I need you so much. . . ."

"You need me?" he said slowly "But . . . I don't understand. . . ."

"Yes," she gasped, "I need you. . . . You told me to come to you when I wanted help; and you can help me. . . ."

The train slackened speed, and stopped. A signal was against them. Katherine's heart was big with misery. "He is going away; he is going away," was all her thought. She put out her hand entreatingly. "Oh, Mr. Franklin, don't go away. . . . I can't let you go unless . . . unless . . . I go too. . . ."

Franklin stared at her. What did she mean? What was all this emotion? . . . He could not understand her. . . . Here was yet another mood to bewilder him.

"You go too, Miss Katherine?" he said, with a constrained laugh. "But that is impossible . . ."

"Ah! it is not impossible!" she cried. "I would go with you because . . . oh, don't you know? . . . because . . ."

Her shrinking attitude and broken voice, the pain in her eyes, found his heart. . . . His face whitened. . . . A great wave of pity for her caught and swept him off his feet. In that bewilderment it seemed that he loved the girl trembling before him. . . .

But no; this feeling was not love. The stir and tumult of passion were wanting.

He had long since decided that she was nothing to him. It would be foolish to yield to a mere sentiment of pity. . . . He mastered the impulse of tenderness, crushing down the feeling that had almost conquered him.

"It is weakness, absolute madness," he said sternly to himself. Then he turned to Katherine and, in spite of himself, his eyes were full and tender.

"Let us both forget that you have told me this," he said gently.

He saw the life die slowly out of her face and leave it old.

"You mean? . . ." her voice shuddered.

He looked his sorrow, but he would not yield.

"Yes, I mean that."

All at once the muscles round her mouth stiffened. Across her lips the words came cold and hard, dropping one by one like shot falling.

"You . . . don't . . . love . . . me? . . ."

Franklin's silence surged over him like another wave, beating him down, snatching the breath from him. Not Katherine, but he himself was drowning in the cold depths of that silence. . . . Did he love her? Was this overwhelming pity love? . .

She felt the rigid aloofness of his attitude, and sank crouching in her corner and covered her face. "I thought you loved me; I thought you loved me," she moaned.

Franklin walked to the other end of the carriage, and stood there fighting with himself. He saw nothing of the purple waves of heather that lapped the edge of the line and flooded the moorland to the distant firs. The piney breath of autumn was round him, but his senses were dull. What could he do? How could he close this

dreary scene? It was impossible to speak; it was heartless to be silent. "I thought you loved me; I thought
you loved me," rang in his ears.

Why did she think so? Had he ever given her
cause to suppose she was more to him than any other
woman?

His survey of the past told him little. At the moments when he had felt most tenderness for her she
had always repelled him. . . . Certainly she had moved
him, and more than once. . . . In that milking scene at
the farm. But then she had taken him unaware, at a
time when Mark's honeymoon had turned his thoughts to
sentiment. And immediately after she had opened his
eyes to his mistake. . . . He might have loved her then,
but . . . Besides, was her attitude towards him the
attitude of a woman who loved? She had always quarrelled with him, disagreed with him, charged him with
misunderstanding her. . . . And now she thought he loved
her! In all his forty years he had never given a woman
a thought; and should he end by marrying an hysterical
girl who had attracted and repelled him, repelled and
attracted him ever since he had known her?

His mind spun round like a wheel, revolving the
question of what he was to do. The central point, the
pivot on which the question revolved, was his own repeated
assurance that he did not love the girl. . . .

It seemed that hours passed while he stood there.
Then he crossed to his old seat and leaned forward.

"Miss Katherine, I want to thank you for telling me
this. I shall never forget. . . . I wish it had been possible. . . . But . . . I have never thought. . . . All my
life . . . it never seemed likely . . ."

She lifted her head and her eyes, sunken with anguish,

stretched out to him, and laid themselves about his heart. . . .

He made a gesture towards her. But she shrank away. Her face was suddenly strong.

"Don't!" she cried sharply. "I wasn't asking you for pity. I need no one's pity. . . . Love doesn't mean giving for giving, not the best love. . . . There is a love that will give itself, though it can have nothing in return. . . . I am glad I have known you. . . . I shall always be glad for much. . . . I would have made your life brighter, if you would have let me. . . ." Her lips trembled. . . . "Perhaps, some day, you may like to remember that someone cares for you. . . ." She smiled palely and held out her hand.

Franklin could not speak. He took her hand and stroked it softly, all the time fighting a fight in which his conception of Katherine warred against the Katherine that stormed his heart, taking it by force, tearing down his banner of self-sufficingness.

It was she who drew away at last, and began with gentle dignity to talk of other things,—Parliamentary news, the topics of the Labour world. Half-reluctant, half-relieved, he suffered himself to be led away from personalities. Her self-command startled him. He looked wonderingly at her, trying to get behind the cold white expression that she wore like a mask. He felt chilled, now that he was outside the warm circle of feeling, but her commonplaces kept him there. For the rest of the journey he did not catch sight of the woman whose passionate abandon had stirred him in strange fashion.

He left Katherine at Grimple; but he waited on the

platform, looking after the vanishing train with eyes that contradicted the cynical twist of his mouth.

Left alone, the mask dropped from Katherine's face, showing the quivering, smarting flesh, the torn heart, the dreadful eyes. The pain of that terrible hour threw its shadow forward across her whole life. "How shall I bear it? How shall I bear it?" she moaned.

She gazed stonily from the window. The moon was a little silver boat sailing across the blue, wafted by the breath of pine and heather The firs stood solemnly by the purple waves that met the purple rim of the sky, and earth showed wide and free and beautiful. The soft folds of nature wrapped around the woman battling with pain and the treachery of the heart and the vanity of life.

CHAPTER IV.

THERE IS ALWAYS A WAY OUT.

THE post had come in. Tom had read Tonina's letter with stormy face, and had gone out without a word. Katherine had scarcely noticed him. Tom was of little account beside the disaster in her own life.

Franklin did not love her. Like a knell the words tolled in her brain: "He does not love me; he does not love me!"

She hardly felt the pain of it. An aching emptiness in her heart was all that remained of the agony with which she had struggled through the night. But her face was pinched and wan behind the everyday purpose of its expression. The strong pitilessness of nature had overtaken her. She knew herself to be a woman, with a woman's heart and a woman's need and a woman's denial.

She had wrestled with the great god Love, and had not prevailed; and to the end of life she would go haltingly on the shrunk sinew where the Divine had touched her.

She felt no regret at her own self-betrayal. A year ago she might have been ashamed at finding that she had given love unsought. To-day, larger and freer, her nature stood proudly unabashed.

"Thou shalt not confess thy love" had been written for the smaller woman whom conventions ruled. Katherine obeyed a higher law-giver; and while the woman in her shrank, wounded by Franklin's scorn, the greater nature crowned itself with its pain and triumphed.

She could not cease to love him because he had no love to give her. . . . Gentle thoughts of him silenced the tolling words. She cried softly to herself for her great pain and her great pride. . . .

But she had no time for weeping. She must work. The men were waiting for their orders. There were tomatoes to be picked, the pollen to be transferred from flower to flower. Katherine acted the part of bee and butterfly in the tomato-frames, and so secured a good yield of "love-apples," as Martha called them.

She set aside her thoughts of Franklin, and went to give Mrs. Fleming her plans for the day. She had only lately begun to consult her mother on the working of the farm. But she was learning to respect her position, and to bear with her petulance. To-day she gave her a new tenderness. A woman who had lived and loved and lost demanded the sweetest pity of life.

Mrs. Fleming felt the difference at once, and was curious to account for the change.

She questioned Katherine about her journey to town, Mark's wife, the flat, the furniture, Tonina's friends

Katherine's thoughts swung back to Franklin. She answered shortly, and Mrs. Fleming sighed over the unsatisfactoriness of motherhood.

"I am not clever like you, Katherine," she said plaintively; "but I'm your mother. And I think there should be confidence between mother and child."

"I think so too," said Katherine, brusquely. "Mother, why has there been so little confidence between us? I know nothing of your life with father. . . . You never talk of him. Were you happy with him? Did you love him very much?"

For the first time Mrs. Fleming realised that Katherine was not a child. A faded blush showed on her cheek as she answered,—

"He was very good. I would have been happy with him, only . . ."

"Only what?" said Katherine, pitilessly.

"Only I had loved someone else before."

"And why didn't you marry the one you loved?"

Mrs. Fleming shrank away from Katherine's compelling eyes, and twisted her hands together. "I am sure I don't know why you should catechise me like this, Katherine," she said nervously.

"I am not catechising," Katherine said. "Only it is always interesting to know why people marry each other, or why they don't. It seems to be the one subject in life that doesn't lose its interest," she added wistfully.

"I was very fond of Colonel Jacob," said Mrs. Fleming, "and I thought he cared for me, and would ask me to marry him. . . . But he never did. . . . He went abroad without a word. . . . Then, after I was married, he upbraided me and said he had always loved me."

"Why didn't he tell you that before?"

"Oh, Katherine, how can I tell? men are so strange. They like a woman and don't find out that they love her till they can't have her. . . ."

"I wonder—" said Katherine, quickly, her eyes flashing. . . .

She checked the words. She had seen a rift in the cloud, and beyond a glimpse of blue. . . . It might be that Franklin loved her after all, and did not understand himself. . . . She had been so certain that he cared; and

Tonina had seen his interest. . . . The thought flashed a bright and shining light into dark places; the gleam of hope remained with her.

"I wonder what became of Colonel Jacob," she said softly.

"It was a great blow to him," said Mrs. Fleming, sentimentally. "He remained in Afghanistan, and I have heard nothing of him for more than twenty years."

"Mother, do you love him now?"

Mrs. Fleming's eyes faltered. She plucked at the folds of her gown.

"Really, my child, what strange questions you ask," she quavered. "It is thirty years since we met, and so many things have happened. . . . I should scarcely call it love, and yet . . ."

A weak little tear hung on her eyelashes. Katherine saw it, and stooped down and kissed her.

"Poor little mother!" she said tenderly.

"Oh! Katherine," Mrs. Fleming sobbed. "Be thankful that you don't know what it is to be fond of anyone. After all these years the pain is as great as it was in the beginning. . . ." She wiped her eyes furtively. "And yet I married your father. . . ."

"That was wrong," said Katherine, stoutly. "That was where you were wrong. There would have been no pain if you had had the right to love him still."

"I was so lonely . . . And I thought he didn't love me, Katherine. But I think your father guessed there was someone else. That was why he made that strange will. He knew I would never oppose the boys."

"If I had been at home he would never have made it," said Katherine, scornfully.

"But you see, Katherine, you thought it more im-

portant to get through your examination than to come
home. . . ."

Katherine reddened. Yes, it had seemed more important then to get a "first" than to nurse the father
whom she had scarcely known. . . . And now what part
had "firsts" in her life?

"Poor little mother!" she said again.

She kissed her with a sudden comprehension of the
long pain borne in silence these thirty years. How hard
life was for women! Would her fate be the same,—the
hungry longing for love denied growing and growing
until, desperate, she stayed her heart on a mockery of
love?

Her face was haggard when she went from the room;
but her heart was more pitiful and tender towards her
mother than it had ever been. She felt a new respect
for her. Only a strong woman would have suffered in
silence.

She wondered at the contradictions of our manifold
nature. Here was a nature tossed hither and thither by
the lightest breeze of disappointment that had stood
firm under a tempest fury of grief;—a tree ruffled by the
wind, whose roots were immovable deep down in the
heart of the ground.

Going from the room she met Tom. His eyes were
furious. He scowled as he saw her and stopped.

"Look here, Kit, I've told Peggy I won't marry her.
I wouldn't, not if there wasn't another woman in the
world. What right had she to send you with tales to
Tonina? . . . And what right had you to interfere?
Tonina's thrown me off, and that's all that your con-
founded meddling has done!"

He glared passionately at Katherine.

"Oh, Tom!" she said beseechingly, "think of Peggy....
You must marry her now. . . . You can't . . ."

"I tell you I won't,—so there! Hang you, let me
pass, will you!"

He pushed her aside roughly, and she did not try to
keep him. There was something in his manner that told
her she could not prevail against the obstinacy of weakness. She stood where he had left her, with terrified
eyes gazing at the tragedy of the situation,—no less tragic
because the pain and horror were not the fruit of crime,
but of a weak will and a shallow passion. . . .

Her heart was heavy when she went into the farmyard to give her orders for the day. Then, as usual, she
went on to the tomato-frames. But the sight of the fruit
reddening among the green leaves gave her no pleasure.
In each love-apple she saw Peggy's bleeding heart. It
made her own pain small to realise the girl's trouble. . . .

At last Katherine threw down the camel-hair brush
with which she had been carrying the pollen from flower
to flower, and ran into the house. . . . She must go to
Peggy and comfort her.

It was raining, but she was used to being out in all
weathers. Walking quickly, she crossed the green, which
looked bedraggled and untidy in the windy turmoil. The
storm had shaken down the autumn leaves; and the
discs that in sunshine would have patterned the grass
with a bright mosaic were curled up and sodden and
grey.

The rushes in the pond were torn, broken by wind
and rain. The pollard willows that edged the water
lifted yellowing rods to the clouds. Here and there the
flame of the burning bushes glowed in the distance
through thinning foliage.

The houses stood round the green, forlorn in aspect, and the ceaseless fall of the rain beat on Katherine's ears with a sound of weeping. The hopelessness of the stricken year set itself to the grief within. Her heart had bidden good-bye to summer

She remembered the day when she had come back to Plimpton and had crossed the green in all the glory of the May sunshine. It was Peggy who had set her footing it merrily,—the same Peggy that weighted her feet now with bewildered sorrow. She wondered at the bitterness with which she had renounced her London life. Surely she had made much ado about nothing. Bitterness? Ah! she had never tasted the bitterness of life until now.

The churchyard gate stood open. She could see the new red earth of Collop's bed where he had lain two days already. . . . "Already!" But she had lived years since she had listened to the rector's reading of the burial office, with Susan Parkin's boys standing open-mouthed gazing, and Martha's eyes watching them behind her handkerchief.

Susan Parkin had said there would soon be a corpse at Great Lowlands. She shook off the uncanny remembrance, half wishing that it could be true for her. Her heart was wounded to death, but she knew she would live still as if she had never known the anguish of yesterday. . . .

She hurried on towards Peggy's cottage. It was a tiny place; two rooms and an attic served for parlour, kitchen, and bedroom.

An oak dresser stood in the kitchen; and some old oak chairs were ranged round the distempered walls. A Henry VII. table stained with age made a shadow on the red brick floor. A bowlful of copper leaves stood

on the table. The only picture in the room was Watts's
"Love and Death."   Blue plates and dishes in a rack
ornamented the opposite wall.   Over the chimney-piece
was a collection of pewter mugs in a frame of riding-
whips.   Everything was very clean.   Peggy lived alone
and did her own housework.

She was not here, but Katherine found her in the
parlour.   The furnishings here were as simple as those
in the kitchen, but there were more pictures.   Botticelli's
"Spring," with its atmosphere of flower-crowned happiness, struck a crude contrast with the "Iphigenia" front-
ing it.

Peggy was on her knees, rubbing the brasses.   She
lifted a hot, red face to Katherine.

"Cleaning day," she said tersely.   "Sit down.   You
can talk while I polish the tongs."

The tension on Katherine's face gave way before the
commonplace words.   Peggy was not fretting then.   "They
look bright enough," she said.

"Hm!" Peggy grunted, looking at them critically.
"Well, yes.   But, you see, an extra rub now means an
extra shilling when they're sold."

"Oh, Peggy!   You would never sell those lovely old
tongs?"

"You never know what you'll do," said Peggy.

"If . . . if you want some money, . . ." Katherine
began.

Peggy let the tongs fall with a rattle and stood up,
her arms akimbo.   Her manner was unconcerned, but
there was a hunted look in her eyes.

"Don't be stupid, Kit.   If I wanted to borrow I wouldn't
beat about the bush.   I'd ask you at once."

"I . . . I knew Tom had been here," Katherine stammered, flushing. "It struck me . . . I thought you might wish to go away." . . .

Peggy smiled grimly.

"So you thought that, too? Tom hinted that I might clear out of Plimpton altogether."

"I didn't mean that—I thought. . . . There's your uncle . . ."

Peggy burst into a loud laugh. . . . "Poor old Uncle Jacob! Imagine it . . . an old bachelor, too!"

She laughed till she cried. Katherine was crying too. If Peggy would only be sad it would be easier. . . .

The rain beat on the windows. The wind shook the house, and roared around them as if to tear from their hearts the thing that kept them silent and constrained. . . . The silence hurt Katherine, but she could not break it, and Peggy would not.

"Who is your uncle?" Katherine said baldly at last.

"Colonel Jacob of The Moat, Chester. Would you recognise him now I have described him, Kit?"

"Peggy, you don't treat me well," Katherine said reproachfully. "I have done my best to help you; and I thought I had succeeded. Don't hold aloof from me like this. . . . Let me help you to bear it."

"Thanks," said Peggy, airily. "For the future I shall manage by myself. There is no help for any one of us but in ourselves."

Round her mouth the lines hardened; the hunted look in her eyes set its strain on the muscles of her face. Seeing her, Katherine's eyes filled again. Peggy stood and looked at her with an immovable smile that mocked the howling of the wind and the steady drip of the rain.

"Kit, you might have saved this," she said suddenly.

"I know, I know," Katherine whispered; "if only I had seen in time."

"Tom thought all the world of you once, and he is easily led" . . . said Peggy; "else he would not . . . Ah, well! it's too late now," she sighed. "But, Kit, you ought to help him. . . ."

"I will try," said Katherine, humbly; "and perhaps . . . in the end . . . everything will come right. . . ."

"I wonder," . . . said Peggy. Her eyes darkened: then she shook off the momentary weakness. "No, it can't be," she said, and laughed grimly. "Kit, the hounds have been baying round here a long time. . . . Well, they've unearthed their fox at last. I shall have to leave my hole. . . ."

"What do you mean? what hounds, what hole, Peggy?"

"The hounds of remorse," she said lightly. "Laburnum Drive is the hole."

Her glance travelled about the room. Suddenly she twisted round to Katherine, and there was a wistful note in her voice.

"It's a jolly little crib, isn't it? But now I think I should be lonely. . ."

"You were not lonely before," Katherine said.

"Good gracious, child, when were you born?" said Peggy, briskly. "Don't you know that a woman who loves is never lonely? It is only when she knows her love is hopeless that the loneliness eats into her life."

The brisk manner made the words more pathetic. Katherine turned away her white face, and caught her breath with a sob. If she could speak of her hopeless love it might help Peggy to bear hers. . . . But she could not unveil her heart. She remained silent, listening to the falling rain. "Was this tragedy in every woman's life?" she thought bitterly. "Must the love sown in pain be reaped not by life, but by death?"

Back to her mind came the voice of the rector read-ing the burial office·—

"'It is sown in dishonour, it is raised in glory; it is sown in weakness, it is raised in power; it is sown a natural body, it is raised a spiritual body That was not first which is spiritual, but that which is natural; and afterwards that which is spiritual The first is of the earth, earthy; the second is the Lord from heaven.'"

The words carried a confused meaning, seeming to answer her question, but vaguely, and in a way she hardly understood. Perhaps, after all, there might be some glad sequel to the love that never found its earthly close,—some sheaves of rejoicing for the sowers.

"I should wish you to have that picture of 'Iphigenia' when I go away. . . ."

Peggy was speaking. Katherine's mind came leaping back; it had gone far in the silence.

"I bought it because I used to think sacrifice was the greatest thing in life," Peggy continued. . . . "There's 'Spring,' too, but it ought to have been Autumn. Well, I shall be away from Plimpton when I reap my har-vest."

Katherine lifted her eyes.

"Peggy," she whispered, "I think that love sown in dishonour may be raised in glory. . . ."

Peggy stared at her.

"I don't understand it, anyway"

"It seems true," said Katherine. "The thing that perishes, that earth claims, is only that part of love that belongs to earth. There is a part of it that lives. 'The first is of the earth, earthy, the second is the Lord from heaven.' "

"Good gracious! I never heard you talk like that before," said Peggy.

A gust of wind shook the cottage, and the rain rattled like shot on the window-pane. Peggy looked out at the storm. The havoc in her garden, the bedraggled plants, the sunflowers beaten down where all had been so trim the day before, deepened the pain she was hiding even from herself.

"I wonder if there is any glory, any 'Lord from heaven,' in love at all?" she cried sharply.

"Oh, there must be!" Katherine exclaimed passionately. "The pain and the disillusion and the emptiness can't be all that comes from the strongest thing that our hearts feel. There must be good to follow sometime."

"Remorse is a good thing, I suppose," said Peggy. "But it is an awful thing to feel its teeth in your flesh." . . . She lifted her head, strangling the sob in her throat. "Kit, I have taught Tom the road to ruin," . . . she said, with ashen face. Katherine turned away her head to hide the pain she could not control.

"How would you like to have to stand by helpless, and see a person going to ruin?" said Peggy, sharply; "see him, and know it was you who had sent him that way?"

"I wouldn't stand by helpless," said Katherine, with a touch of scorn in her voice; "I'd do something to turn him out of the way."

Peggy shrugged her shoulders. "If you are in a tight place yourself, and the way out is blocked?"

"There is always a way out," said Katherine, looking up in time to see a light kindle on Peggy's face.

It was the light that streams out on a dark midnight, showing the boiling sea and the sharp-edged rocks. . . . Katherine remembered that they had spoken before of "a way out." She put out her hands entreatingly.

"Oh, Peggy! you wouldn't. . . ."

"Don't be afraid, Kit," Peggy smiled. "I feel horribly alive. If a hundred teeth in my heart won't kill me, a hundred horses won't."

Words and manner reassured Katherine. She rose slowly, her face subdued and full of pity, in which there was no dread.

"I'll come round again later," she said. "Don't decide anything, Peggy. I'll see Tom, and try to persuade him. . . ."

What more could she say to drive that hunted look from Peggy's eyes? She was silent; and the wind howled about the walls, and the rain beat with unsteady pulse in the quiet.

"Kit, why don't you despise me? . . . It is I who have made a mess of Tom's life," Peggy said suddenly. "I was a brute to blame you. He would have tired of me. . . . Men only amuse themselves with love. From the day Tonina came he changed. . . . But I thought that now . . . when he knew" . . . She turned away her face. "What a fool I was!" she laughed.

Katherine could not bear the ring of pain in her voice. She walked quickly to the door, and under the dripping laburnum arches to the gate. The first time she had seen them the branches had been weighted by golden chains. Now they bent under a load of brown and withered seed-pods,—an unlovely harvest for the blossoms of the sun.

Peggy stood under the trees, unconscious of the

snatching winds, and of the rain beating on her bare
head.

She saw nothing of the long country road, vanishing
until it lost itself in the common that in the distance
looked like a sea of mist. Her gaze fell heedlessly on
the cottage roofs. The outer world did not exist for her
any more. Her world was within. At last she shook
her face free of doubt, and her face became resolute.
She lifted her eyes on tree and earth and mist and rain,
and she shivered in the cold, and turned back into the
cottage.

She climbed slowly to her bedroom and remained
there a long time, touching the things with caressing
fingers, lingering over them, stroking them softly.

When she came down she was in her habit. Her
face was pale under the hat-brim.

She glanced up at the picture in the kitchen,—the
closed door, the helplessness of Love against Death.

"It is all wrong," she said aloud. "It is Life who
is helpless against Love. It is Love who calls in
Death."

She went out, taking her way to the stable. At the
sound of her step the horse turned his head and whin-
nied. A frightened look came into her eyes. She flung
her arms round his neck and leaned against him.

"Oh, Sambo! oh, my poor boy! I have to go away
and leave you! There is no other way. . . . And you
will find another mistress;—but I think Kit will take
you. . . . Sambo, do you know it is our last ride?"

Sambo turned his head and looked round at her,
and Peggy wiped away her tears, smiling to think he
understood.

She saddled him herself, fastening buckle and strap

with reckless trembling fingers. With her own hands she fed him until, satisfied, he scattered the corn she held to his mouth. She loitered over her task, and even laughed when he nosed the food disdainfully. And when she rode through the gate the smile was still on her lips.

But it faded away as she rode, and her face grew set and hard. "I wonder if I shall ever see it again," she said, her eyes moving over field and meadow. Her gaze lingered about the lanes where she had wandered with Tom; and she tossed up her head, and caught her breath with a little moaning noise. . . .

Then her mood changed. She set spurs to Sambo and dashed along the road and down the hill, laughing harshly. Sambo turned the whites of his eye, and passed the white gate with a dancing sidelong motion that tightened Peggy's hold on the reins. . . .

All at once a new look was on her face. It was as if thought, galloping, had been thrown back suddenly on its haunches. . . . She set her lips in a thin red line, and lifted her head jauntily. . . . "I'll make him do it, if I die for it!" she said recklessly. "Who cares? If there is a way out I'll find it!"

She twisted sharply round, and went at a gallop towards the gate.

——— — —

CHAPTER V.

ON THE EVE OF DEFEAT.

ALL the day following his journey from town Franklin's thoughts were engaged with Katherine's confession. No woman had ever claimed his thoughts like this.

The son of a dissenting minister in Hull, he had spent a lonely boyhood in his father's library, avoiding the Xantippe that was his stepmother. Later, until he found work in the Labour Movement he had passed his days in his book-shop in Hull, and had only known of his housekeeper's presence by the tyranny of her cleanliness.

Then had come a great dock-strike, and the cry of the starving dockers had been heard in the land, even in the book-seller's den. Franklin could not silence the sound. Outside his door he saw the men grouped, pipeless, hopeless, undaunted. They were the soldiers in the Labour war,—a war that slays its heroes though not a drop of blood be shed.

He could not get away from the memory of their faces. They whitened the pages of his books; rugged and worn they looked at him from every cover.

He came out from his shop to study these human books, and the study fascinated him. It led him into the homes of the people, where women hid their sufferings that men might fight the power that crushed them. He saw the strike from the workers' point of view, and all his sympathy went with the dockers.

He set up a soup kitchen; and during the hungry weeks that followed he beggared himself to feed the women and children.   When the war was over he stood among book shelves as empty as the shelves in his larder. . . . A pamphlet on strikes bridged him over the next weeks, and drew the attention of the Labour world to him.   He was already known as a somewhat quixotic partisan of the people; the pamphlet showed him a thinker.   He was offered, and he accepted, a secretary-ship, and went up to town, where his education and enthusiasm made him a force, and attracted to him all the younger men, among them Mark Fleming.

Perhaps it was owing to Franklin's steadfastness that Mark had remained so long in the Movement.   It was to strengthen the weak knees that Franklin became his friend. And now Mark had left the cause, and all that the friendship had brought forth was this unwelcome confession from Mark's sister.

Franklin wondered how it had come about.   He walked up and down the parlour of the Wheat Sheaf at Grimple, biting his moustache, and asking himself how she had come to think he loved her?

He was not a little disturbed by the episode.   He paced the floor, his brows darkening and dismayed. How could he, a crusted old bachelor, have attracted an unformed girl, little better than a child?   It was absurd! Certainly he had not misled her by admiration.   She was frankly unreserved.   She had none of the alluring mystery of the womanly woman, the reticence, the modesty he admired.   She was proud of her independence and vaunted herself.   He had not scrupled to show his disapproval of her qualities. How then could she have supposed that he loved her?

He paused in his walk, and stood drumming discontentedly against the window.

It was market-day in Grimple, and the people were passing the Wheat Sheaf on their way to the High Street. The crowded pavements reminded him of Goodge Street. He stood once more at the window of Mark's lodgings, his heart pitiful for the girl weeping on the sofa.

Her passion had been that of a child; she had not vaunted herself then. He could almost hear her sobbing. . . . He turned round, half expecting to see a girl huddled up on the sofa. Then he smiled constrainedly, conscious of a softer feeling stirring him.

"Poor little thing!" he said to himself.

She had cried then over her fallen ambitions. Would she be crying now over her fallen hopes?

He took off his *pince-nez* and swung it slowly round and round in his fingers. . . .

Perhaps, after all, she would not be fretting. There would be her farm-work to do,—the cows must be milked. . . . How sweet and dainty she had been, driving the cows across the field. She had not looked like a strong-minded woman then, but like a simple, wholesome country girl. . . . Yes, she would be hard at work; the old cowman was dead. . . . The thought of Collop took him back to Sunday night and Collop's cottage. . . . He looked through the window, and saw her sitting lonely in the shadowy kitchen, the puppy pressed to her cheek, her eyes dim with yearning. . . . But that could not be the true Katherine, the girl he had called unwomanly, who was not soft and gentle. The real Katherine was a quite different person. How had he seen her last?

There flashed before him the picture of an artificially lighted room, and women and men as artificial as the light; and, standing among them, a girl straight and tall, with the fresh air all about her, and the sun burnt red on her cheeks, claiming as friend the shabbiest man in the room. . . . Yes, this was the fearless, frank Katherine of whom he disapproved.

At the last word he jerked up his thoughts. . . . How could he disapprove of her for the warmth of that generous greeting, for the frankness that set her miles away from those simpering dolls? She had been the only true woman among them all; the only one who had a heart and was not ashamed to show it. And it was this brave heart that he had disdained. . . .

Franklin frowned. But his vexation at himself only made him bent on justifying his action.

After all, if a man loved a woman wouldn't he tell her so? She had no right to force a man into a position in which he must look foolish if not ungenerous. . . . Why could she not be content with friendship and the help he had offered? . . . All at once he remembered that she had said she wanted his help, and had begged him not to leave England. He had almost decided to accept that colonial appointment, and yet . . .

Well, he could advance the cause better if he remained in England, and represented his party in the House. He must find out what this trouble was in which she needed help. The girl was lonely enough; an ineffectual mother, Mark absorbed in his wife, and a happy-go-lucky brother,—she stood practically alone. Poor little thing! No wonder she had turned in her need to a man that she trusted. . . . And after all, she had not done anything very terrible. According to the Fabians and to

progressive thought, she was quite within her rights to
show her feeling for him. A wistful look chased the
frown from his face. Why should he be vexed, because
she had shown him such favour? A man was fortunate
indeed to win the love of a woman who shared his interests, and would be comrade as well as wife.

He thought of his grim lodgings in Battersea. How
much cosier than his Mark's rooms in Goodge Street had
always seemed! Was it because of Katherine's presence
there? And did that account in any way for his own
frequent visits to Mark? He did not go so often to the
gaudy flat where Tonina ruled. . . .

Poor little Katherine! It was hard that Mark
should have turned her adrift. She had felt it too;
she was a passionate little soul, and her feelings were
deep. . . .

Someone came noisily into the inn-parlour. Franklin
turned round. When he saw Mark he felt like "a guilty
thing surprised." His air was almost apologetic as he
went forward.

"Well, old man, I didn't expect to see you here," he
said, with a gaiety that was its own accusation.

"Confounded nuisance coming," grumbled Mark.
"Pilchard's making a mess of it, isn't he?"

Pilchard was the Labour candidate.

"More or less," said Franklin. "The game is nearly
up. I always said he was the wrong man. . . . And now
Dawson knows it."

His manner was more natural. Mark had evidently
no personal reason for his visit.

"I know that," said Mark, eagerly; "but I heard
something at the office to-day that would alter all that,
and give Pilchard the pull over Dawson. I've come down

on purpose to tell you. I have a sneaking fondness for the cause yet."

"Of course you have!" said Franklin, heartily. "But you might have sent me a wire."

Mark shook his head. "Too risky. The thing is a dead secret, a personal thing, awfully damaging to Dawson. I got it in confidence at the office, you see, and it's as much as my place is worth to tell it. Still, you're as safe as Pharaoh; and it's touch and go with Pilchard unless Dawson's crippled. . . . Well?"

He sat astride the sofa and looked inquiringly at Franklin. But Franklin shook his head, pursing up his lips.

"Don't you want to know?" Mark said impatiently.

"No," said Franklin.

Mark sprang from his perch. "Well, what in the name! . . . And after I've come down on purpose!" . . .

"The fact is," said Franklin, tossing back his head, "I don't believe in getting a pull over Dawson by foul means. Everything must be straight and aboveboard."

"Pack o' nonsense!" Mark exclaimed. "What's that to do with it? Look here, you're in charge of this business, aren't you?"

"Well?" said Franklin.

"And if Pilchard doesn't get in you'll be blamed for it."

"Well?" said Franklin again.

"Well, look here! It's a hanged certainty that he won't get in unless you can check the other man's move. What I can tell you gives him over to you. Pilchard walks in; and the credit is yours."

"The discredit, you mean," said Franklin, quietly. "Mark, my boy, you meant to do us a friendly turn; but Pilchard mustn't get in by fraud."

"Moonshine!" said Mark, roughly.   "Everything is fair in war."

"I won't do it," said Franklin.   "Pilchard gets in without fear or favour, or not at all."

"You are a fool!" said Mark, his thin face flushed and dark.   "And you're the only man I dare trust with the thing. . . . I daren't risk a libel action for the *Hour Glass,* else I'd tell Pilchard. . . ."

"No use;" Franklin shook his head.   "If you're betraying confidence I won't hear."

"Then I've come all this way for nothing?" Mark grumbled.

"Not a bit of it. . . . You're in the nick of time for to-night's meeting.   Give us a speech."

"Not I!   I'll take the last train up."

"How is your wife?" said Franklin.

"Violin-mad," Mark said, with unnecessary bitterness.   "She's at it all day until she fairly drives me out of the place.   And at night she is generally playing somewhere, so we don't see much of each other."

"Sounds accommodating," said Franklin, drily.

There was an ugly twist about Mark's mouth.

"These professional women are the very deuce; they have a will of their own, and get it.   Poor little Kit was a tame cat compared with Tonima."

"How is your sister?" said Franklin, with elaborate ease.

"Flourishing, I believe.   But I must go; there's just time for that train."

He glanced at the clock and went out of the parlour.

Five minutes after, another man put his head in.

"Hillo, Brace!" said Franklin, rousing himself.   "How are things going?"

Brace came in, tossed his hat on a chair, poured out a glass of water from the carafe on the table, drank it, then spoke. "All's up with Pilchard. Only a miracle will get him in."

"I always thought so," said Franklin, with a grim smile. "We must make a big effort to-night."

"The fellows are saying you've made a mess of the canvassing."

"That's not true," said Franklin, quietly.

"Well, to-night will decide things. . . . By the way, don't ask me to speak."

"You must," said Franklin. "Everything depends on this meeting."

"I know that; but 'pon my word, it's impossible. I've had a nasty shock, and can't get over it."

"What has happened?"

"I was going through Plimpton, and just as I passed that old farm-house the other side of the common a girl came tearing out, riding bareback. Her face was like the grave, but I recognised her at once as Fleming's sister. You will remember her; she used to speak for us in town. . . . Fine girl, capital speaker. I stood watching her, wondering how she stuck to that horse without a saddle; and half an hour after . . ."

"Well?" said Franklin, impatiently.

"I passed the house again. They were carrying in a stretcher with the girl . . ."

"An accident?" Franklin interrupted. He started up from his chair, and stood, his hand gripping the back of the seat.

"Yes, she had been thrown. She was dead before they picked her up."

"*She was dead before they picked her up?*" Franklin

repeated in a strange, hoarse voice. Both hands gripped
the back of his chair. The room was spinning round.

Brace poured out another glass of water and drank
it very slowly.

"I'd give anything not to have seen it," he said.
"They had covered her face with the skirt. She always
wore green, I remember. It will be a nasty shock for
Fleming; he thought a lot of her. I rather admired her
myself. . . . I'll never forget a speech she gave in the
Park one Sunday. I couldn't speak to-night without thinking of it, and making an ass of myself. . . . It's a rough
business. Poor little girl!"

Brace passed his hand over his forehead and gulped
down some more water. "This will make a difference to
Fleming's prospects, I fancy. He told me his father had
left a curious will,—the farm to be the girl's so long as
she didn't marry, or something like that."

"Yes," said Franklin, in a dazed manner. He walked
to the window and stood with his back to the room.
He dared not look round. The silence was an open
grave. . .

"I hope she wasn't a friend of yours," said Brace at
last, awkwardly.

"I don't think I ever knew her," Franklin answered.

The truth of the words held the sting of death for
him. He had never known her. . . .

The room seemed to spin again. He was in town
at Ludgate Circus. The noise of train and traffic hurtled
round. . . . The shouts of men trying to stop a runaway
horse deafened him. . . . He saw Katherine spring forward, right in front of the flying hoofs. . . .

Once again he stood in a horrible paralysis The
woman he loved was in peril of life, and he was power-

less. . . . "The woman he loved?" . . . Ah, yes! he knew it now. . . . Then all was dark. There was a rushing and surging in his ears, a thunder of words. "The horse had thrown her. She was dead before they picked her up." . . .

From that noise and tumult Franklin groped his way painfully back to the present. He turned to Brace. . . . The words came slowly and haltingly. "Thank you for telling me this. I shall not forget"

CHAPTER VI.

THE WHITE GATE.

KATHERINE was going down the drive, when a lad, mounted on one of their own horses, came galloping up to say that Peggy had been thrown. She was in the hillside field.

All at once Katherine was marble; and the hard cold voice was like her face.

"Is she much hurt . . . dead?"

The boy widened his mouth, dropping the under lip.

"Her back's broke."

"Get off!" Katherine cried.

She almost dragged the boy from his seat, took his place, and flew along the drive and down the road towards the hillside field, spurred on by words that tore her memory. "When life gets too hard I will take the leap. . . . There is always a way out. . . ."

A group of men guided her to the place. Where the white gate had stood there was an opening. Her face blanched as she rode through.

Peggy lay where she had been thrown. Katherine knelt on the wet grass, and lifted the dead face to her bosom and held it there, the men watching stolid and silent.

She looked up, and her lips moved, but no sound came. The men turned away, and examined Sambo, lifting his legs and speaking under their breath.

Katherine laid her burden down, straightening the habit. She folded Peggy's hands on her bosom, and wiped the mud from her face before she lifted herself.

"Bring her home to Great Lowlands," she ordered, in a high strained voice.

Before they raised Peggy, one of the men folded his coat on the gate, which they had taken off its hinges. . . . The straight, uncovered form pleaded for seclusion. Katherine slipped off her skirt and laid it over face and figure, and the bearers lifted their burden.

Under the horror that froze Katherine her thoughts moved swiftly. The life struggled in her heart like a caged creature throwing itself against the bars of its prison; but her mind was free, and it hovered about Peggy's need.

She remounted, and rode quickly to the farm, leaving the men to follow.

White as the dead, she met them again at the door, and led them up to her room, where she had made her own bed ready. . . . She had sent one of the servants for her mother, who was at the rectory; the other had gone for the doctor. Alone in the house, Katherine did for Peggy what Martha had done for her old man. When the doctor came Peggy lay shrouded and peaceful, and there was no need to disturb her.

Tom had not been at home since the morning. The thought of him lay a heavy terror on Katherine's mind. Every fresh arrival at the house made her tremble to hear his voice.

Death had crashed through the quiet of Great Lowlands. People were coming and going. There would have to be an inquest. Katherine had to see everyone, to answer questions, to make arrangements. She had not a moment for grief. There were letters to be written, telegrams to send.

Coming into the hall, Mrs. Fleming saw on the table the telegram addressed to Colonel Jacob, The Moat, Chester. The name had vaguely pricked Katherine's memory; it stood before Mrs. Fleming as the ghost of a dead love. Forgetting the tragedy at her gates, she sank into a chair, agitated and trembling. Katherine found her there crying.

The girl came forward in the marble coldness that had held her since her ride to the hillside field. The horror was in her eyes; her face was still and white.

"Mother dear, you must not let it upset you," she said gently.

Mrs. Fleming wiped her eyes, looking up.

"It's a terrible thing," she sobbed. "I always said she would kill herself riding those young horses. . . . Katherine . . ." Her tone changed to an eager curiosity, "Katherine, how did you know where to find Colonel Jacob?"

"Peggy told me," said Katherine. Her voice shook. She knew now why Peggy had told her.

"It must be the same," Mrs. Fleming said quickly. "I wonder how she knew . . ."

"He was her uncle. The telegram is to tell him. . . . I have asked him to come here. . . ."

Mrs. Fleming got up, shaking. "It must be the same. Her uncle! . . . You take too much upon your-self, Katherine," she quavered. "You should have con-sulted me first. . . . Not but what I shall be pleased to see him," she added, a weak smile breaking through her protest.

"There was nothing else to be done," said Katherine,

gravely. "Peggy is here . . . it would have been lonely at the cottage. . . ."

Mrs. Fleming began to cry again: "Oh, Katherine!" she said reproachfully, "to bring her here, when I am so ill and nervous! . . ."

"She is in my room, mother, away from everybody."

The thought of Peggy's uncle soothed Mrs. Fleming's fears. "He will feel it very much, I am sure," she said, pressing her handkerchief to her eyes. . . . "And my poor son too."

"Where is Tom?" Katherine asked.

"Gone to town . . . You must break it to him gently, Katherine. I believe he was sincerely attached to the girl, though I never thought her a suitable match for a Fleming. . . . Of course if I had known she was related to Colonel Jacob I could have put up with her coarseness and unladylike . . ."

Katherine snatched her hat from the rack and ran from the house, her heart bursting.

She passed the people, standing in knots on the green talking over the accident. She saw them nudge each other, and grow silent, and stare as she went by; but she took no notice, and walked on furiously to Laburnum Cottage.

The rain was over. A stormy sunset crimsoned the pools in the road, and flashed red lights to meet her from the windows of Peggy's cottage.

The door was not locked. She opened it and went in; and the silence in her heart filled all the empty rooms.

The orderliness in kitchen and parlour made her catch her breath and tread softly. She was in the house of death. She stumbled up the stairs to the bedroom,

Here, too, everything was prepared for Peggy's going
away, except that the bed wore clean linen, as if in ex-
pectation of a guest. . . . Katherine's heart rose in her
with a great cry. . . . She swayed and clutched at a
table to keep herself from falling. With a clatter it came
to the ground, scattering the contents of a drawer
wrenched open by the fall.

Katherine gathered together the dainty needle-work,
her eyes full of terror and love and pity. Only a few
hours before, Peggy's fingers had lingered tenderly among
them; but the look on her face had been the look of the
woman who sees the fruit of her body dead before
her. . . .

Katherine did not replace the things in their hiding-
place. She carried them to the stove in the kitchen, and
setting fire to them, watched them burn till Love and
Death guarded the ashes that held Peggy's secret.

Her face was grey like the ashes when she took her
way home through the dusk; and the weight of life and
death bent her figure so that she walked like an old
woman. The green was shrouded in mist. It clung to
her face in dank folds.

Mrs. Fleming had gone to her room. The maids
stood at the door talking to Susan Parkin. . . . With a
fierce joy Katherine's hand closed over the key in her
pocket. It belonged to the locked door, behind which
Peggy lay. She passed Susan with a shudder, remembering her prophecy. At ten o'clock she sent the maids to
bed. She would sit up for Tom.

She threw herself on the sofa, and lay there with
white face and eyes staring at the dead thing the day
had brought forth. At last it became intolerable. The
sight of Peggy herself would be less dreadful. . . .

Katherine crawled upstairs to her room and lighted a candle, and sat down beside the shrouded figure. And as she sat there the dead spoke. Peggy's silence arraigned her.

The day had been charged with wounded love and helplessness, with pain and disappointment; but striking through the agony came now the sharp thrust of a keen-edged thought,—

"Kit, you might have saved this."

Katherine lifted herself in quick denial that stopped on her lips. . . . The dead compelled the truth. . . . She shrank back humbled. . . . Was she guiltless?

Had she not taken Tom's one duty from him, and set him free to drift into any entanglement he pleased? Had she tried to redeem him from his idleness? Had she not feared lest he should interfere with her management? . . . She might have saved this final disaster. . . .

In the anguish of that stroke her heart lay open. Dazed as she was, she saw herself, her pride, ambition, self-seeking, the strong compelling forces of her conduct. Her ears heard the mute reproach of dead lips. In the quiet it thundered round her, awful, irresistible, filling the room.

The silence in her soul surged with the words: "You might have saved this." And in her heart the truth rolled and echoed. again: "You might have saved this." The night was full of the thunder of her impeachment. As it crashed round her, she cowered, and sank on her knees, and covered her face before God.

Footsteps were on the stairs, but she did not hear them. The door opened, and Martha tiptoed in.

"Missie," she said in a loud whisper, "I be comed

to help you with the poor lass, but I doubt I'm over-late. . . ."

Katherine rose from her knees, strangling the sobs in her throat.

"It's all done, Martha; just as you did it on Sunday night."

"Ay, poor dear! And you've forgot nothing? . . . Well, I'll come along for the coffining, and so no tongues shall wag over the poor heart. Yes, her were a hearty lass. I couldn't but admire her frank ways."

She turned back the sheet with reverent fingers and looked at Peggy, her face twitching with grief.

Katherine took the old woman's hand. "Let us go downstairs," she said gently.

In the kitchen Martha wiped her eyes, and was immediately her old bright self.

"You're killing yourself fretting, duckie," she said, "and fretting never mended no broken bones. 'Tis nature for a man to be roving, we all know. But I telled Mr. Tom many a time 't was well to be on with the new love before he were off with the old. 'T would save a tarrible deal o' pother if men minded that when they went a-sweethearting."

"Will you stay here to-night?" Katherine asked wearily.

"No, duckie; the puppy be sadly, poor dear! I come to arst you to see if you could tell what ailed en. He do suffer tarrible, to be sure;—but it do be late, and missie be tired."

"No, I'll come," said Katherine. "I want to breathe the air. Tom can't be here yet."

"Then come along, duckie. It be time surely. I doubt the poor boy be missing the old woman."

Katherine went out into the darkness. Still she could not think; she could not feel. Life whirled about her. The very earth reeled. Whirled with the reeling world, she had no point of certainty. The one certainty was most uncertain of all. . . . *"Peggy is dead. Peggy is dead."* . . . The thought focussed her mind to the instability of her world. It was not true! How could Peggy be dead? How could Peggy be lying upstairs dead? . . . *By her own hand?* The other world crashing into the present loosened her hold of both worlds. The soul of Katherine stood swaying dazed on the edge from which Peggy had slipped swiftly into the unknown. But the girl Katherine followed Martha with feet that did not swerve or falter.

CHAPTER VII.

A MAN'S LOVE.

KATHERINE was still at the cottage when Tom came in. The room was full of smoke from a flaring lamp, and soot-flakes from the chimney were thick on the cloth and dishes.

"Phew!" Tom grimaced; "a pretty welcome for a fellow! Kit might have waited up."

His temper had improved since the morning. He had gone to Ridgmont Gardens, boiling over with indignation and thwarted passion, and Tonina had met him with open friendliness, and rallied him gaily on his bad temper. Under her gaiety there was something that baffled him. He could not pass the barrier of her sisterliness.

While he sulked and smarted at the change, she chirped on about his "soul" for music, until he began to think his admiration of her had only been admiration of her art, the awakening of a real passion for music. He confessed to a voice; and she made him sing to her, and went into raptures over his ordinary baritone, turning his head with her praise. The flattery softened those other words in which Tonina had scarified those "men who helped women to make mud-pies of their married life." Tom had winced at the veiled reproof, but had had manliness enough to see that he deserved it.

And immediately after she had made him forget the sting in allusions to his horsemanship and the splendid figure he cut in the saddle. From this she skilfully led the talk to Peggy, her spirit and courage and originality, until Tom's thoughts harked back to Peggy's smartness, that had first attracted him. . . . He began to see also that his feeling for Tonina changed with her changed tone. Peggy's conscious eyes stirred him more than Tonina's sisterly glances. . . . Because she no longer belonged to him he wanted her. . . . By the time he left Ridgmont Gardens he had swung round into a half-formed wish to keep faith with his old love. . . . "With Peggy a fellow is a man; Tonina makes you feel as if you were a whipped schoolboy." . . .

He hung up his hat and coat in the hall.

"I suppose Kit's gone to bed huffed because I went to town in spite of her. Well, I'll go upstairs and have a talk with her. I may as well let her know I'm going to make it right with Peggy. I know she isn't asleep."

He had seen the light in her window. It had been almost the only one in the village, and it had shone with a kindly ray, guiding him home.

"I'll go up now and tell her," said Tom.

Whistling softly, in great good-humour with himself, he went along the passage, his steps echoing in the sleeping house. A thread of light from the door Katherine had left unfastened lay across the landing and guided him up the stairs. He knocked at the door, and hearing nothing pushed it open and went in. The candle had burnt low, and the small flame flickered, casting thick shadows. Tom saw nothing but the outline of the figure on the bed.

"None of your shamming, Kit," he said gaily. "I know you aren't asleep, and I want to have a talk with you"

He went closer, and stooped down, and met the white face of the dead. . . .

Even in that dim light he recognised the thing he saw; and he stood staring down, shocked into numbness,—thought, sensation, emotion suspended.

"Peggy!"—the name was in his memory, but it was strange to him. It did not belong to the face that looked up at him from the pillow, to the glassy eyes half-closed. . . . Then fear came crashing through the paralysis What did it mean? what did it mean? Who was this lying in Katherine's bed, still and pale and awful? . . .

His dry lips moved. "Peggy . . . Peggy . . . Peggy!" . . . The words dropped one by one into the silence and plumbed its depth. . . . Drops of terror chilled his forehead. . . . He put out his hand and touched her. . . .

At the cold of that frozen form he staggered back against the wall where he stood, his eyes fascinated by the dead face. Was this Peggy whom he had loved and forsaken,—Peggy whom he still loved, and would not forsake? . . .

Like a moth his glance crossed the shadow and flitted about the light of that white presence. His eyes burnt and were shrivelled as he looked, but his gaze fluttered about the pillow and could not die. . . .

"Peggy!" he groaned, "I love you. . . . I was a fool. . . . I was going to tell you I love you. . . . Tonina's nothing to me. I only love you."

It was true. Peggy lying dead and beyond his reach forever was dearer to him than she had ever been in life. He remembered the spring morning when she had gone her own way and had whipped his passion into mad desire. . . . And now she had gone her own way by that high road on which he would never overtake her. . . . Passion flamed in him again, fanned by remorse and regret and unattainable longing. . . .

The candle burnt low; the room was suddenly dark but for the pale glimmer of the clouded moon.

The changed light was as though sound had conquered silence, and it roused Tom He stumbled to the door, but on the threshold he looked back. . . .

The face shone white where all was shadowy white, and it drew him again into the room. . . . It was cruel to leave her staring up into the darkness. . . . He covered her, but the sheet clinging to her face seemed more cruel than the darkness. He drew it away, and threw his arms about her.

.   .   .   .

Katherine followed Martha through the orchard. The moon was hidden, and the trees loomed dark, holding out towards them ghostly branches on which the apples hung unseen. The women's footsteps made no sound as they went over the sodden moss. Cloaked and hooded, the two passed like mysterious Fates where the gods had rioted.

They came out of the orchard into the meadow. In the distance the glassy face of the pond looked blankly up at a stormy sky Beside the bank gleamed the light from Milkmaid Cottage.

The puppy was lying in a basket beside the kitchen fire. His eyes were dull, his limbs limp; his tail moved feebly at the sound of Martha's steps.

"Ah, poor Jockie!" she sighed. "Lie still, duckie, mother do be come now. Mother will soon make her boy well. Deary, deary, his little body be as tight as a nut!"

"Is he very bad, Martha?" Katherine asked pitifully, stooping over him. Then she looked up: "You must get oatmeal and make him a poultice."

Martha eyed her dubiously.

"I doubt Jockie would sooner have the poultice inside than out," she began.

"Don't waste time. Get it at once," Katherine said in her old masterful manner.

A curious twinkle was in Martha's eye as she made the poultice ready. When Jock's head fell helplessly over the bandage she wrapped him in a shawl and gave him to Katherine.

The girl sat holding him, her heart pitiful for his helplessness, something like mother-love stirring in her. It soothed the pain of her suffering, and lessened the tension of her dread. Thought steadied itself She remembered Peggy's love for dumb things, and her dive into the water to save the drowning puppy. The memory flickered in her heart like a flame trembling to life . . . Was it possible that tender-hearted Peggy could have wilfully sacrificed two lives to her despair? Had she not intended to leave Plimpton, and riding recklessly in that last ride met her death?

The frost about Katherine's heart melted, and the icy bands that had held her were unbound. Her feet stood on ground that did not yield. Grief took the place of horror and dread and intolerable fear. She could bear the thought of an accidental death. . . . It lifted the heaviest weight of anguish. . . . At last she roused herself, and gave the puppy to Martha. "I must be going back. . . . Tom will be coming home."

The sharp old eyes searched her face.

"I'm sure you've cured the baby, duckie. I couldn't a-bear to lose en. I'd ha' missed my old man tarrible bad but for Jockie. . . . Ay, women be a poor box o' tools for shaping love! that be the man's work; but they be well enough for keeping it together once 'tis made."

"I think they know more of love than men," said Katherine, her weary eyes grown wistful.

"Lor no, missie!" said Martha, disparagingly. "You thinks so because you doesn't know men and the ways of 'em, which it ain't seemly that you should, being a young maid. A woman be like stone fruit with just the one love in her; but a man be as full of love as a pumpkin be of seeds. . . . And he can't help hisself, for 'tis nature do give him the advantage over the woman."

"I suppose only a woman remains faithful to one love?" said the girl, sadly.

"Ay, poor, weak fools, they doesn't know their privileges! . . . You looks a sight betterish than when you comed in." Martha gave another of her keen glances. "More spunk about you like."

"Yes, I feel better," said Katherine. "It doesn't look so hopeless. Good-night, Martha."

Martha waited till she heard the garden gate click. Then the lines of her face puckered and twisted. She chuckled delightedly as she lifted Jock out of the poultice. She held him up by his forepaws and laughed aloud when his head fell to one side.

"Poor heart!" she said, her sides shaking. "Mother's treated her boy shameful He be as drunk as a lord; and I dunno what missie would say to the old woman if her knowed 'twas only a gill of whiskey that ailed en. But lawks! who'd ha' thought of a poultice for to make a puppy sober? . . . Ah, well, poor lass! it's done en good and roused en a bit. I've knowed a sick chicken keep a maid from breaking her heart for love; yes, I have. . . . And missie'll never know the baby ailed nothing but a drop o' Glenlivet. . . . Dear heart, he took en as prutty and nat'ral as a dandy. To be sure, Fan be pure Scotch; and we knows what be bred by the flesh will go to the devil. . . ."

Katherine walked back to Great Lowlands. A trail of light from a broken cloud was on the pond. It was as though a sleeping face had awakened. The turmoil in her calmed. She grew strong again. Nerve and muscle knit. There was even a spring in her feet as she walked. The land lay submissive under its burden of night, patient for the slow coming dawn. Soon the shrouded form would stir, the strong limbs thrill, and Earth blush under the eyes of her bridegroom coming out of his chamber, rejoicing as a strong man. . . .

Katherine drank the midnight strength, her lips at nature's breast, and courage came to her.

The wind swept through the silence like a melody, bringing remembered words:—

"Temple thou hast none,
Nor altar heaped with flowers;
Nor virgin choir to make delicious moan
Upon the midnight hours;
No voice, no lute, no pipe, no incense sweet
From chain-swung censer teeming;
No shrine, no grove, no oracle, no heat
Of pale-mouth'd prophet dreaming."

Her face woke. Determination took the place of grief and humbleness. She would build a temple to night, to pain, and sorrow, and minister there. She would plant her grove of human trees. . . . Tom should be the first. It was not too late. She would set herself to save his soul.

The zest of resolve thrilled her; she tried to control it, reproachful at her heartlessness. Not an hour ago she had been stricken to death, dazed, bruised, humiliated; yet the horror of great darkness was passing from her. Already dawn was breaking. . . . She hurried her steps through the orchard and came breathless to the house.

She went quickly into the parlour, but there was no sign of Tom. The supper table was covered with blacks; the lamp smouldered offensively. . . . She went to the kitchen, cosy with dancing firelight, and spread supper there, making coffee against Tom's coming in.

When all was ready she took a candle and went up to lock the door that she had left unfastened. It was wide open, and she paused on the landing. The light ran before her into the room. Tom sat on the bed, holding Peggy in his arms.

Katherine stood frozen, gazing at Tom's dazed white face, the whiter face on his breast. Peggy's bosom rose and fell with his heavy breathing.

Katherine turned away her eyes and stepped back.

. . . But she could not leave him like that. . . . She went into the room, setting down her candle.

"Tom," she said softly, "Tom, dear . . ."

He started, and life flashed back to his face. He laid Peggy down with trembling hands and stood up, his knees shaking. The strength of his unavailing passion had made him weak.

"What is it? . . . how was it? . . . who has done it?" he said brokenly.

"Sambo threw her," Katherine whispered. "She was quite dead. . . ."

He turned himself from Katherine's eyes. . . .

"Then it wasn't me? . . ."

She went to him and put her arm round him silently.

"I thought it was me," he said hoarsely.

Katherine shook her head. She couldn't speak.

"And now it's too late," he said, as if to himself. "And now it's too late . . ."

"It was over in a minute," Katherine said in a low voice. "She couldn't have felt anything."

Tom crossed to the bed and stroked Peggy's disarranged hair. His hands lingered about her.

"I'd give anything if I had known sooner," he groaned. "And I was hard on her. . . . Kit, do you think she had got over it before . . . before? . . ."

"I was with her," Katherine faltered. "She spoke kindly of you. . . ."

"Ah, she wouldn't bear malice! she had a good heart. . . . I was mad . . . And now it's too late. . . ."

"It is not too late," Katherine said gently. "It may come right yet, Tom."

Her lowered voice sounded hollow in the hush about them.

"How can it come right?" Tom burst out. "Peggy is gone, my one love . . . The only one who loved me. . . . Don't you see that she is gone? . . . I have nobody left. How can it come right?" . . .

Katherine shrank back from his fierce eyes; then she put her hand on his arm.

"I love you, Tom And I loved Peggy, too. . . ."

Tears were pouring down her face. He stared at her, and roughly drew away.

"You! you!" he cried. "You love nobody but yourself. It's you that came between me and Peggy. I'd never have broken with her if you hadn't interfered. . . ."

He dashed the tears from his eyes, biting his lips.

"Oh, Tom, I can't bear to hear you say that!" Katherine sobbed. "But it is true. . . . It was my fault. . . . I only thought 'of myself. . . . I didn't help you. . . ."

"I didn't help myself; you weren't to blame for that," he said. "Don't cry, Kit," he added more gently. "We won't quarrel before her. . . ."

"She wished us to be friends," Katherine said humbly. "Tom, won't you be friends?"

He made no answer. But he let her take his hand, and they stumbled down the dark stairs into the light.

CHAPTER VIII.

REAPERS.

ONCE again Great Lowlands was astir. There were sounds in the house; the outdoor life forced an entrance through open windows. Noises from field and byre, harvesters shouting to their teams, bleating of sheep, lowing of cattle, mingled with the voices of the maids, busy in removing the traces of Peggy's sorrowful outgoing. Katherine had gone to the grave to weep there. Tom was in the orchard, watching moodily while the apples were gathered. The question of the new cowman had been settled. Jim would take Collop's place.

The autumn day was glorious. Among the rhododendrons a thrush piped to the orchestra of grasshoppers that twanged away in the grass. The sunshine burnished the leaves of apple and pear and cherry tree, until all along the orchard the russet branches stood in brave ranks,—an army with banners. It burnished the stubble from which the stooks were being carted, and flaunted with the poppies in the half-reaped furrows. It made splashes of red and blue and yellow on the kerchiefs of the women following the scythes. They sang as they worked, and their voices sounded sweet in the distance. Everyone was out of doors and a-field this morning; only Peggy "Home had gone and ta'en her wages." Even Mrs. Fleming was out, walking with Peggy's uncle—a cheery soul—among the reapers.

The gay morning had brightened her, bringing colour to her cheeks, and freshening the brown of her hair. Her face was like an autumn leaf through which the sun shines. When she passed through the fields into the meadows a new spring was in her gait, a hint of youth in her carriage. Now and then she glanced at her companion with the shy adoration of a girl.

He was a little old man, clean-shaven and red-faced, with a short, turned-up nose and twinkling eyes behind gold-rimmed spectacles, not a figure to provoke admiration, though Mrs. Fleming gave it him abundantly. A trail of bramble had caught her dress. It delayed her as she went through the kissing gate.

Colonel Jacob stooped and freed her, a smile broadening his broad mouth.

"You have found a sweetheart, you see," he panted, raising himself.

The colonel was over sixty, and stout. He had sacrificed himself to do this little service.

A faint tinge, the ghost of a blush, showed on her cheek.

"You always called the bramble so, I remember," she smiled.

"Because it had a way of sticking to the woman to whom it was attached." He laughed with boyish glee at his own daring.   .

"I think it was because the thorns hurt so," she answered, her mouth trembling.

"Now, Jessica, now, my dear," he said, taking her hand and patting it softly.

They walked on hand in hand,—a pair of autumn lovers quaint to see: she tall and graceful and yielding; the little man solidly compact.

He shuffled into step with her, on his face an air of delightful importance and proprietorship. His eyes were radiant behind his spectacles. . . . He gave her a shy look. She was crying. . . . Concern chased the importance from his face. He stopped.

"Now, my dear Jessica, now, now."

With fumbling haste he found his handkerchief, a generous one of yellow silk, and raised himself on tiptoe to wipe away her tears. He did it roughly in his nervousness; then he drew her face down and kissed it. . . .

He set a yard or two between them. . . .

"I . . . I beg your pardon, Jessica. . . . I did not know what I was doing. . . . I really could not help it. . . . I hope I have not vexed you. . . ."

His pleased air ran ahead of the penitent words.

"I am not vexed, Colonel Jacob," she stammered.

He set his glasses straight on his nose, and looked up at her, beaming more than ever.

"Let me offer you my arm," he said, crooking the limb funnily. His face brimmed over with pleasure and importance and vanity; his body rounded out with gratification. . . . He measured his steps with her longer ones.

"I wonder what you are thinking?" Mrs. Fleming timidly broke the silence.

"I was thinking that Jacob waited fourteen years for his wife. . . . But he got her at last."

His eyes looked fiercely over the rim of the spectacles.

"It is thirty years, . . " she faltered.

"But he got her at last!" He jerked her arm closer to his side, jerked himself up, and kissed her again.

"Colonel!" Mrs. Fleming protested.

"I'll have one for each year I've waited," he chuckled.

They were in sight of Milkmaid Cottage. She drew her arm away, and they walked on demurely.

Martha stood at the door, watching Jock asleep with the cat under the lavender pincushion. She waited for the two, and made her obedience.

"Glory be to goodness that I had on a clean print!" she said to herself. From behind the privet hedge she followed them with her eyes.

"That be the poor heart's uncle. . . . Well, to be sure! the mistress do look beside en like the willer-tree beside the soft-water tub in the back garden. . . ." She raised herself on tiptoe . . . "Oh, lor, if they ain't sweethearting!" she gasped. "I might ha' knowed it. There be the look on 'em the very ducks and drakes has when they be courting. . . . Oh, be ashamed of herself! a widder with a first family. . . . Now if 't was missie he had a fancy for—fresh and young and tender as a chicken . . . and I knows Miss Katherine would enjoy a gentleman. . . . Lord! what fools men be, to be sure! But there, sweethearting do be in season the whole year round. Here be one pair parted yesterday, and another be making to-day; and so the world do wag. Though little 't will wag if the men passes the maids for the widders; and a lean-to like the mistress in partikler. . . . It minds me o' what Mr. Tom used to call stale-mate in the play of chess."

CHAPTER IX.

SHALL WE TASTE THIS WONDERFUL WINE?

THE South Hants election was over. The speech Franklin had made on Friday night under tension of emotion had turned the scales in favour of the Labour candidate. Pilchard had leaped the hurdle that barred his return, and had run in before Dawson, who was sauntering idly into the constituency.

Franklin had had no leisure to dwell on his grief. There was a grim humour in the telegram he had sent to Mark: "Am deeply grieved. Let me have details of accident and funeral arrangements."

Mark had wired in return: "Thrown while riding. Death instantaneous. Funeral Tuesday, twelve o'clock."

Tuesday was the day of the election, and Franklin had had to remain in Grimple.

On the Sunday he debated with himself whether he should go over to Plimpton, but he decided against it. He had no right even to demand a last look.

Memory lashed him, using for whip the scene in the railway carriage. Why had he not known then that he loved her? . . . She had read his love better than he, who had not been able to interpret the writing on the wall of his heart. And now love's feast was over. Death's hand had written in the house of life, "God hath numbered thy kingdom, and finished it. . . ."

He went through his work like a man whose thoughts

weie in irons. When the election was over, Brace and
Pilchard said the contest had made an old man of him.

His opponents noticed his altered appearance. They
had seen him sturdily working, cheerfully leading the
forloin hope, keeping his paity together by sheer force of
will; and now, when he had got his man in, he looked as
if he had a ciime on his conscience. Dawson set himself
to find a reason for his own defeat and Franklin's
despondency.

Before returning to London, Franklin wrote a letter
recalling his refusal of that colonial appointment. . . .
Then he went over to Plimpton to see the place where
they had laid her. . . .

Like a man in a dream he climbed the hill from the
station. His consciousness seemed to be held in the
hollow of the flame that scarred his heart; it could not
pass the walls of fire.

The birds sang along the way; the hoarse croak of
frogs came up from the ditch. Hips and haws and scarlet
arbutus laughed in the hedges, honeysuckle horns blew
fairy blasts. He heard nothing and saw nothing.

He crossed the green, merry with children's voices.
The pond was flecked with white wheie the ducks were
busy, diving, wagging tail and bill, having domestic
disputes. . . . Beyond the pond the churchyard was
flecked with white too. . . . But the stones were motion-
less.

The lych gate was a bower of ivy. . . . He paused
under it. . . . Had she rested at this little inn before
continuing her jouiney? There had been a wedding that
day, flowers still strewed the path. He stepped carefully so as not to tread on them. His wavering gaze
was caught by a mound of white beside newly turned

earth. . . . His feet dragged as he went towards it.   The
flowers were drooping in the sun, but a hum of bees
shook the silence over the grave.   A butterfly balanced
lightly on a wreath of immortelles.   There was a card,
black-bordered, tied to the wreath, "From Martha Collop,
wishing Comfort with Respecks."

A crown of blood-red geraniums caught his eye; there
was a card too on this.   Franklin stooped and lifted it.
"From Tonina with . . ."

He let the pasteboard drop, and his face was grey.
. . . Yes, this was the place. . . .

He stood there silently, with bared head . . .

Thought and feeling whirled giddily round. . . . They
had strewn flowers for her bridal with death.   And that
turf . . . That was the green skirt laid over her face—she
always wore green. . . .

A strong pain made a pivot for the whirling thoughts.
. . . She had covered her face on that railway journey,
and he had been glad not to look on her. . . . And there
was nothing here he could bear to look on. . . .

Thought twisting rapidly seemed to stand still. . . .
Now he was back in his boyhood,—a little lad in the
dissenting chapel at home, hearing his father preach.
The whitewashed walls were splashed with sunlight; the
hum of bees came drowsily through the open window, a
background for the preacher's voice: "The kingdom of
God is within; isn't that enough?"

It was his own voice speaking.   He was talking to
Katherine in Collop's cottage. . .   The walls were covered
with book-shelves, the room looked small, and dark but
for the one candle.   She sat in the chair opposite him,
holding a child in her arms, and listening while he read
from the little brown Keats,—a first edition, too.

"I will be thy priest, and build a fane
  In some untrodden region of the mind,
    Where branched thoughts new-grown with pleasant pain
  Instead of pines shall murmur in the wind.
  And in the midst of this wide quietness
  A rosy sanctuary will I dress
  With the wreath'd trellis of a working brain;
  With buds, and bells, and stars without a name.
  And there shall be for thee all soft delight
  That shadowy thought can win;
  A bright torch, and a casement ope at night
  To let the warm Love in! . . ."

He looked across at Katherine and smiled. . . . The chair was empty. Wife and child were gone. . . .

Then his sun went down while it was yet noon. . . . The earth under him yielded and sank. . . . He crushed the flowers as he fell. . . .

In the darkness that gathered, Katherine came to him; and he saw her in a dream as Milton saw his "late espousèd saint." She laid her hand on his heart, and it beat again. Her tears fell on his face, and life came back. The touch of her lips set the blood swinging in his veins. . . . His eyelids fluttered apart. A golden haze like a curtain made a dimness round him. . . . He stirred. . . . The curtain lifted, showing him Katherine's face, red as the geranium wreath, and close to his. . . . Contented, he sank again into the dream that gave him back his love. . . . He was on his feet again, faint from the smell of the flowers. When the mists cleared he saw Katherine's face, pale and fearful, across the grave.

"Katherine!" his voice trembled. "But it can't be Katherine! . . . 'The wingèd Psyche with awakened eyes.'" . . .

His glance groped blindly towards her.

She came round to his side. "You are ill!" she cried anxiously.

His shaking fingers fumbled with his glasses; his look was strange.

"Then I've been dreaming; and you aren't dead? . . . And you weren't here just now?"

The colour flamed in her face. She stooped and picked up his hat, and held it to him with a hand that shook.

"Please let me take you home. You are very ill," her voice shook too. She touched his arm. "Mr. Franklin, you must come with me at once," she said urgently.

At her touch consciousness leaped its prison walls. He put his hand to his head in a bewildered fashion.

"Who is buried here,—in this grave?"

"Peggy, Tom's *fiancée*. . . . Surely you knew? . . . You wired to Mark. . . ."

"She was dead when they picked her up," he said vaguely.

"Yes."

"The day after I saw you. . . ."

The colour fell away from her face; she remembered their last talk.

"You will come and see my mother?" she said, shrinking from the eyes that flashed upon her with a strange gladness.

He tossed up his head, throwing off his sorrow and his doubt at once.

"Yes, yes," he cried. "Let us go away from the graves. . . . For this my love was dead and is alive again. . . . She was lost, and is found." He hurried along the path; in his haste trampling down the flowers that strewed the way.

"We won't go indoors," he said excitedly. "I couldn't

bear a roof over me. I want to be in the air and breathe. I want to see you and feel that you are alive on the earth."

Katherine shook her head gravely. "You ought to come in; you were unconscious when I found you. You have been very ill. . . "

"Ill? not I!" he cried, a triumphant ring in his voice. "Don't look so frightened, dear; it is only that much gladness doth make me mad. They told me that you were dead. Look at me, Katherine. . . . Tell me I am not dreaming. . . ."

His look claimed her face. Her eyes found his, and nestled there. . . .

"I am not ill now," he smiled contentedly.

"Ah, yes! you look so old. . . ."

"I've lived a hundred years in one week, Katherine . . . But I am old, child, over forty. . . . Are you sure you can love an old man?"

"You must find out," she said shyly, smiles bringing back youth to the face that had also grown old in a week. Then she resumed her practical manner. "But I am a busy woman. I have to see Martha about the chickens. . . ." Then the soft light rushed back to her face and made her eyes tender. "Please come with me," she said, blushing prettily. "You must tell me why you thought I was dead."

As they walked he told her of Brace's mistake, and his own sorrow. His love was a secret that eye and voice and manner cried from the house-top. To Katherine it was a call to prayers and praise. "Love has come! Love has come!" she cried triumphantly.

She told him of Peggy's end, and they were grave as they came to Milkmaid Cottage.

Martha saw them from the window, and put down her work to watch them. She dropped back when they came to the garden gate.

"Oh, my good fortune! If there ain't another two sweethearting! Lawks! it might be spring-time, and all the birdsies and the beastsies a-pairing and a-mating. . . . But lor! missie have chosed a sour un! I likes the looks of her ma's gentleman better'n him; yes, I does! Little Tubby ain't so personable, but he do have some spunk with en. He knows what he wants, and he do laugh till he gets en. . . . But this chap be all of a rough-and-tumble, and sour like a cow with the colic. . . . But Lord love us! a man be a man if not a mouse, and not to be despised." Then she was at the door, smiling and making her obedience. . . . "And would missie please to walk in, and the gentleman too, and taste her gooseberry wine, that folkses did say was a rare thing for breeding love between couples. . . ."

Franklin looked at Katherine with a laugh in his eye.

"Well, shall we go in and taste this wonderful wine?"

CHAPTER X.

MARTHA'S ADVICE IS SOUND.

COLONEL JACOB was on his way to Milkmaid Cottage. He had struck up a friendship with Martha Collop and her excellent homemade wine; and the cottage offered a refuge from Tom's silence and Mark's obstinacy.

He regretted to leave Jessica to fight with those overbearing young cubs, but it was a delicate affair, and he was better away. Besides, Miss Katherine was on her

mother's side, and she was a better man than either of
her brothers.

But it was preposterous that the sons should oppose
the marriage. Great Heavens! what would the world
come to if the younger generation was to have a say in
its guidance! . . Pish! a couple of callow youths!   .
Poor Jessica was so conscientious and easily led—it was
always the people with consciences that were willing to
be guided—they might persuade her it was her duty to
give him up. And all because of a foolish clause in a
foolish will,—Great Lowlands to the girl if the widow
married again! Did ever anyone hear the like? And
what had Fleming meant by it? That the boys could
not keep the farm together without their mother? Or
did he mean to give them a reason for objecting to a
second marriage? . . It was a shameful and preposterous
thing! . . . "'Pon my soul, it's well my dear niece didn't
live to be tied to a Fleming! Poor girl! I owe her a
grudge too; for if she had told me of her engagement
I'd have discovered Jessica a year ago. To think she
has been a widow six years! 'Pon my soul, I have a
mind to get a special licence and marry her out of
hand! . . ."

He walked on angrily, and the quick pace took away
his breath. He stopped to rest at the wicket. He was
really quite puffed by that little walk from the house;
and it was downhill too.

"Bless me, I can't be growing old yet," he said to
himself. "A man is in his prime at sixty, especially if
he isn't married and has no domestic cares to worry
him. . . . Domestic cares? A—a—ah!" He drew a long,
considering breath, then he pulled himself together,
relieved   "No, impossible, *quite* impossible. But she is

not strong. I always thought her a delicate girl. . . .
'Pon my soul, it would be a risk for me to marry a
delicate woman! The whole thing has been too sudden.
It's taken me unawares. A bachelor of sixty should think
twice before he lets a woman have a finger in his life.
A woman in a house is an awful nuisance,—tidying here,
and clearing away there. . . . And you mustn't smoke indoors because of the curtains; and you mustn't smoke
out of doors because it ain't respectable. And you mayn't
wear slippers in the drawing-room because she is there;
and you mayn't take 'em off in the parlour for the same
reason. You mustn't tell a good story because she's a
lady; and you mustn't sit silent because it ain't polite to
the woman. . . . No, no, marriage is a company where the
liability is limited to one; and that one is the man. . . .
I'm rather afraid it's too late for me to draw back now;
but I hope to goodness the sons—sharp, sensible lads
both of 'em—will persuade their mother against a second
marriage."

He walked briskly up the path, and rattled his stick
against the cottage door. Martha opened it, bobbing and
smiling while she tied on a clean apron.

"Well, Mistress Collop, I thought I would look in as I
was passing."

Martha was used to the formula. She curtsied again.

"You're welcome as flowers in May, sir. Would you
be pleased to walk in?"

"Well, since you press me, for a minute; only for a
minute, Mistress Collop."

He shuffled into the parlour and took the chair she
dusted for him.

"And would you be pleased to taste my gooseberry
wine, sir?"

"Well, since you press me. . . . But it must be only one glass. . . ."

Martha knew this formula also. She bustled into the kitchen and took a half-empty bottle of wine from the cupboard. She tipped it on one side, eyeing it doubtfully.

"He have had three bottles already; 't would serve him right if I put a drop o' water to this one. Lawks! it do be as strong as a lion; he'd never know no difference."

She carried the bottle to the pump; but she shook her head and turned back into the kitchen. "No, I can't do it; not if 't was ever so! I respecks good wine too much to water it. . . . But pray goodness the wedding come soon, else my cellar be empty, and not a sixpence to show for it."

She hobbled into the parlour, carefully protecting the cobwebs round the bottle she carried

"There, sir! Now, if that ain't a pictur'?" she said proudly. "Ah, you may trust a spider for scenting out the best bottles! There be a glass for you, sir, which is wishing long life, a pleasant wife, and pleasure."

"Thank you, Mistress Collop; ah, thank you!"

He hid a red face behind the glass, which he set down empty.

"It's better wine than they had at the funeral," he said.

"Oh, go along, sir! 'T would be wasting good wine for to have it at a burying. Them what do be mourning sincere don't know if the wine be good or bad. And them what ain't be mourning honest wouldn't have it knowed as they had the onfeelingness to fancy the wine or not to fancy it. . . . But I sees you are a knowledge-able gentleman for wine, sir."

She filled the glass a second and a third time.

"Can you tell me the difference between a funeral and a marriage, Mistress Collop?" The colonel was critically considering the bottle.

"Surely, sir; for the one do end life and the other do mend it."

"No, no; the one rends life, and the other darns it."

Martha chuckled, shaking her sides.

"Lawks! I sees you are a jocular gentleman, sir, with your jokes and naughty words. But 't is said hereabouts that death be naught, and love be naughty. . . ."

The colonel's face was like one of Katherine's "love-apples."

"Ah, a man may well hesitate. . . . What was it that young dog Mark said to-day about degrees in love? 'Courtship is bliss, and marriage is blister.' And Miss Katherine retorted smartly that the bliss was positive while the blister was only comparative. . . ." He absently filled the glass again. . . . "Yes, yes; a man may well hesitate before setting sail on the sea of matrimony."

"And if you hesitates long there be little o' my gooseberry wine spared for another couple," said Martha to herself. She twisted a knot in her apron and hung her head coyly. "If I were a young gentleman thinking of 'Marnkay and the United States, I'd sooner steam than sail, sir; yes, I would!"

The colonel's eyes twinkled. "Very good,—ah, very good, indeed! But when a man's single, Mistress Collop, he'd better remain so."

He drank his fifth glass slowly and thoughtfully.

"Oh, go along with you, sir!" Martha cried, her eyes on the bottle. "A mole could see as a gentleman like you were intended to make a lady happy, if not two, only you've wasted your chances."

A gentle, genial warmth stole through the colonel. He lingered about the subject.

"So you don't believe in bachelors, Mistress Collop?"

"Bachelors? Lord love you, no, sir! poor weak tools! For what's a man without the woman but the half of a pair of scissors, neither knife, nippers, nor good screw-driver. . . . And all because he ain't got the spunk to face the screw as would jine the two halves together. Lord! I do never have no patience with a man without a pardner."

"But a bad partner,—an unsuitable partner, Mistress Collop?"

"Oh, go along, sir! A man may play timid all his life, and in the end a woman do get him. . . . Lord! I've seen seventy eagerer to be a groom than seven-and-twenty. You can't be locking the door against nature. If her don't come in decent by the door, her do jump down the chimbley, bringing the soot with en."

"Then you don't recommend single blessedness?" he said drearily.

"What be single blessedness," she said scornfully, "but butter-milk as won't make butter, though you churns yourself giddy! Blessedness be sing'lar enough in this weary world, but it do take more 'n one to make en. Lawks! if the Lord sent the beastsies two and two into the ark, saving the lady with the gentleman, it be useless for man to kick against the pricks. My old man said them words, and there never was a happier man mated. Love were as fresh the day we parted as the day we paired, and that were forty year."

She poured out the last glass of wine and did not notice that it was the last.

"You have lost your husband, Mistress Collop, yet you enjoy life."

Martha did not resent the colonel's irony.

"Lawks, what be the use o' fretting? 'T would never bring my old man back! Widders as sees their husbands comforrable in the ground has a deal to be thankful for."

"That is true," said the colonel, cheerfully. "The grave ends many an unhappy marriage."

"Ay, that it do," Martha sighed. "But lawks! we never knows if it be to begin again on the other side. We can but leave it. . . . Parson do say, 'Cast thy burden on the Lord, and thou shalt find it after many days.'"

Colonel Jacob's little twinkling eyes were grave behind the glasses.

"It would undoubtedly be a relief to know that a wife would not meet her first husband in another life," he said hesitating.

"Ay!" said Martha; "and I put the question to missie, but her couldn't give the answer. But lor! my mind do be settled now; for if Collop and me knows anything on the other side we'll know to come together again. And if we knows nothing 't will be the same to both."

"And what do you think of second marriages, Mistress Collop?" said the colonel, blowing his nose noisily.

"I be thinking a empty bottle will hold four gills o' wine just as well as four gills o' emptiness," she answered. "If you be for marriage, marry quick, says I; for the pears that hang on into the winter the frosses do nip. . . ."

"Not a single glass more!" said the colonel, rising suddenly. "No, I will not be persuaded. . . . I must go back to see that those overbearing young cubs don't force their dear mother into doing as they wish. . . . You are a sensible person, Mistress Collop, a very sensible person. Your advice is as sound as your excellent wine. 'If you marry, marry soon.'"

"Ay!" Martha sighed, "my thoughts runs on marriages after a burying. And if what I hears be well informed there will soon be a wedding at Great Lowlands."

"What! what!" Colonel Jacob turned again into the room and looked fiercely at her.

"The new cowman, sir, as be stepping into my old man's dead shoes. Missie do say as he'll wed the servant lass where he come from. And Milkmaid Cottage be the home for the new pair, so the old woman be cuckoo'd out of her nest, and forty year in en . . ."

"Dear, dear," said the little man, sympathetically. "That is hard; that is hard indeed, Mistress Collop."

"Lord love you, no, sir! 't is nature," said Martha, briskly. "What be Jenny Wren wanting wi' nesses now Cock Robin be dead? . . . I be but a leaking tub to fret over it. . . "

"And where will you go to?" said the colonel, anxiously.

"There be two places certain sure in this life," said Martha, cheerily, while her face worked. "Them be the Union or six foot o' churchyard, and the old woman can take one or t' other. Glory be to goodness! the club 's paid Collop's grave, and 't will pay my burying, so they can't do me out o' my little clay shanty."

"Nonsense! nonsense!" said the colonel; "it is not to be thought of. Dear, dear, what a waste of talent it would be! You could not make your excellent wine in the Union, and still less in the churchyard. No, no, Mistress Collop, there's the cottage I bought for my dear niece, furnished too; I'll put you in as caretaker. You shall

have it rent free as long as you live; and a trifle for
keeping it, say five shillings a week."

"Oh, lawks!" Martha gasped, and fell suddenly into
a chair. She threw her apron over her head and laughed
aloud. Then she stood up and made her obedience.
"Heaven bless you, sir, and send you long life, a pleasant
wife, and pleasure!"

She sat down again, swaying backwards and for-
wards.

The colonel tiptoed softly to the door, glancing back
over his shoulder at the old woman sobbing behind her
apron. He closed the door gingerly, and his fat little
legs went at a run down the garden path. At the gate
he stopped, and flourished his handkerchief about his
hot face.

"I'll get a special licence!" he panted. "Long life, a
pleasant wife, and pleasure! . . ."

Martha lifted the tray with the bottle and the glass.

"I doesn't grudge him a drop!" she said stoutly; "not
a single blessed drop, though it do be four bottles. . . .
Furnished! and rent free! . . . and five shillings a week
till my old bones be laid with Collop's and the club pays
the burying! . . . And all of a bottle of o' gooseberry
wine and a heart soft with courting! . . . Oh, Lord! what
fools men be!"

. . . . .

Mrs. Fleming and her children were still in the
breakfast-room. The French window stood open, showing
lawn and shrubbery and flower-beds. Away in the distance the fields lay newly reaped on the hill crowned by
the dead tree that marked the western boundary of the
farm.

Katherine faced the window, and eyes and thoughts

were far away in the sunshine with the joyous reapers
and with her own glad harvest-time. Smiling, she recalled her thoughts, but still they ranged beyond the
window and beyond the present to the morning after her
return to Great Lowlands. The fir-tree in which the
thrush had sung was deserted now; but the autumn day
had its minstrels too. A robin whistled in the holly
hedge; the bees hummed about the sweet peas. From
the meadows came the bleat of this year's lambs. In
the sky was a living, wavering cloud and the twitter of
gathering swallows. The mellow fruitfulness of the day
sang of hope realised. Eighteen months ago all had
seemed so hopeless, and to-day she looked on the work
of her hands and saw that it was good.

The house wore a different air; the garden was jocund
with flowers,—daisies and dahlias, sunflowers and asters.
Marigold and nasturtium lit beacon fires on the heights
of the raised beds. Last week the linden-trees had been
wind-worn and tattered; now the yellowing leaves tossed
their sunshine back to the sky. All was gay and glad
outside, and gay and glad in Katherine's heart. It was
not only Franklin's love that had wrought the change.
She had risen from the old life of ambition, pride, and
self, and was seeking higher things. Peggy's death had
been an earthquake shock releasing her from the bonds
of a living death. She had come forth from the tomb
bound by the graveclothes of her old life; and, freeing
herself, had worn only the garments of her humiliation.
But in her shame she had heard a Voice: "Bring forth
the best robe and put it on her, and put a ring on her
finger and shoes on her feet. For this my love was dead
and is alive again. She was lost and is found. . . ."

It was another Katherine who had gone from that

Voice into the old workaday world. Her hands were busy still, her feet never idle. She planned and arranged as before; but in place of the self that had filled her horizon there were three figures,—mother and brother and friend.

Mrs. Fleming was going about, a pathetic happiness on her face, giving Katherine confidences about her old love, to which the girl responded heartily.

Tom was more difficult, and Katherine could not break down the stubborn gloom that had encased him since Peggy's death. She beguiled him into a grudging interest in the good harvest; but he shunned her society and went about the fields sulking and morose.

Colonel Jacob's presence at Great Lowlands irritated him. It kept open his wound in the eyes of the villagers. He hated to know that they were pitying him, and looking and wondering "how he do be bearing up."

Peggy's uncle, bustling about the village, cheery and good-tempered, joking with the mason when he chose a stone for the grave, laughing while he paid the under-taker's bill, only made them pity "young mester" the more. Under his breath Tom swore at the colonel, who comforted him with gay sympathy and cheery reminiscences of "poor Peg."

Nothing damped the colonel's spirits. He had snapped his fingers at Mark's anger at the engagement; but now Mark had come himself to add force to Tom's sullen opposition to the marriage. The sons had a reason for their opposition. If Mrs. Fleming married again the farm would be Katherine's. They would not consent to the marriage, and Mrs. Fleming would not marry without their consent.

"Katherine, won't you speak to your brothers?" she asked, weeping.

The voice woke the girl from her dreams, and she looked up. It vexed her to see Mark's dictatorship and Tom's sullenness. The old hardness glittered in her eyes.

"If mother chooses to marry again, Mark, why should you object?" she cried. "It is pure selfishness that makes you stand in her way."

"You have nothing to do with this," said Mark, quietly. "The affair is between mother and Tom and me."

"But I can't sit here and see you make mother miserable," Katherine protested.

"It is quite easy for you to go away," said Mark.

"Oh, Katherine, don't leave me!" sobbed Mrs Fleming. "Your brother is so hard. . . . He can't understand a woman's feelings."

Katherine went to the sofa and sat down beside her mother. She threw her arm round her and faced Mark with eyes blazing.

"Now, Mark, say what you have to say and let us end the scene."

Mark angrily walked to the mantelpiece, and propped his back against it. Tom was stretched in an arm-chair, his legs straight before him, his chin on his breast. He kept a gloomy silence, and took no notice of the combatants.

"If mother marries again she simply burdens the farm with another person," Mark said frowning. "Of course he will control her income; and what sort of a lookout would there be for us? We don't want any more masters here. . . . Besides, mother is better off as she is."

"She loved him years ago, . . ." Katherine began.

"You talk like a schoolgirl," Mark interrupted testily. "She only loves him because she didn't marry him. Marriage will cure any love."

He laughed cynically, and dug his hands into his pocket. Katherine gave him a look that did not miss the unpleasant light in his eyes and the sneer on his thin lips. How hard he was! how changed from the Mark of Goodge Street days. He bore her gaze with a hardened nonchalance.

"Listen to me," he said firmly. "You are all for sentiment. I am protecting mother against herself. A week after the marriage she would wish herself free again. . . ."

"I don't know why you should say that," Mrs. Fleming bridled, and made a feeble protest.

"That is not the point," Katherine said to Mark. "Mother can judge for herself. Why should there be all this fuss? I for one would be glad to know she was happy. . . ."

"Twaddle!" said Mark, vigorously. "If anyone has not made mother happy it is you. She has not been able to call her soul her own since you came to the place."

Katherine's eyes fell. She had deserved the hard thrust.

"I should be thankful for someone to love me," said Mrs. Fleming, plaintively; "and Colonel Jacob would not be in your way. He is independent, indeed, well off; and we should live at Chester."

Tom looked up at the words. "I am not going to stay here alone and work the farm by myself," he put in sulkily.

16*

"There's your sister," Mrs. Fleming quavered.   "She
could not think of leaving the farm to go to ruin again.
She is necessary here, but I am not.   I have been set
completely on one side."

Katherine had a sudden comprehension of what she
had done.   The responsibility of success was on her.
She must be tied to Great Lowlands because she had
saved it.   She had chosen to manage by herself, and
now she must be left to manage alone.   Her ability
had come home to roost,—a bird that fouled its own
nest.

"As long as Kit stops it will be all right," Tom said.
"But what's to hinder her from marrying too, and leaving
the farm on my hands?"

A quick shiver passed through Katherine; a white
cloud fell across her face.   She had not thought this
marriage would affect her own future.   She knew that
Franklin loved her.   Some day he would claim her.
Would she have to give up his love and stay with Tom?
How could she give up what was more than life to her? . .
She argued the point.   She was not free to choose.   She
owed something to Franklin, and something to the people
for whom they would work together. . . .

The last plea was silenced by a voice: "It would be
better to help two sweethearts to be happy together. . . ."

These two, her mother and her lover, had waited thirty
years for happiness,—to be denied at last? . . .

Katherine thought of the promise made to Peggy, that
she would help Tom.   She could only help him by
staying here.   She confronted her duty with a stoical
quiet, facing it with set mien that gave no sign of her
tortured heart.   She was learning the wisdom of life.   She
could lift the cup of renunciation with steady hand, and

drink the bitter draught without change of front. . . . She
stared before her, and did not see the flowers that made
a rainbow round about the window. . . . The solitary
figure of a woman toiled up the hill towards the tree that
spread its arms crosswise on the summit. In the silence
she drained the cup. . . . The coldness of death was in her
voice when she spoke,—

"If mother marries, I shall stay here with you, Tom. . . .
So that need not interfere. . . ."

"It doesn't matter who goes or stays," Mark fumed;
"the thing is out of the question. I for one won't consent
to losing my rights in the land."

Katherine went to the table and stood leaning against
it. Her breath came quickly, her face was white and
passionate.

"Mark, haven't you any feeling? Haven't you any
pity for women who break their hearts? She has loved
him thirty years. . . . She might be happy now if you
would let her. . . ."

"I am not going to lose the property that ought to
be mine," said Mark, doggedly.

Katherine leaned heavily against the table. Should
she leave things alone and give Mark the responsibility of
keeping her mother at the farm, and freeing her to go to
Franklin? . . .

It was a short, sharp struggle; and then she spoke.

"If mother marries, the place is mine. . . . Well, then,
Mark, give your consent, and I will hand over the farm
to you and Tom. . . ."

For a long minute there was silence. Then Mark's
dark face flushed. He lifted himself from the mantelpiece with an awkward laugh.

"I'm agreed," he said. "But you'll have to sign it away legally before witnesses. . . ."

"Hang the whole confounded business! I'll have nothing to do with it!" Tom cried, and flung angrily out of the window.

Katherine did not speak again. She walked unsteadily from the room, and climbed the stairs and threw herself on her knees beside the bed where Peggy had lain. . . . She faced her resolve quietly, and did not strive or cry. She would put Franklin out of her life. . . .

Two years ago she had fought with all her strength against a lesser sacrifice. To-day she put away from her life and the joy of life, and no one knew what she had done. But the soft gladness died from her face, and pain stood sentinel before her barred eyes.

CHAPTER XI.

VIGIL.

AND now it was winter. A special licence had given Colonel Jacob his wife almost before the engagement was a settled fact. Katherine was high in favour with her step-father.

"She shall not suffer for giving up the property," he said to himself. "When I make my will we shall see. . . . Good, unselfish girl, she shall not suffer."

His bridesmaid's present to Katherine was a cheque for £100. Katherine put it in the bank against a rainy day.

There were other changes at Great Lowlands besides Mrs. Fleming's absence. The new cowman and his wife were at Milkmaid Cottage, and Martha was living at Laburnum Drive. She had not accepted Katherine's offer of a home with her.

"No, no, missie; when Mr. Right do come you'll be off at a gallop, and then the old woman do be turned out. This little shanty be all I wants. I've gotten Collop's bed what he died on, and I'll put en in the lean-to. 'Twill make me a good warm bedroom with the kitchen neighbourable. Lawks! think o' me with a parly and best bedroom like a lady in the land!"

"But why shouldn't you use the bedroom, Martha?" Katherine asked.

"Lawks, duckie! I couldn't sleep comforrable on any

bed but Collop's When I wakes o' nights I lays thinking
of he, and I sees his poor old head on the piller, and
him dying as quiet as a mouse, and it do cheer me tarrible well, and be company for me."

So Katherine was alone at Great Lowlands with Tom.
She had attained her goal; she was acknowledged head
of house and farm, and the goal was only the picturesque
entrance to a wilderness where the springs were waters
of Marah.

Tom was working with her on the farm,—he the little
wheel of the bicycle, she making the great revolutions in
management. She kept their interests linked while they
worked; but after work they went different ways. Katherine sat with knit brows making up accounts and
puzzling out schemes of drainage and tillage, while Tom
lounged on the green, or loitered at Milkmaid Cottage
talking to Jim and Sarah, whose cockney smartness
flavoured the talk.

It was the same thing over again. Katherine forged
ahead, absorbed in her plans, and left Tom to devise his
own schemes of amusement. She carried out her resolu-
tions only as far as they fitted in with her own necessities.
She was not any nearer to Tom than she had been before. She knew nothing of the moods when, gloomy and
remorseful, he walked by himself, thinking miserably of
the past. She accepted his reckless merriment for a sign
of returning content, and did not try it to see if it rang
true. . . . She had plucked out her right eye and cut off
her right arm to save her brother, and, satisfied with
her mutilation, had gone her way, leaving him un-
saved.

She raised a barrier of work round her to hide from
view the places where the gods walked. Franklin's love

went with her through all her busy days, but she would not suffer herself to be led into the fair places to which it beckoned her. His letters were the points of light in her life. They were full of hope, and of vexation at the uncertainty of his plans. Katherine blessed the uncertainty; knowing that this alone kept Franklin from speaking of their marriage, and kept her from putting an end to his hopes.

Franklin waited for the decision of his committee, secure in the thought of Katherine's love. Through the winter days life blazed with light and warmth for him. Foggy London, the Labour world groaning and travailing in pain, were swept out of his consciousness. Katherine made his world, where summer reigned.

Outwardly he was still quiet and reserved; but there was a snap and a sparkle in his eye that signalled an awakening.

Coming into his rooms one night he showed plainly the new man in him. Dissatisfaction had gone from his face; cynicism was there yet, but poised lightly, ready for flight. He held himself straight, seeing his goal near. That air of youth had not been supplied by his tailor. His clothes were shabby still,—not clothes for a man with whom the world went very well. That eager youthfulness should be tricked out bravely,—silver buckle and silken hose, scarlet doublet, a plumed hat for love's cavalier.

Franklin threw himself into his favourite chair, lit his pipe, leaned his head back, and sent his thoughts to Katherine. His eyes were glad, watching the rings of smoke he puffed into the air. . . . They were wedding-rings, of course. . . . Ah! if she sat here beside him, close so that he might touch her, he would be the happiest man in London. . . . How had those humdrum days in

the old bookshop ever contented him? Peace and leisure
forsooth! A man would get enough of those in the
grave. . . . Books! Had books ever taught him as much
as he had learned from one look into Katherine's eyes?
Had any book ever thrilled him as he had been thrilled
by the touch of certain little fingers? Love was the only
culture! . . . And there was no law to divorce a man
from his reading because he married a wife. It would
make his reading richer to share it with Katherine. . . .
His thoughts lingered about the confused picture he had
seen of Collop's cottage that was yet his little house in
Hull, and Katherine sitting with the child in her arms
while he read Keats to her, giving

> "All soft delight
> That shadowy thought could win."

Ah! that first edition had been offered up on the
altar of the Labour agitation. . . . Well, well! he could
not grudge anything to the Movement that had given him
Katherine.

It was on a Labour platform that he had seen her
first. The clever little face had pleased him. He had
asked who she was. . . . But that could not have been
the reason of his friendship for that uncertain quantity,
Mark Fleming?

Franklin blushed like a girl at this impeachment of
his motive, and threw back his head, and laughed self-
consciously because he saw its truth.

It was she who had taken him to Goodge Street from
the very first, and he had not suspected it. He might
have known it before, if he had not guarded his heart by
a prickly criticism of her. . . . How could he have been
so hard on the child? Her sentiment and enthusiasm

were trailing vines gracing the strong nature whose roots
were deep.   And what if she hadn't ability to write that
History?   Who wanted a woman to be all intellect?   It
was enough if she was all heart. . . . Ah, well! some day
they would write that History together.   He could supply
the knowledge and judgment, and she would give it form
and structure. . . . What a marriage theirs would be,—a
true comradeship!   No mere humdrum existence!   She
had too many pointed opinions of her own meekly to accept his views. . . . He would never tame his shrew. . . .
But he didn't want to tame her!   The conventional
woman—an india-rubber doll grimacing and squeaking at
a husband's will—was intolerable.   He admired force
and ambition and self-guidance in a woman.   Katherine
was his ideal. . . .

His thoughts were interrupted by the postman's knock
at the house door.   The letter carried his appointment
as secretary to the Labour Organisation in the West
Indies.   He must be prepared to start in a fortnight.

His face was suddenly grave.   That was sooner than
he expected.   Would she consent to an immediate marriage?   A fortnight!   It scarcely gave her time to buy an
outfit.   And, now that he came to think of it, they were
not even betrothed. . . . The formality had not seemed
necessary.   He had to go to Glasgow to the Conference
to-morrow night, else he would have run down to talk it
over.   He would write at once, of course; but he wished
he could have given her more time. . . .

He puffed his last smoke-ring into the air, and with
considering eyes watched it float away and fade into no-
thingness.

While Franklin was seeing wedding-rings in the smoke
Katherine was crouching over the fire, listening to the

howl of the storm outside. She was alone, sitting up for Tom. It was a wild night. The rain pattered on the window. She could imagine it swathing the darkness, wrapping and clinging to the night. . . . That gust shook the house. It must have torn the thin film of the rain into tatters. . . .

Suddenly the storm was inside; the lamp flamed up; a rushing mighty wind filled all the room. The rain lashed the carpet; the fire leaped in the grate. . . . Katherine sprang to her feet. The French window had swung wide; a wind-battered figure was driven in from the garden.

"Oh, Martha! how you frightened me, coming in like a ghost! And you are wet through! come to the fire this instant."

"Hush, duckie, hush!" Martha whispered breathlessly. "I wants you; and I doesn't want the serving-maids to know as I do be come. Put on your things, and come along o' the old woman. 'Tis Mr. Tom, he be at The Three Sojers, and drunk as a lord. Jim were with en, but I have started he off home to Sarah. Not a button will Mr. Tom budge. He thinks he be at the Wheat Sheaf, a-courting his poor dead sweetheart. He do be carrying on shameful, and the men be larfing at en and nudging each the other, and leading en on cruel . . ."

Katherine was already in the hall, putting on her cloak. Her mouth was hard; her eyes glittered in sockets grown suddenly hollow. Her heart flew helplessly on the storm, driven with the wind and tossed. There was no ark in sight; underneath were black depths.

She came back into the room, drawing on her hood.

"Come, Martha," she said brusquely, and the two went forth.

They crossed the lawn and found the gate. The road was dark, and a sudden gust blew out the flame in the lantern Martha carried.

They stumbled along, the rain beating them back with its scourge of small cords. Above the churchyard wall the wind howled among the poplars. The trees creaked and groaned, bending towards the ranks of white tombstones.

"Glory be to goodness! Not one o' they ghostses would be getting out o' their warm graves on such a night," said Martha, cheerfully. "And if they did, the wind would tear their poor thin bodies all to shreds before ever we seed them."

They crossed the green, their feet splashing into the pools that had gathered there. A pitchy darkness swathed everything. The light in the inn was the one wakeful eye in all the village. They came near, and Katherine put her face close to the window and looked through a chink in the shutter.

The chimney-piece jutted out into the room, framing the hearth, on which a heap of logs crackled. A settle was ranged on either side, and before each was a narrow, long table with jugs of beer.

The men on the settle had weather-battered faces, to which clung a suggestion of the soil. They were not unlike potatoes or swedes. Tom was leaning forward, his head on the table, asleep.

Katherine's heart beat with noisy throbs. She leaned against the wall to recover herself. Where she stood she could hear the talk.

"Lawks, young mester do sup as much as a young maid and no more. But his belly be fuller than his noddle, I'll be sworn."

"'Tis a true word; but he be shoved out o' 's right-ful place, and needeth small wit. He mun foller young miss like dam and shadder. Lord! young miss be tar-rible hard to beat,—a man all but the breeks."

"They do say her be breeched under her female gowning. Yon day in hillside fields when her shifted off her skirt for the dead maid, her stood knickerbocked, and brazened it without a fall o' eyelashes."

"Ay! 'tis cruel hard to wear a man's masterfulness in a maid's weak frame. My missus were saying there be small woman about en by the way her drives men folks, i' place o' bending the neck to 'em. . . ."

"The new cowman were saying how she stood among her betters i' Lunnon, and spoke up bold as brass. She were a rare one for working-folkses up there; but the whole parish might be starving hereabouts and her wouldn't ever know it. . . ."

"Her were tarrible fond-like o' the dead maid. . . . But what be young mester saying o' his sweetheart?" . . .

"'Tis but boasting in his cups, and not to be enter-tained. The maid were quality, for all her jockeying wi' horses. Young mester were nodding. . . . When the drink be in, the wit be out. . . ."

Katherine drew herself up.

"Wait here, Martha," she commanded.

She went to the door, turned the handle, and stepped inside. The tobacco reek made her fall back an instant, and the men saw a white face thrown sharply against the background of night and storm. They recognised her as she came forward. Her glance mowed down their eyes like a scythe. One after another the men shuffled up and slunk to the door. The landlord watched the scene from the bar.

Katherine called Martha, and together they raised Tom and got him out into the night. Half dragging, half pushing him, stopping every minute for breath, they made their way across the green.

They stopped at the lych gate. "Oh, Martha! we can never get him home," Katherine gasped.

"We mun leave en in churchyard," said Martha, gaily. "And if Mr. Tom do want more sperrits he can dig en up like turnups. Come, duckie, my old bones do ache wi' carrying en; best leave he in churchyard where the dead be dumb."

It was impossible for the two women to drag Tom all the way to Great Lowlands. Katherine sighed with relief when they laid him down on the seat in the porch.

Martha lighted the lantern and showed the key in the church door.

"Now, thank the Lord that do temper the wind to the shorned lamb, and do make parson a forgetful man;" she chuckled.

They raised Tom again, in spite of his incoherent objections, and laid him down on the matting in the aisle.

Martha lifted herself with a sigh. "Now then, duckie, he do be safe. We mun leave en to hisself, and pray goodness he come to a better man."

"I shall stay here with him," Katherine said quietly; and Martha was obliged to obey the girl, and leave her alone with Tom.

The great door swung heavily to, and silence fell about the place where Katherine sat watching Tom, who had fallen asleep. And as she sat there the devil came to her, tempting her. To what purpose was this waste

of strength and love and devotion? Was she to break
the vase of love for the anointing of life's fool, when the
king himself knelt for the consecrating oil? Tom was not
worthy of the sacrifice. He was not only going to ruin
himself, he was leading Jim to ruin. . . . A sharp pain
thrust through the pain of her shame. Jim had been
steady and sober until she had brought him here to be
led into temptation. . . . Sarah's happiness was a burden
of responsibility she had placed upon herself. She must
stay on at Great Lowlands to deliver Jim from her brother
and Tom from himself. . . .

The lantern threw long shadows across the aisle, and
the pillars sprang out of the darkness, stony guardians
of the silence. At the eastern end was the tomb of the
crusader Fleming. Katherine could see the pale glimmer
of the marble against the dusk. As she sat there, the
mystery and awe of her childhood returned to her.
She felt once more the aspirations of the little girl
dreaming of great deeds like those of that far-off
ancestor.

The years passed; and she sat in the family pew,
her eyes, wistful under the confirmation veil, straying towards the marble figure while she vowed to be a true
soldier of the cross. The ecstasy and exaltation of the
hour came back to her.

Then, later, she stood beside the tomb, and vowed
herself to the Crusade of the poor.

All the old influences thronged round her like ghosts
of the dead. She had kept none of those old vows; she
had lived through many phases of renunciation, and
still she sought herself, and only herself. And here at
her side was another battle to be fought; the prin-
cipalities and powers of darkness were to wrestle with,—

the kingdom of a man's soul was to be redeemed from the enemy. . . .

She lifted her lantern and walked to the end of the church, where the Flemings of long ago kept their ancient pomp and state. The figure of the Crusader stood out whitely against the darkness, and the light she carried struck the crossed hilt of the sword. "The cross is mightier than the sword," Katherine whispered, with a swift thought of One, surely the greatest among the Gods, who had conquered by love. Standing there, she vowed herself to this new Crusade with a humility and a passion that had not touched her former vows. Holding the lantern high, she lingered a moment on the chancel steps before the altar. As the light streamed round, the darkness fell like tattered banners about the lonely figure of the girl.

CHAPTER XII.

WHERE TWO LOVE TRUE.

FRANKLIN sat on the platform in the great public hall at Glasgow, seeing the throng of faces gathered into one little face held in a hard and conflicting silence. They had just handed a letter to him, Katherine's answer to his urgent appeal against her decision.

"No, she could give him no other answer. She begged him not to try and see her."

The tones of Brace's voice drummed in his ears; but the voice was Katherine's voice. . . . He crushed the letter in his hand, and thrust it deep into his pocket.

His face had not lost the shock her first letter had given him three days before. It was still drawn and haggard, and very tired. He leaned back in his chair, and his thoughts swept about the girl to find a reason for this repulse.

She had said she could love him with no hope of winning love again. . . . If she loved him, would she refuse to give him a reason for her conduct? He could not believe she did not love him. . . .

She was clever at a pose, he knew; but she had not been acting in that scene in the railway carriage. He saw the piteous eyes, the soft shrinking glance, the entreating hands. . . . She could not have deceived him then

And she had not repulsed his love when he had

found her at Peggy's grave. Her eyes had not lied to
him then.

Yet when, confident in her love, he had written to
claim his wife, she had thrown at him a cold denial hard
with finality. . . . Even his last pleading letter had failed
to move her. She could not write again. She begged
him not to see her. . . . She had cast him off with the
heartlessness of a heartless woman. . . .

Brace's voice droning on carried him back to the inn
at Grimple. He was dazed and stunned; and it was
Brace speaking: "The farm is the girl's as long as she
doesn't marry." The words startled him to comprehension. . . .

Here was motive for this repeated refusal. She loved
rule and the means of power. The farm gave scope for
both. . . . When she had to decide between love of him
and love of power the man must go. . . .

His lips curled. She had always loved power, and
confessed it. He remembered that scene long ago in
Goodge Street.

"Anything is worth doing that gives power," she was
saying.

"And what will you do with your power if you should
ever get it?" he asked.

"I will make you recognise it."

"I think you would not be so cruel," he had
laughed.

He laughed to himself now very bitterly; and the old
cynicism captured his face and put iron bands round it.
. . . Anything was worth doing that gave power . . . even
if in doing it she broke a man's heart.

His anger gathered with the swiftness of a summer
tempest. Eyes and brow were black with storm.

"Fool! to have trusted a woman! . . ."

Did he not know the treachery of women? He had seen the arts of his stepmother, the trickery with which she forced his father's hand. . . . He had found out his housekeeper's frauds, lying, petty meanness, theft. . . . The only women he had known had been dishonest. . . . Even Katherine had once played the eavesdropper. Pah! they were all alike. . . .

His distrust had warned him; yet he had allowed her to caress it to sleep. She had played with him as a cat plays with a mouse, after she had caught him. This letter was the tardy, final nip in which she took his life.

His lips twisted bitterly. . . . She could hardly be blamed for it; it was the woman's instinct of capture. Now his love was dead, and he stood beside her grave. The flowers were red with the red deed she had done. . . .

Ah, well! no woman should ever come into his life again. He would never again play mouse to any feminine cat. . . .

It was his turn to address the meeting. He rose and spoke easily and fluently, but his sarcasms bit. While he spoke, the hand in his pocket tore Katherine's letter to shreds, rolling up the pieces into little pellets. He did not know he destroyed the postscript that, written overleaf, he had missed:—

"I love you with all my heart. Tell me you will trust me till I can explain."

.   .   .   .   .   .

Katherine walked with drooping head in the sunshine. She carried the *Daily Chronicle,* which told her Franklin had sailed from Southampton. He had never

answered her last letter. He had not told her he would
trust her. . . . She was glad he had not tried to see
her; she could not have trusted herself to keep to her
purpose. . . . But if she could have seen him . . .

She walked on. . . . But she had been right not to
give reasons for her refusal. Even if Franklin misunderstood her silence she could not blazon out the sacrifice
she was making. . . . If he could not trust her, he might
even have thought it another pose, renunciation for effect.
. . . Her lips trembled. . . . Yes, she had been right
to remain silent. . . . She said it again and again, silenc-
ing her own doubts. . . . But she had thought he
would understand. . . . She had thought he would trust
her love. . . .

The red fields were furrowed and scarred with the
plough. In the distance a green haze showed the springing corn. Beyond were the pines she had planted "for
the immortal gods."

She steadied her white lips, smiling faintly.

Life was not over; love was not gone forever. There
were human trees to plant,—a temple to build for the
immortal gods. And while she loved she could not lose
the love she had lost.

"Who loves, has," she whispered, half-sobbing. . . .

She took the road to Peggy's cottage. Martha was
in her sprigged print, standing on a chair, fastening a
curtain before Botticelli's "Spring." She looked down at
Katherine.

"Bide still, duckie, I be just finishing. Yes, I mun
cover up they shameful hizzies. I be bashful to look at
that young woman a-wearing a figured bedgown in broad
daylight."

The light came leaping back to Katherine's eyes. "Oh, Martha! that is not a shameful hizzy. It is perfectly beautiful. Don't hide it."

Martha drew the curtain across the picture and came down from the chair.

"Beauty or no beauty, it be no picture for a decent woman. Lawks, it do mind me o' Susan Parkin in drink when they warmints o' boys dressed en up, and drummed en on the green. Come to the kitchen, duckie; it do be unseemly for a young maid to sit looking at that curtain."

"And have you covered up the picture in the kitchen, Martha?"

"Why for should I?" Martha said snappishly. "What be there ondecent about en?"

"There's the little Love," said Katherine.

"Ay! he do be a little Love, prutty boy! No, I wouldn't cover he up; not if 'twas ever so."

"He hasn't on even a bedgown," Katherine laughed.

"And why for should he? Flesh ain't ondecent; 'tis the bits o' rags, hiding a leg here, and showing an arm there, what do make ondecency. I allus feels if there was no clothes there'd be nothing shaming; but 't was Eve knowed better than her Maker, dressing up wi' fig-leaves! . . . Sit down, duckie, I've just had Mr. Tom a-calling."

"What did he want?" Katherine asked.

"A bit o' talk; he do be kind o' lonely-like. I spoke en fair and sound, telling en 't were ill to scandalise the dead; and he were that shamed-like. . . . No, he'll never go nigh The Three Sojers no more. . . . And here be Jock, pleased as pleased to see his lady . . ."

Katherine lifted up the puppy, holding her chin high to avoid his kisses, while Martha looked on, chuckling.

"Ay, kiss en, Jockie! missie's face be long as a garden rake to-day."

"You are cheerful enough, Martha," said the girl, reddening. "Don't you miss poor old Collop?"

"Miss my old man? Lord love you, no, duckie! I knows he be well covered up in churchyard; but where two loves true it takes more than two yards o' earth to part 'em."

"But life parts them," said Katherine, sadly.

"Not a bit on't!" said Martha, gaily. "When man and maid do love they'll come together through fire and flood."

"But many who love never marry," said Katherine.

"Lawks, duckie, that ain't love! When love's true there be enough strength in man and maid to shove sun and moon and stars out o' the road so they meets. . . . Yes, the unborn child fights for life; and them what God calls together comes together."

"I wish I could believe that, Martha."

Martha darted a sharp look at the girl.

"And why do Mr. Right leave you hanging your head like a chicken wi' the pip?"

"Who is Mr. Right, Martha?"

"Why that old Sober as was here in harvest. . . . Oh, I seed what you be up to! I knowed you was his lady and he your gentleman. 'Tis ill hedging and ditching wi' love, duckie. Gather your rosebuds when roses be budding. Them that be meant to marry marries though they tarries, like your ma and the Angel Jacob.

Mind, duckie, time makes a show in front, but he be bald behind."

"I can't leave Tom," said Katherine, passionately. "I'll never leave him alone."

"Lord bless the poor simple heart of a maid! Why, you'll be wedded and bedded ere Mr. Tom have lost the taste of his sweetheart's burying."

CHAPTER XIII.

A MECCA-WINDOW IN THE TEMPLE.

SOMETHING unusual in the Plimpton landscape thrust itself through Mark's brooding. He lifted his sullen eyes to the man driving the gig.

"That's a capital crop of peas. . . . But I always thought the ground hereabouts was waste swamp," he said.

"So it were," the driver answered. "But the ground be redeemed and turned fruitful since young Mester Fleming ha' drained en. . . ."

"I shouldn't have given him credit for doing it," said Mark, curtly; and sank back to the recollection of the waste Tonina had made in his life.

The horse dragged slowly up the hill from the station; and the two men were silent.

Presently they drew to one side to let a drove of cattle pass. Mark eyed them with the glance of the prospective farmer.

"Good country for pasture about here," he remarked.

"Well, that depends if the beastses gets the pasture," said the driver, stolidly.

"Those have nothing to complain of," said Mark, with a backward twist of the eye at the drove.

"No, that be true this year. But two year since you could ha' putten your hand 'tween the ribs o' every one o' them same beastses; they was that clemmed and lean-like."

"Whose fault was that?" said Mark carelessly.

"'Twere young Mester Fleming what had the blame. He had the wit to know better, 'twere sure, but he wouldn't turn hisself to en. There be a mighty great change at Great Lowlands sin' he ha' settled his mind to the farming."

"I thought it was Miss Fleming," said Mark.

"Well," said the driver, slowly, "they do say 'twere her showed young mester the way. But now he do be farming like a great wise man, and young miss be handi-ful wi' the women folk and childer in Plimpton. She be a rare un for helping folkses to help theirselves, be young miss."

"She might have helped Tonina and me," Mark thought bitterly.

He wondered how he would explain his sudden return to Great Lowlands; and when he reached the house an explanation seemed necessary.

"Where has Tonina gone?" Katherine asked when he had finished.

"To Italy, with her confounded fiddle," said Mark.

His words were nimbler than his eyes. They moved slowly, weighted by care.

"Can't something be arranged?" Katherine asked. "Is the separation final?"

"Of course it is! She won't give up playing, and I can't work at home."

"Mark, why did you give up the office work?"

"I had to. It was that South Hants election. Dawson stalked me down, saying it was the information I gave Franklin that won the seat for Pilchard. I had to resign, though he could prove nothing. . . ."

"And what are you going to do now?"

"Turn farmer," he laughed awkwardly. "That will set you free to go back to town, Kit. You can take rooms; and there is the furniture you warehoused. . . ."

"I gave it to Miss Rowe," said Katherine, quickly. "Her rooms in Charlotte Buildings were so bare; but I don't quite understand, Mark. Are you driving me out of Great Lowlands?"

"Of course not!" he answered sharply. "I'm only setting you free to take up your work again. You should go down on your knees and thank me for liberty."

There was a queer little smile about Katherine's mouth. She did not speak. Her eyes were full on Mark where he stood, cringing and sheepish and mean. . . . Then she softened towards him. She curbed the quick retort on her lips.

"I daresay you mean kindly, Mark," she said gently. "If I had been free to leave the farm I would have gone before without your permission."

There was a little break in her voice. . . . Last winter freedom would have meant a new heaven and a new earth to her.

"But I thought Tom was running the farm now," said Mark, surprised. "I thought he was doing so well since Peggy died."

"He is doing splendidly," said Katherine, with a

proud smile; "but I have other work here that I can't leave."

It was true. The criticisms that she had heard at The Three Soldiers had opened her eyes to work in the village. It was not only in London that the poor suffered. . . . There were birth and death and pain and poverty—all the persons of the drama—on the stage of Plimpton life. The tragedies were not mounted with the scenic effect of the London boards, but they were no less tragic.

There were Labour questions in the village as urgent, as insistent, as those in London. The great cure might be applied as well here to the few as there to the multitude. She could be emptying her can of milk a gill at a time. Improve the condition of the labourer, and you improve the conditions of labour.

She had gone in and out of the homes, meeting the women as a woman who had loved and suffered and lost, and learned to make the best of life.

Tom had helped her to start a working-man's club. There was a smoking-room where he was always ready with a good song; and in the gymnasium he taught fencing and athletics.

Katherine had the women's side of the club, where the mothers sewed while she lectured on household topics, or read to them or sang. The club had taken root in the village. If she left it, it must wither and die. And there was Tom. The club filled up his evenings, and led his interests into healthy channels. She could not launch him on Mark's society with any confidence that he would not lapse into the old reckless idling. . . . No, she could not leave Plimpton, though Mark's presence at the farm might set her free to go elsewhere. But where

could she go?—Her mind flew round the village and
lighted on Martha's cottage; on bedroom and parlour
still empty. . . . Its doors swung on hinges of freedom and independence. There the fetters of the big
house would fall from her. She would burst the bonds
of domestic affairs. Her heart leaped up with a joyful
cry. . . . She was free at last to write her History of the
Labour movement. At last the aloe had blossomed. . . .
She had planted her human trees; she was building her
temple. The book should be the Mecca-window in her
temple,—it would face the man she loved. She had
her life-purpose in her grasp. . . . The moment made
turmoil in her veins. Hope stood a-tiptoe in an eager
outlook, seeing life; and life was good. It trailed clouds
of glory with it; it was golden with rays of Godhead.
. . . What if love never found its earthly close? It was
good to have loved. . . . What if her temple was empty?
She could keep the sacred fires alight. What if she
must die in the wilderness? She could plant her groves
for the immortals. . . . She looked back on the past,—
on its pain, its disillusion, its failure, and behold, it was
very good. . . . Out of the eater had come forth meat,
and out of the strong sweetness. She would write her
book and send it to Franklin, and he would know that
she was true to him. There was a sound of bells in
her voice when she spoke,—a distant tinkle as of the
herd coming home from the pastures, udder-laden and
willing.

"We can talk about my leaving afterwards, Mark.
You look so tired! Won't you come into the dining-room
and let me get you some lunch?"

Mark lifted his brows surprised. This was not Katherine as he had known her. . . .

During the day he watched her. She looked more
womanly, older too; but added years did not account for
that equable tone in all that she did and said, for her
ordered calm.

When the men came for direction there was no sharp
command from her. It was Tom who answered, she who
asked his advice.

She listened to an interminable tale in the kitchen
while her soup cooled in the dining-room. But she came
back smiling; and "Tom, I wonder if the club would run
to flannel for Susan Parkin's rheumatism?"

He missed the impetuous Katherine, but he saw the
strength in everything she did. Later in the day he
caught a glimpse of the girl.

Going into the barn he stumbled over a score of
babies playing "Nuts in May," with Katherine leading.
Her hair was tousled, her dress tumbled; her eyes leaped
and laughed. She looked the biggest baby of them all.
Sarah—an old friend from Goodge Street, nursing a baby
of her own—explained that on Thursdays there was a
mother's tea at the club; and Miss Fleming always took
charge of the children so as to free the women for the
afternoon. "She's a friend to the whole village," she
finished, looking proudly and fondly at Katherine. "It's
her as helps poor women, and makes their homes happier-
like."

Mark went out of the barn whistling. He found
Tom, and laid his plans before him; and long before the
interview was over he was staring at the manliness and
self-direction Tom had developed.

When Katherine came in from the barn with roses on
her face and a gay prankishness in her eye, he addressed
her solemnly;—

"Kit, I've been thinking over matters."

Katherine jerked her thoughts back from "Gathering Nuts in May," and looked at him, her face a-blossom with fun.

"Yes, Mark," she smiled.

"Look here, Kit, I don't want you to go away. You must stay with us. I haven't forgotten how well we used to get on. . . . I've had a talk with Tom too. He won't hear of your going. And he says he'll have nothing to do with the land unless you have a third of the profits."

Katherine's face was undefended from its feeling.

"Tom is a dear!" she said heartily. "It was generous of him to say that."

"And I'm quite willing to agree," said Mark, loftily. "We'll share and share alike, and you'll stay on."

"I'll stay on in Plimpton," said Katherine, joyously. "But I will go to another house where I shall be free to write."   •

Her eyes glowed; her face became strong and earnest. Yes, she would write her book. And she would send it to Franklin; it would bridge the silence that was a deep gulf between them. Her work would be the fruit of these years of struggle and pain, of wrestling and defeat, of courage waxing and waning, of a reed shaken by the wind. . . . Ah, it was good to have lived the years in which she had eaten the fruit of the knowledge of good and evil in herself,—which had taught her the anguish and the ecstasy of life.

She had learned the difficult patience of denial. She had learned too the humble dignity of the common day. The light in her eyes was a flaming torch that swept present and past and future.

Her thoughts sang. The words on her lips were grave:—

> " With aching hands and bleeding feet,
>   We dig and heap, lay stone on stone;
>   We bear the burden and the heat
>   Of the long day, and wish 'twere done.
>   Not till the hours of light return
>   All we have built do we discern."

CHAPTER XIV.

THE BOOK IS A MASTERPIECE.

THE year kept the feast of Spring. In every garden banners were fluttering; the meadows were spread with cloth of gold. Hawthorn swung its censer by field and fence where earth heaped her green spaces with white billows, matching the cloud billows heaped above in the blue spaces. From the blue came the rapture of the lark; from the green the bleat of young lambs. Looking from Martha's cottage, the common in the distance with its yellow gorse seemed to be a colour echo of the laburnum glory in the garden. The living sunshine laughed up to the living sun.

Two figures crossed the light. Mark and Tom were going to the common to play golf. Jock sat on the window sill, and barked recognition. He looked wistfully after them. Why must a dog sit indoors when there were geese to chase, rabbits to hunt, balls to find? The eye he turned to Katherine held a melancholy question in its depth.

Katherine caught him and tossed him up, and kissed

him for sheer gladness.   Her heart kept the feast.   The
winter of toil was over. . . . She had built her temple;
she had written her book. . . .

Her heart clashed cymbals and danced before the
festive company of her thoughts.   They went in procession to the temple.   The Mecca-window was open to
airs of heaven. . . . She could write to Franklin now, and
send him her History.   She would send also that letter
from the Chairman of the Labour Congress, which said
the book would do more for the cause than all the agitation of the past six years.   And Franklin would reply
kindly . . . and then. . . . Yes, her work at Great Lowlands was over, and she was free to go to him.   There
was no fear of Tom's lapsing now.   This last year had
established him.

Katherine's life in the cottage had proved a restrain-
ing influence.   He could not visit her without being reminded of Peggy; and if he stayed away he missed the
petting and spoiling that Martha and Katherine and
Jock gave him.   He went every day, and did not know
how strong the women were to keep him in safe paths.
He had Mark's companionship at home and at the club.

To rid himself of the burden of leisure Mark had
strolled into the club.   Its interests seized him; he was
once more under the tyranny of Katherine's earnestness.
He lectured on Labour topics until he had swung round
to his old position and views.   Katherine laughed happily
when she told him he had come to Great Lowlands to
be a Labour leader.

The club and Tom could spare her now.   She saw
her wilderness aflame with golden success; and Love sang
its lark's song in the sky.

The History she had written owed everything to

Franklin. His theories and ideas ran like a pattern through the warp and woof of facts. His judgment weighted every sentence. Her own research in town, and experience in the country had been blossoming plants; Franklin's mind had transferred the pollen from flower to flower, and made the plants fruitful. She told herself fancifully that her History of the Labour Movement—that unappetising thing!—was a love-apple!

Then she kissed Jock joyfully, and agreed with him it was too good a day to stay indoors. It was a high day and a holiday. She would go and play golf with the boys; and he might come too and chase the balls.

She swung along with a frolic happiness, tossing her club and humming to herself. And the song was Ambrose's "Schlüsselblume." But though she carolled his verses, she gave never a thought to the poet. He had come to Plimpton last summer to see Katherine "where the roses blow."

He had found her superintending the afternoon tea of a litter of pigs, crown and glory of Martha's establishment.

He had suffered many things from the draped Botticelli, from "Love and Death" desecrated in the kitchen; from Martha's gooseberry wine, and from Jock, who licked the shine off his patent-leather shoes.

It was horrible to see that when Katherine was not feeding pigs she was soiling her hands with the Labour Question. He had sniffed at her History. . . . The club with its coal societies and clothing societies, its dominoes and drum-and-fife band, made him shudder. Katherine herself, sunburnt and healthy and wise, was not his ideal of the dainty feminine. . . . He had taken the next train

back to town without offering to her the rondel that held
his heart. He had gone out of Katherine's life as lightly
as he had entered it. She sang his verses and gave him
never a thought.

She overtook her brothers on the common. Tom had
a letter for her that he had forgotten to leave at the cottage. Katherine's heart saw Franklin's writing before her
eyes skimmed the envelope. She carried off her letter to
read it alone. Her feet sprang with the turf. He had
written at last! . . . "For lo! the winter is past. The rain
is over and gone; the flowers appear on the earth; the
time of the singing of birds is come. . . . Arise, my love,
my fair one, and come away."

What would his letter say? No need to break the
seal; she knew! "Arise, my love, my fair one, and come
away." He had loved and trusted her through that long
silence as she had loved and trusted him. . . . And now
the winter of silence was over. . . .

She hid herself under a burning bush of gorse. The
flowers flamed about her, but the bush was not consumed.
The thorns pricked her hands as she crept among them.
What matter!

She loitered over the letter, reading the address, criti-
cising the writing, bruising the grape of anticipation before
she would yield it wholly to tongue and palate.

Ah! how merry was this gay world, where love
shrilled high unseen, and success blossomed abroad! . . .
And those two figures with silver shafts in the sun, were
they not the young gods come at last to earth? . . .

She broke the envelope, and drew out the letter, smiling tremulously.

Dear Miss Fleming,—I send you the MS. of a History of the Labour Movement that I have written. Bates and Bullen have agreed to take it; but you may possibly care to see it before it goes to press.

Yours truly,

Richard Franklin.

National Liberal Club,
London, W.

.   .   .   .

Katherine sat there still, holding the letter. There was even a smile on her face,—the afterglow of the sunset. . . . She had taken her heart in her hand, and was watching it gasp out its life. That red stain where the gorse had pricked her was its life-blood. . . .

Franklin had written a History too, so her work would be useless. In any case it would be eclipsed by the brilliance of his. The success she had sighted would never be hers. . . . What did that matter! She could see a hundred successes go, and snap her fingers at the retreating figures! . . . But Love had gone. . . . She had built her temple. And as she had builded, the walls had sprung up of marble overlaid with gold. The great spaces had been flooded with light from a mystic Presence that she had thought was Love himself. . . . And Love had not come to his temple. Long ago she had seen the vision of the gods threading the spaces of the moonlight. And when day came she knew it had been only mischievous boys tearing down the flowers. It was the same thing over again; he had torn down all her garlands. . . .

Was this the letter of a man to the woman he loved? and after those long months of silence and separation?

18*

There was no love here; friendship even would have given more than those chill words. . . . She had asked bread, and Love had given her a stone. . . .

And the winds howled and the rains beat and the floods came; and the house she had built fell. And great was the fall thereof.

.   .   .   .

She found Franklin's manuscript at the cottage, and she took it away to read undisturbed.

It was merely a long pamphlet, a somewhat inadequate *résumé* of the story of the Labour Movement; the sort of thing Katherine herself might have written before she had made her elaborate Museum research. It showed the threadbare garments that covered the people; but its proposals for patching and mending were unpractical, even sentimental. Some of the sentences had a familiar ring in her ears; but she did not recognise them as echoes of her own speeches, the emotional utterances of her platform days. . . .

The alertness on her face steadied itself, poised between security and dread. . . . Franklin could not fail. . . . His failure was before her. . . .

She did not guess that the strong intellect had been warped by his brooding distrust; that loss of faith in the woman had worked to slackened faith in the cause he had loved. Franklin's heart had reacted on his brain to the disadvantage of the book. It was unworthy of his knowledge and power and enthusiasm. It could not greatly affect the cause. An ineffectual arrow, it fell short of the mark. Many such had already been aimed at the bull's eye of the Labour Question. Katherine revolted at the thought that Franklin should fail like other men . . .

If she could only substitute her work for his! But that was impossible. Her book would never be published now. . . . She would not flaunt her triumph in the face of Franklin's failure. . . . Even though her History would do more for the cause than years of agitation she would suppress it. . . . She could not humble the man she loved. . . .

She remembered the Sunday in the Park when the people had listened to her and not to him. . . . His failure had hurt her then; and she loved him a hundred times more to-day than she had loved him then. Yes, though his letter might say he had ceased to love her, she loved him still. . . . She could not deal him a blow in order to help on any cause. The people must give way before the individual.

She got up wearily and began to pace the room. The stinging thoughts buzzed about her. Was it right to sacrifice the people merely in order to spare Franklin's feelings? The picture of Iphigenia, Peggy's last gift, followed her steps. She could not get away from it.

Peggy herself stood in the room. Katherine could hear her speaking: "The best thing in life is sacrifice. . . . Love means sacrifice. . . ."

Katherine's eyes were dark with struggle. She threw out her hand passionately. "I could sacrifice myself," she cried, "but I can't sacrifice him. He is a proud man; it would be bitter to him to see that I could succeed where he failed. . . . Let the people go! What do I care if the cause suffers? Movements can do without the individual; men and women are only necessary to each other. I loved him first; my love for the people came second. . . ."

Again the silence spoke, but now it was her own voice answering: "The first is of the earth, earthy; the second is the Lord from heaven." Then came Peggy's wistful accents: "I wonder if there is any Lord from heaven in love at all?"

Katherine shrank back. There could be nothing god-like in her love that could not renounce itself. And she had once believed in renunciation. . . . A far-away echo came to her from the old days before Newnham. . . . "Go where thou wilt, seek whatever thou wilt, thou shalt not find a higher way above nor a safer way below than the way of the cross. . . . The cross is always ready, and everywhere waits for thee. Thou canst not escape it whithersoever thou runnest, for wheresoever thou goest, thou carriest thyself with thee, and shalt ever find thyself."

.   .   .   .

Franklin sat in his room and read Katherine's letter again But by this time he knew every word in it.

DEAR MR. FRANKLIN,—I have read your book, and you will forgive me if I tell you frankly it does not do you justice. I am sending you a History that I have written. You will see that whatever is of value in it is due to you. Please tell me which of the two shall be published. I would have suppressed mine in order to make way for yours, but it seems wrong to let my wishes influence me in a matter of this sort. Have you quite forgotten your old friend? I have not forgotten you. I long to know that you are well and happy.

Faithfully yours,
KATHERINE FLEMING.

Franklin smiled a grim smile that much use was wearing down to a pleasant one. . . . But he hardened his heart again. "She can afford to be conciliatory," he said; "the book is a masterpiece. . . . She can even afford to remember the wretch she grinds under her car-wheels...."

Still he could not convince himself that it was the letter of a woman triumphing. She had not forgotten him. . . . Had he for a single moment let her slip from heart or mind? This very book had been written to please her, in spite of his sore sickness. She had inspired it. In that far country where he had fed on the husks of love's denial he had been prodigal of thought for her. He had dressed a rosy sanctuary "With the wreath'd trellis of a working brain." . . . And now she said the book did not do him justice. . . . Ah! there peeped out the cloven foot. She was clever, but nature betrayed her. Could a woman be critical where she loved? . . . No, he would not risk a second denial. He barred and locked his heart against her.

He looked grey and worn, a man old before his time. His eyes were dull. He showed the marks of the fever that had sent him home invalided. . . . Even if she loved him, what had he to offer to any woman,— the wreck of a man? No, he must not imperil his resolution. He would return her manuscript, and then . . . No, even friendship was impossible. . . .

Katherine read the slip of paper with white face.

"You must publish your History. It is a most valuable contribution to the literature of the movement.
"R. F."

She looked round her piteously. Jock put up his head and licked the tears from her face. Katherine laid her face against his shaggy coat. Even a dog's love may be an angel at the tomb. . . . But there was no abandonment in the purpose of the clear eyes she lifted again.

Love sprang to its old seat; and faith—poised lightly above the whirling doubt and evasive circle of the moment—sped onward to meet the future. She could wait; and while she waited she could work for the people.

———

CHAPTER XV.

THE GODS ARRIVE!

"Ay! I sees you picking my white clover!" said Martha. "You doesn't dig, but you ain't ashamed to pluck."

Katherine raised herself, laughing, from the garden-plot.

"The flowers are so sweet, Martha," she said, a dainty deprecation in her tone.

"Sweet? ay, sweet enough! but sour enough oftens. White clover be *Memories*. I sets it with the balm, what be *Sympathy,* and beside the foxglove *Sincerity*. . . . They makes a prutty posy for the dead, meaning 'Sincere sympathy with remembrance.'"

"Have all your flowers a meaning?" Katherine asked.

"In course they has, duckie. The bluebells be *Constancy,* and the voylet leaves stands for *Love*. The blossoms be past, but there's seeds setting, and next year, please God, we'll have a rare show. . . . I plants en close to the veronica, meaning *Faithfulness,* and not so far off I puts yellow heartsease, which be *Waiting*. That bit o' dead heather do mean *Solitude*. It had used to grow under the bay-tree, which be *Glory,* but the leaves killed en. The blue salvy you be wearing is *Knowledge*. The plant be like to choke up the flax, meaning *Fate*."

"Oh!" said Katherine, with a little delicate, unexpected laugh. "To think that I have had this grand company about me, and never knew it!"

"Lawks!" said Martha, "we be poor fools, for we doesn't see to understand the meanings that nature do stick into the life she fetches up out o' the ground. Who'd ha' thought to find Love a-hanging his head under the leavses, and hiding behind them clover-tops? And missie herself minds me of a whole posy o' meanings; yes, you does."

Katherine made an inarticulate noise in her throat, and the red flooded her face. She stooped and added some violet leaves to the posy in her belt. . . . She lifted herself, and her eyes sought the blank road. It was more than a week since Franklin had returned her manuscript, and she was still expecting him. . . She had looked into her life, and found it empty. All that lay there were the napkins she had bound about her love,— the times of her achievements, the hours of her triumphs, the great moments big with promise. Love had no need of these. He had risen. . . . Soon, in some shining grey dawn, he would meet the woman seeking him. She had found him once on Peggy's grave, and her kiss had wakened him. . . .

Suddenly her eyes darted forward and eagerly questioned the distance. Where the road twisted round from Great Lowlands a cloud of dust came sweeping down the wind. Katherine's face fell; not one, but a troop was coming. . . .

She could hear them singing. The familiar tune bore the words far:—

"Here we come gathering nuts in May, nuts in May, nuts in May;
Here we come gathering nuts in May so early in the morning."

The village children were making holiday. Katherine's eyes gladdened. She hummed the tune herself, tapping

her foot. Who could be sad on a spring morning, with
the sun in his best mood, the south wind attending,
earth laughing, children singing, and the lark high on
the wing? Not Katherine, though only a fortnight had
passed since that day when she had cowered under the
thorny gorse. The flame that encircled life had not consumed the joy of life.

> "Is it so small a thing
> To have enjoyed the sun?
> To have lived light in the spring,
> To have loved, to have thought, to have done?
> To have advanced true friends, and beat down
>   battling foes?"

She said the words smiling, and there was a bloom
on her smile, the purple soft indefiniteness of a royal assurance.

> "Who will you gather for nuts in May, nuts in May, nuts in May?
> Who will you gather for nuts in May so early in the morning?"

The shrill voices came nearer, the treble questioning.

> "We'll gather a maid for nuts in May, nuts in May, nuts in May,
> We'll gather a maid for nuts in May so early in the morning,"

the boys sturdily answered.

"Lawks! I quite forgot 't were White Monday," said
Martha, running to the fence. "Bless the little mites!
I loves to see 'em, boys and maids together as nature
meant."

> "Who will you send to fetch her away, fetch her away, fetch her
>   away?
> Who will you send to fetch her away so early in the morning?"

The thin treble soared high, the refrain sounding like
the beat of ascending wings. Martha and Katherine

could see the children's faces now.   Jock got up from
his nap on the doorstep, and cocking his ears sauntered
condescendingly to the gate, to watch also.

The children walked two and two, carrying flowers
tied on poles, and wearing garlands of May and lilac and
laburnum.   As they came on, the boys' strident voices
took the road:—

"We'll send young Love to fetch her away, fetch her away, fetch
    her away;
We'll send young Love to fetch her away so early in the morn-
    ing."

"They Parkin boys be marching first," said Martha,
"and the young warmints has gotten they rosydondrons
from our orchard, I'll be sworn."

Katherine ran to the gate and leaned over to see
them pass.   Susan Parkin's lads headed the procession,
their heads crowned with chaplets of rhododendron
leaves.   They had only flowers enough for the poles, it
seemed.

Behind them came more boys, carrying branches of
palm and willow catkins.   They wore clean smocks and
stepped out, challenging and bravely bashful, before the
girls.   Nimble and eager and shy the little maids followed, their aprons filled with flowers.

". . . send young Love to fetch her away . . ."

The singing trailed off to the end of the column, where
the babies lisped on "Fetch her away, fetch her away,"
not knowing that their elders were dumb.

The boys had caught sight of Katherine, and were
openly conscious.   They pulled their forelocks, grinning;
the girls made their obedience, smiling with soft eyes.
Leaning over the gate under the yellow laburnum bloom

Katherine kissed her hands to them. "Dear little hearts! Bless you! bless you!"

When they had all passed beyond the thin screen of the dust Katherine looked down the empty road. There was a peculiar quality in her glance,—freedom, a noble deliverance that gave dignity. The young faces, free and glad, facing the future—gods that feared not—had sent her thoughts back to the children of the city, who toiled and strove and suffered, not knowing if there was any God at all.

A great yearning was in Katherine's heart to go to these with her message of joy, and the hope of life and good to crown the year. She, too, would gather nuts in May that there might be food for these poor souls. . . .

"Martha," she cried, "I must leave you. I am going to London to live. I must take the nuts I have gathered here for those that are hungry."

Her voice broke. She swung round from Martha.

"Oh, be ashamed o' yourself! Crying and reddening your eyes for a pack o' nonsense! What be the good o' old nuts that do require salt to make 'em tasty? Wait till the young nuts be ripe."

Katherine dashed away her tears and turned to the old woman, her voice broken outright beyond control.

"Ah! haven't they eaten the salt?" she cried shrilly. "They have eaten the salt; they have eaten the salt, and have never tasted the nuts!"

.   .   .   .   .

She took her hat and went forth to think alone over her resolve. Her eyes were composed and steady and confident. There was no appeal, no uncertainty in their depths. They held the fruits of autumn in the lap of summer's maturity. Determination straightened her figure, but the strong pole was crowned with flowers. Her face was garlanded with a holiday happiness. She was free at last to give herself wholly to the service of the people. She would go to her work; and when she was worthy Love would walk with her there.

Unconsciously she had taken the road to the station. Thought set its screen between her and things outside. She did not see the man toiling wearily up the hill.

Franklin's love was dead; but he could not go away without coming to see the place where she was laid. . . .

While she was yet a long way off he saw her, and he knew that his love was not dead. He would have run to meet her, but he was still too weak; only his eyes pressed on and embraced her.

They feasted on the grace and freedom of her walk. She swung her hat in her hand, and the hair stood out round her head like a halo. He could not see the posy she carried in her belt. The salvia and veronica and clover were hidden, but the wind bore to him the strong smell of the sprig of balm. Joy and strength were as gods that walked with her.

She came nearer. . . . A flashing happiness in his eyes lighted a torch to greet her.

"For this my love" . . . he began. . . .

But she was close now. She must see him if she recalled those distant eyes. . . . How grave and earnest she looked! . . Had he ever doubted that face? . . . He could trust her with honour itself . . . Now she had seen him! . . . No, her gaze passed beyond him! . . .

Katherine's mind was behind the screen, in the past. This was the same road that had brought her to Great Lowlands three years ago. She remembered the morning she had toiled up the hill, bearing the burden and heat of the day, her heart bitter, joy dead, the temple of hope in ruins. . . . Peggy had helped her on her way. . . . There was the white gate; it had been the gate of death and the gate of life. . . .

She had raised another temple, and had built for the gods. . . . But they had not come to their temple. . . . One Figure had entered. His scourge of small cords had driven out those that bought and sold. He had over-turned the tables of the money-changers. He had no form nor comeliness; his visage was marred more than the sons of men. . . . She had called him Death, not knowing the strong Son of God. . . . And now the house she had built was empty of guests. She would go out into the highways and hedges and compel them to come in that her house might be furnished. She would fill the place with the halt and the lame and the blind. The temple she had built should be a home for the People. . . .

A great light shone on her face.

Franklin stopped. . . . She had recognised him! . . . No, not yet. Her eyes gazed beyond him as if they saw a vision of angels.

THE END.

PRINTING OFFICE OF THE PUBLISHER.

April   1898.

TAUCHNITZ EDITION.

Each volume 1 Mark 60 Pf. or 2 Francs.

This Collection of British Authors, Tauchnitz Edition, will contain the new works of the most admired English and American Writers, immediately on their appearance, with copyright for continental circulation.

Contents:

Collection of British Authors, vol. 1—3274   *Page 2-14.*
Collection of German Authors, vol. 1—51 .   „   15.
Series for the Young, vol. 1—30 . . . . .   „   15.
Dictionaries . . . .   „   16.

Latest Volumes:

The War of the Worlds. By *H. G. Wells,* 1 vol.
The King with two Faces. By *M. E. Coleridge,* 2 vols.
The Skipper's Wooing. By *W. W. Jacobs,* 1 vol.
His Grace of Osmonde. By *Frances Hodgson Burnett,* 2 vols.
A Fair Deceiver. By *George Paston,* 1 vol.
Rough Justice. By *M. E. Braddon,* 2 vols.
The Chevalier d'Auriac. By *S. Levett-Yeats,* 1 vol.
The Christian. By *Hall Caine,* 2 vols.
The Tragedy of the Korosko. By *A. Conan Doyle,* 1 vol.
Jerome. By *Mary E. Wilkins,* 2 vols.
Another's Burden. By *James Payn,* 1 vol.

Collection of British Authors.

Rev. W. Adams: Sacred Allegories 1 v.
Miss Aguilar: Home Influence 2 v.
The Mother's Recompense 2 v.

H. Aïdé: Rita 1 v. Carr of Carrlyon 2 v.
The Marstons 2 v. In that State of Life 1 v.
Morals and Mysteries 1 v. Penruddocke 2 v.
"A nine Days' Wonder" 1 v. Poet and
Peer 2 v. Introduced to Society 1 v.

W. H. Ainsworth: Windsor Castle 1 v.
Saint James's 1 v. Jack Sheppard (w. Port.)
1 v. The Lancashire Witches 2 v. The Star-
Chamber 2 v. The Flitch of Bacon 1 v. The
Spendthrift 1 v. Mervyn Clitheroe 2 v.
Ovingdean Grange 1 v. The Constable of
the Tower 1 v. The Lord Mayor of Lon-
don 2 v. Cardinal Pole 2 v. John Law
2 v. The Spanish Match 2 v. The Con-
stable de Bourbon 2 v. Old Court 2 v.
Myddleton Pomfret 2 v. The South-Sea
Bubble 2 v. Hilary St. Ives 2 v. Talbot
Harland 1 v. Tower Hill 1 v. Boscobel
2 v. The Good Old Times 2 v. Merry
England 2 v. The Goldsmith's Wife 2 v.
Preston Fight 2 v. Chetwynd Calverley
2 v. The Leaguer of Lathom 2 v. The
Fall of Somerset 2 v. Beatrice Tyldesley
2 v. Beau Nash 2 v. Stanley Brereton 2 v.

Louisa M. Alcott: Little Women 2 v.
Little Men 1 v. An Old-Fashioned Girl
1 v. Jo's Boys 1 v.

Thomas Bailey Aldrich: Marjorie
Daw, etc. 1 v. The Stillwater Tragedy 1 v.

Mrs. Alexander: A Second Life 3 v.
By Woman's Wit 1 v. Mona's Choice 2 v.
A Life Interest 2 v. A Crooked Path 2 v.
Blind Fate 2 v. A Woman's Heart 2 v. For
His Sake 2 v. The Snare of the Fowler 2 v.
Found Wanting 2 v. A Ward in Chancery
1 v. A Choice of Evils 2 v. A Fight with Fate
2 v. A Winning Hazard 1 v. A Golden
Autumn 1 v. Mrs. Crichton's Creditor 1 v.
Barbara, Lady's Maid and Peeress 1 v.

Alice, Grand Duchess of Hesse (with
Portrait) 2 v.

Lizzie Alldridge: By Love and Law
2 v. The World she awoke in 2 v.

Grant Allen: The Woman who did 1 v.
"All for Greed," Author of—All for
Greed 1 v. Love the Avenger 2 v.

F. Anstey: The Giant's Robe 2 v. A
Fallen Idol 1 v. The Pariah 3 v. The
Talking Horse, etc. 1 v. Voces Populi 1 v.

Matthew Arnold: Essays in Criticism
2 v. Essays in Criticism, 2nd Series, 1 v.

Sir Arnold: Light of Asia (w. Port.) 1 v.

Miss Austen: Sense and Sensibility 1 v.
Mansfield Park 1 v. Pride and Prejudice
1 v. Northanger Abbey 1 v. Emma 1 v.

Baring-Gould: Mehalah 1 v. John
Herring 2 v. Court Royal 2 v.

Lady Barker: Station Life in New
Zealand 1 v. Station Amusements in New
Zealand 1 v. A Year's Housekeeping in
South Africa 1 v. Letters to Guy, etc. 1 v.

F. Barrett: The Smuggler's Secret 1 v.
Out of the Jaws of Death 2 v.

J. M. Barrie: Sentimental Tommy 2 v.
Margaret Ogilvy 1 v.

Miss Bayle's Romance, Author of
—vide W. Fraser Rae.

Rev. R. H. Baynes: Lyra Anglicana,
Hymns and Sacred Songs 1 v.

Beaconsfield: vide Disraeli.

A. Beaumont: Thornicroft's Model 2 v.

Currer Bell (Ch. Brontë): Jane Eyre 2 v.
Shirley 2 v. Villette 2 v. The Professor 1 v.

Ellis & Acton Bell: Wuthering Heights,
and Agnes Grey 2 v.

E. Bellamy: Looking Backward 1 v.

F. Lee Benedict: St. Simon's Niece 2 v.

Benson: Dodo 1 v. The Rubicon 1 v.

Walter Besant: The Revolt of
Man 1 v. Dorothy Forster 2 v. Children of
Gibeon 2 v. The World went very well then
2 v. Katharine Regina 1 v. Herr Paulus
2 v. The Inner House 1 v. The Bell of St.
Paul's 2 v. For Faith and Freedom 2 v.
Armorel of Lyonesse 2 v. Verbena Camel-
lia Stephanotis 1 v. Beyond the Dreams of
Avarice 2 v. The Master Craftsman 2 v.
A Fountain Sealed 1 v.

W. Besant & James Rice: The Golden
Butterfly 2 v. Ready-Money Mortiboy 2 v.
By Celia's Arbour 2 v.

A. Bierce: In the Midst of Life 1 v.

E. Bisland: vide Miss Broughton.

William Black: A Daughter of Heth
2 v. In Silk Attire 2 v. Adventures of a
Phaeton 2 v. A Princess of Thule 2 v.
Kilmeny 1 v. The Maid of Killeena, etc.
1 v. Three Feathers 2 v. Lady Silverdale's
Sweetheart 1 v. Madcap Violet 2 v. Green
Pastures and Piccadilly 2 v. Macleod of
Dare 2 v. White Wings 2 v. Sunrise 2 v.
The Beautiful Wretch 1 v. Mr. Pisistratus
Brown, M.P., in the Highlands 1 v.
Shandon Bells (w. Portrait) 2 v. Judith
Shakespeare 2 v. The Wise Women of
Inverness, etc. 1 v. White Heather 2 v.
Sabina Zembra 2 v. Strange Adventures
of a House Boat 2 v. In Far Lochaber
2 v. The New Prince Fortunatus 2 v.
Stand Fast, Craig Royston! 2 v. Donald
Ross of Heimra 2 v. Magic Ink, etc. 1 v.
Wolfenberg 2 v. The Handsome Humes 2 v.
Highland Cousins 2 v. Briseis 2 v.

The price of each volume is 1 Mark 60 Pfennig.

The Black-Box Murder 1 v.

Richard Doddridge Blackmore: Alice Lorraine 2 v. Mary Anerley 3 v. Christowell 2 v. Tommy Upmore 2 v. Perlycross 2 v.

"Blackwood," Tales from — 1 v.— *Second Series* 1 v.

Isa Bladgen: The Woman I loved, and the Woman who loved me, etc. 1 v.

Lady Blessington: Meredith 1 v. Strathern 2 v. Memoirs of a Femme de Chambre 1 v. Marmaduke Herbert 2 v. Country Quarters (with Portrait) 2 v.

Baroness Bloomfield: Reminiscences of Court and Diplomatic Life (with the Portrait of Her Majesty the Queen) 2 v.

Rolf Boldrewood: Robbery under Arms 2 v. Nevermore 2 v.

Miss Braddon: Lady Audley's Secret 2 v. Aurora Floyd 2 v. Eleanor's Victory 2 v. John Marchmont's Legacy 2 v. Henry Dunbar 2 v. The Doctor's Wife 2 v. Only a Clod 2 v. Sir Jasper's Tenant 2 v. The Lady's Mile 2 v. Rupert Godwin 2 v. Dead-Sea Fruit 2 v. Run to Earth 2 v. Fenton's Quest 2 v. The Lovels of Arden 2 v. Strangers and Pilgrims 2 v. Lucius Davoren 3 v. Taken at the Flood 3 v. Lost for Love 2 v. A Strange World 2 v. Hostages to Fortune 2 v. Dead Men's Shoes 2 v. Joshua Haggard's Daughter 2 v. Weavers and Weft 1 v. In Great Waters, etc. 1 v. An Open Verdict 3 v. Vixen 3 v. The Cloven Foot 3 v. Barbara 2 v. Just as I am 2 v. Asphodel 3 v. Mount Royal 2 v. The Golden Calf 2 v. Flower and Weed 1 v. Phantom Fortune 3 v. Under the Red Flag 1 v. Ishmael 3 v. Wyllard's Weird 3 v. One Thing Needful 2 v. Cut by the County 1 v. Like and Unlike 2 v. The Fatal Three 2 v. The Day will come 2 v. One Life, One Love 2 v. Gerard; or, The World, the Flesh, and the Devil 2 v. The Venetians 2 v. All along the River 2 v. Thou art the Man 2 v. The Christmas Hirelings 1 v. Sons of Fire 2 v. London Pride 2 v. Rough Justice 2 v.

Lady Brassey: A Voyage in the "Sunbeam" 2 v. Sunshine and Storm in the East 2 v. In the Trades, the Tropics, etc. 2 v.

The Bread-Winners 1 v.

Bret Harte: *vide* Harte.

Rev. W. Brock: A Biographical Sketch of Sir H. Havelock, K. C. B. 1 v.

Shirley Brooks: The Silver Cord 3 v. Sooner or Later 3 v.

Miss Rhoda Broughton: Cometh up as a Flower 1 v. Not wisely, but too well 2 v. Red as a Rose is She 2 v. Tales for Christmas Eve 1 v. Nancy 2 v. Joan 2 v. Second Thoughts 2 v. Belinda 2 v. Doctor Cupid 2 v. Alas! 2 v. Mrs. Bligh 1 v. A Beginner 1 v. Scylla or Charybdis? 1 v. Dear Faustina 1 v. [Indeed 1 v.

Broughton & Bisland: A Widower John Brown: Rab and his Friends 1 v.

E. Barrett Browning: A Selection from her Poetry (w. Port.) 1 v. Aurora Leigh 1 v.

R. Browning: Poet. Works (w. Portr.) 4 v.

E. Bulwer (Lord Lytton): Pelham (w. Portr.) 1 v. Eugene Aram 1 v. Paul Clifford 1 v. Zanoni 1 v. The Last Days of Pompeii 1 v. The Disowned 1 v. Ernest Maltravers 1 v. Alice 1 v. Eva, and the Pilgrims of the Rhine 1 v. Devereux 1 v. Godolphin and Falkland 1 v. Rienzi 1 v. Night and Morning 1 v. The Last of the Barons 2 v. Athens 2 v. Poems and Ballads of Schiller 1 v. Lucretia 2 v. Harold 2 v. King Arthur 2 v. The New Timon, St Stephen's 1 v. The Caxtons 2 v. My Novel 4 v. What will he do with it? 4 v. Dramatic Works 2 v. A Strange Story 2 v. Caxtoniana 2 v. The Lost Tales of Miletus 1 v. Miscellaneous Prose Works 4 v. Odes and Epodes of Horace 2 v. Kenelm Chillingly 4 v. The Coming Race 1 v. The Parisians 4 v. Pausanias, the Spartan 1 v.

Henry Lytton Bulwer (Lord Dalling): Historical Characters 2 v. The Life of Viscount Palmerston 3 v.

J. Bunyan: The Pilgrim's Progress 1 v. **"Buried Alone,"** 1 v.

F. H. Burnett: Through one Administration 2 v. Little Lord Fauntleroy 1 v. Sara Crewe and Editha's Burglar 1 v. The Pretty Sister of José 1 v. A Lady of Quality 2 v. His Grace of Osmonde 2 v.

Miss Burney: Evelina 1 v.

R. Burns: Poetical Works (w. Port.) 1 v.

Richard F. Burton: Pilgrimage to Mecca and Medina 3 v.

Mrs. B. H. Buxton: "Jennie of 'The Prince's,'" 2 v. Won! 2 v. Great Grenfell Gardens 2 v. Nell—on and off the Stage 2 v. From the Wings 2 v.

Lord Byron: Poet. Works (w. Port.) 5 v.

Hall Caine: The Bondman 2 v. The Manxman 2 v. The Christian 2 v.

V. Lovett Cameron: Across Africa 2 v.

Mrs. Campbell-Praed: Zéro 1 v. Affinities 1 v. The Head Station 2 v.

Carey: Not Like other Girls 2 v. "But Men must Work" 1 v. Sir Godfrey's Grand-Daughters 2 v. The Old, Old Story 2 v.

Thomas Carlyle: The French Revolution 3 v. Frederick the Great 13 v. Oliver

Cromwell's Letters and Speeches 4 v. The Life of Schiller 1 v.

A. Carr. Treherne's Temptation 2 v Egerton Castle. Consequences 2 v "La Bella" etc. 1 v.

Charlesworth: Oliver of the Mill 1 v.

M. Cholmondeley. Diana Tempest 2 v "Chronicles of the Schönberg-Cotta Family,"Author of—Chron.of theSchönb.-Cotta Family 2 v. The Draytons and the Davenants 2 v. On Both Sides of the Sea 2 v. Winifred Bertram 1 v. Diary of Mrs. Kitty Trevylyan 1 v. Victory of the Vanquished 1 v. The Cottage by the Cathedral 1 v. Against the Stream 2 v. The Bertram Family 2 v. Conquering and to Conquer 1 v. Lapsed, but not Lost 1 v.

A. Clark: The Finding of Lot's Wife 1 v.

Mrs. W. K. Clifford· Love-Letters of a Worldly Woman 1 v. Aunt Anne 2 v. Last Touches 1 v. Mrs Keith's Crime 1 v. A Wild Proxy 1 v. A Flash of Summer 1 v.

Frances Power Cobbe. Re-Echoes 1 v. Coleridge. The Poems 1 v.

C. R. Coleridge· An English Squire 2 v.

M. E. Coleridge· The King with two Faces 2 v.

Charles A. Collins· A Cruise upon Wheels 2 v

Mortimer Collins: Sweet and Twenty 2 v. A Fight with Fortune 2 v.

Wilkie Collins: After Dark 1 v. Hide and Seek 2 v. A Plot in Private Life, etc. 1 v. The Woman in White 2 v. Basil 1 v. No Name 3 v. The Dead Secret, etc. 2 v. Antonina 2 v. Armadale 3 v. The Moonstone 2 v. Man and Wife 3 v. Poor Miss Finch 2 v. Miss or Mrs.? 1 v. The New Magdalen 2 v. The Frozen Deep 1 v. The Law and the Lady 2 v. The Two Destinies 1 v. My Lady's Money 1 v. The Haunted Hotel 1 v. The Fallen Leaves 2 v. Jezebel's Daughter 2 v. The Black Robe 2 v. Heart and Science 2 v. "I say No," 2 v. The Evil Genius 2 v. The Guilty River 1 v. The Legacy of Cain 2 v. Blind Love 2 v.

"Cometh up as a Flower," Author of—*vide* Broughton.

Conrad· An Outcast of the Islands 2 v

Hugh Conway· Called Back 1 v. Bound Together 2 v. Dark Days 1 v. A Family Affair 2 v. Living or Dead 2 v.

F. Cooper: The Spy (w. Port) 1 v The Two Admirals 1 v. The Jack O'Lantern 1 v.

M Corelli: Vendetta! 2 v. Thelma 2 v. A Romance of Two Worlds 2 v. "Ardath" 3 v. Wormwood. A Drama of Paris 2 v. The Hired Baby, etc. 1 v. Barabbas 2 v. The

Sorrows of Satan 2 v. The Mighty Atom 1 v. The Murder of Delicia 1 v. Ziska 1 v. The County 1 v.

George L. Craik: A Manual of English Literature and Language 2 v.

Mrs. Craik (Miss Mulock): John Halifax, Gentleman 2 v. The Head of the Family 2 v. A Life for a Life 2 v. A Woman's Thoughts about Women 1 v. Agatha's Husband 1 v. Romantic Tales 1 v. Domestic Stories 1 v. Mistress and Maid 1 v. The Ogilvies 1 v. Lord Erlistoun 1 v. Christian's Mistake 1 v. Bread upon the Waters 1 v. A Noble Life 1 v. Olive 2 v. Two Marriages 1 v. Studies from Life 1 v. Poems 1 v. The Woman's Kingdom 2 v. The Unkind Word 2 v. A Brave Lady 2 v. Hannah 2 v. Fair France 1 v. My Mother and I 1 v. The Little Lame Prince 1 v. Sermons out of Church 1 v. The Laurel Bush 1 v. A Legacy 2 v. Young Mrs. Jardine 2 v. His Little Mother 1 v. Plain Speaking 1 v. Miss Tommy 1 v. King Arthur 1 v.

Miss G. Craik: Lost and Won 1 v. Faith Unwin's Ordeal 1 v. Leslie Tyrrell 1 v. Winifred's Wooing 1 v. Mildred 1 v. Esther Hill's Secret 2 v. Hero Trevelyan 1 v. Without Kith or Kin 2 v. Only a Butterfly 1 v. Sylvia's Choice; Theresa 2 v. Anne Warwick 1 v. Dorcas 2 v. Two Women 2 v.

G M. Craik & M. C. Stirling: Two Tales of Married Life (Hard to Bear, by Miss Craik: A True Man, by M. C. Stirling) 2 v.

Mrs. Augustus Craven: Eliane. Translated by Lady Fullerton 2 v.

F. M. Crawford: Mr. Isaacs 1 v. Doctor Claudius 1 v. To Leeward 1 v. A Roman Singer 1 v An American Politician 1 v. Zoroaster 1 v. A Lonely Parish 2 v. Saracinesca 2 v. Marzio's Crucifix 1 v. Paul Patoff 2 v. With the Immortals 1 v. Greifenstein 2 v. Sant' Ilano 2 v. A Cigarette-Maker's Romance 1 v. Khaled 1 v. The Witch of Prague 2 v. Three Fates 2 v. Don Orsino 2 v. The Children of the King 1 v. Pietro Ghisleri 2v. Marion Darche 1v. Katharine Lauderdale 2 v. The Ralstons 2 v. Casa Braccio 2 v. Adam Johnstone's Son 1 v. Taquisara 2 v. A Rose of Yesterday 1 v. Corleone 2 v [2 v. The Grey Man 2 v.

Crockett: The Raiders 2 v. Cleg Kelly

J. W. Cross: *v.* George Eliot's Life.

Miss Cummins: The Lamplighter 1 v. Mabel Vaughan 1 v. El Fureidîs 1 v. Haunted Hearts 1 v.

P. Cushing: The Blacksmith of Voe 2 v.

"Daily News": The War Correspondence 1877 by A. Forbes, etc. 3 v.

The price of each volume is 1 Mark 60 Pfennig.

Dark 1 v.

R Harding Davis: Gallegher, etc. 1 v
Van Bibber and Others 1 v.

De Foe: Robinson Crusoe 1 v.

M. Deland: John Ward, Preacher 1 v.
Democracy 1 v.

Demos *vide* George Gissing.

Charles Dickens: The Pickwick Club
(w. Port) 2 v. American Notes 1 v. Oliver
Twist 1 v. Nicholas Nickleby 2 v. Sketches
1 v. Martin Chuzzlewit 2 v. A Christmas
Carol, The Chimes; The Cricket on the
Hearth 1 v. Master Humphrey's Clock
(Old Curiosity Shop, Barnaby Rudge, etc.)
3 v. Pictures from Italy 1 v The Battle of
Life; the Haunted Man 1 v. Dombey and
Son 3 v. David Copperfield 3 v. Bleak
House 4 v. A Child's History of England
(2 v. 8° M. 2,70) Hard Times 1 v. Little
Dorrit 4 v. A Tale of two Cities 2 v. Hunted
Down, The Uncommercial Traveller 1 v.
Great Expectations 2 v. Christmas Stories
1 v. Our Mutual Friend 4 v. Somebody's
Luggage; Mrs Lirriper's Lodgings ; Mrs.
Lirriper's Legacy 1 v. Doctor Marigold's
Prescriptions; Mugby Junction 1 v. No
Thoroughfare; The Late Miss Hollingford
1 v. The Mystery of Edwin Drood 2 v. The
Mudfog Papers, etc. 1 v. *Vide* Household
Words, Novels and Tales, and J. Forster

Charles Dickens: The Letters of
- Charles Dickens edited by his Sister-in-
law and his eldest Daughter 4 v

B. Disraeli (Lord Beaconsfield): Con-
ingsby 1 v. Sybil 1 v. Contarini Fleming
(w. Port.) 1 v Alroy 1 v. Tancred 2 v.
Venetia 2 v. Vivian Grey 2 v. Henrietta
Temple 1 v. Lothair 2 v. Endymion 2 v.

Ella Hepworth Dixon: The Story of
a Modern Woman 1 v.

W. Hepworth Dixon: Personal History of Lord Bacon 1 v. The Holy Land
2 v. New America 2 v. Spiritual Wives 2 v.
Her Majesty's Tower 4 v. Free Russia
2 v. History of two Queens 6 v. White
Conquest 2 v. Diana, Lady Lyle 2 v.

L. Dougall· Beggars All 2 v.

Dowie: A Girl in the Karpathians 1 v.

A.C. Doyle: The Sign of Four 1 v. Micah
Clarke 2 v. The Captain of the Pole-Star
1 v The White Company 2 v A Study in
Scarlet 1 v. The Great Shadow, etc. 1 v.
Sherlock Holmes 2 v. The Refugees 2 v.
The Firm of Girdlestone 2 v. The Memoirs
of Sherlock Holmes 2 v. Round the Red
Lamp 1 v. The Stark Munro Letters 1 v.
The Exploits of Brigadier Gerard 1 v

Rodney Stone 2 v. Uncle Bernac 1 v. The
Tragedy of the Korosko 1 v.

Professor Henry Drummond: The
Greatest Thing in the World, etc. 1 v.
The Earl and the Doctor: South Sea
Bubbles 1 v.   [High Latitudes 1 v.
The Earl of Dufferin Letters from
Mrs. Edwardes. Archie Lovell 2 v.
Steven Lawrence, Yeoman 2 v. Ought
we to Visit her? 2 v. A Vagabond Heroine
1 v. Leah: A Woman of Fashion 2 v. A
Blue-Stocking 1 v. Jet· Her Face or Her
Fortune? 1 v. Vivian the Beauty 1 v. A
Ballroom Repentance 2 v. A Girton Girl
2 v. A Playwright's Daughter, etc. 1 v.
Pearl-Powder 1 v The Adventuress 1 v.

Miss A. B. Edwards. Barbara's History 2 v. Miss Carew 2 v. Hand and Glove
1 v. Half a Million of Money 2 v. Deben-
ham's Vow 2 v. In the Days of my Youth
2 v. Untrodden Peaks, etc. 1 v. Monsieur
Maurice 1 v. Black Forest 1 v. A Poetry-
Book of Elder Poets 1 v. A Thousand
Miles up the Nile 2 v. A Poetry-Book of
Modern Poets 1 v. Lord Brackenbury 2 v.

Miss M. B.-Edwards. The Sylvestres
1 v. Felicia 2 v Brother Gabriel 2 v. Fore-
stalled 1 v. Exchange no Robbery, etc 1 v.
Disarmed 1 v. Doctor Jacob 1 v Pearla 1 v
Next of Kin Wanted 1 v. The Parting of the
Ways 1 v.   For One and the World 1 v.
A French Parsonage 1 v. France of To-day
1 v. Two Aunts and a Nephew 1 v. A Dream
of Millions 1 v.   The Curb of Honour
1 v.   France of To-day (2nd Series) 1 v.
A Romance of Dijon 1 v.   The Dream-
Charlotte 1 v.

E. Eggleston: The Faith Doctor 2 v.
Barbara Elbon: Bethesda 2 v.

George Eliot: Scenes of Clerical Life
2 v. Adam Bede 2 v. The Mill on the
Floss 2 v. Silas Marner 1 v. Romola 2 v.
Felix Holt 2 v. Daniel Deronda 4 v. The
Lifted Veil, and Brother Jacob 1 v. Impressions of Theophrastus Such 1 v Essays
and Leaves from a Note-Book 1 v.

George Eliot's Life as related in her
Letters and Journals. Edited by her Husband J. W Cross 4 v

Mrs. Elliot: Diary of an Idle Woman
in Italy 2 v. Old Court Life in France 2 v.
The Italians 2 v. Diary of an Idle Woman
in Sicily 1 v. Pictures of Old Rome 1 v.
Diary of an Idle Woman in Spain 2 v. The
Red Cardinal 1 v. Sophia 1 v. Diary of
an Idle Woman in Constantinople 1 v. Old
Court Life in Spain 2 v. Roman Gossip 1 v

Henry Erroll. An Ugly Duckling 1 v.

The price of each volume is 1 Mark 60 Pfennig.

E. Rentoul Esler: The Way they loved at Grimpat 1 vol.

Essays and Reviews 1 v.

Estelle Russell 2 v.

D'Esterre-Keeling: *vide* Keeling.

Euthanasia 1 v.

J. H. Ewing: Jackanapes, etc. 1 v. A Flat Iron for a Farthing 1 v. The Expiated 2 v. [Brownies, etc. 1 v.

F. W. Farrar: Darkness and Dawn 3 v. The Fate of Fenella, by 24 authors, 1 v.

Percy Fendall: *vide* F. C. Philips.

George Manville Fenn: The Parson o' Dumford 2 v. The Clerk of Portwick 2 v.

Fielding: Tom Jones 2 v.

Five Centuries of the English Language and Literature (vol. 500) 1 v.

George Fleming: Kismet. A Nile Novel 1 v. Andromeda 2 v.

A. Forbes: My Experiences of the War between France and Germany 2 v. Soldiering and Scribbling 1 v. Memories and Studies of War and Peace 2 v.—See also "Daily News," War Correspondence.

R. E. Forrest: Eight Days 2 v.

Mrs. Forrester: Viva 2 v. Rhona 2 v. Roy and Viola 2 v. My Lord and My Lady 2 v. I have Lived and Loved 2 v. June 2 v. Omnia Vanitas 1 v. Although he was a Lord 1 v. Corisande 1 v. Once Again 2 v. Of the World, Worldly 1 v. Dearest 2 v. The Light of other Days 1 v. Too Late Repented 1 v.

J. Forster: Life of Charles Dickens 6 v. Life and Times of Oliver Goldsmith 2 v.

J. Fothergill: The First Violin 2 v. Probation 2 v. Made or Marred, etc. 1 v. Kith and Kin 2 v. Peril 2 v. Borderland 2 v. "Found Dead," Author of—*v.* J. Payn.

Caroline Fox: Memories of Old Friends from her Journals, edited by H. N. Pym 2 v.

Frank Fairlegh 2 v.

Harold Frederic: Illumination 2 v. March Hares 1 v.

Freeman: The Growth of the English Constitution 1 v. Select Historical Essays 1 v. Sketches from French Travel 1 v.

James Anthony Froude: Oceana 1 v. The Spanish Story of the Armada, etc. 1 v.

Lady G. Fullerton: Ellen Middleton 1 v. Grantley Manor 2 v. Lady Bird 2 v. Too Strange not to be True 2 v. Constance Sherwood 2 v. A stormy Life 2 v. Mrs. Gerald's Niece 2 v. The Notary's Daughter 1 v. The Lilies of the Valley, etc. 1 v. Countess de Bonneval 1 v. Rose Leblanc 1 v. Seven Stories 1 v. The Life of Luisa de Carvajal 1 v. A Will and a Way, etc. 2 v. Eliane 2 v. (*v.* Craven). Laurentia 1 v.

Mrs. Gaskell: Mary Barton 1 v. Ruth 2 v. North and South 1 v. Lizzie Leigh, etc. 1 v. Charlotte Brontë 2 v. Lois the Witch, etc. 1 v. Sylvia's Lovers 2 v. A Dark Night's Work 1 v. Wives and Daughters 3 v. Cranford 1 v. Cousin Phillis, etc. 1 v.

D. Gerard: Lady Baby 2 v. Recha 1 v. Orthodox 1 v. The Wrong Man 1 v. A Spotless Reputation 1 v.

E. Gerard (Madame de Laszowska): A Secret Mission 1 v. A Foreigner 2 v.

Agnes Giberne: The Curate's Home 1 v.

G. Gissing: Demos. A Story of English Socialism 2 v. New Grub Street 2 v.

Right Hon. W. E. Gladstone: Rome and the Newest Fashions in Religion 1 v. Bulgarian Horrors, etc. 1 v. The Hellenic Factor in the Eastern Problem 1 v.

Goldsmith: The Select Works: The Vicar of Wakefield, etc. (w. Portrait) 1 v.

Edward J. Goodman: Too Curious 1 v.

J. Gordon: A Diplomat's Diary 1 v.

Major-Gen. C. G. Gordon's Journals, at Kartoum. Introduction and Notes by A. E. Hake (with eighteen Illustrations) 2 v.

Mrs. Gore: Castles in the Air 1 v. The Dean's Daughter 2 v. Progress and Prejudice 2 v. Mammon 2 v. A Life's Lessons 2 v. Two Aristocracies 2 v. Heckington 2 v.

Sarah Grand: Our Manifold Nature 1 v.

Miss Grant: Victor Lescar 2 v. The Sun-Maid 2 v. My Heart's in the Highlands 2 v. Artiste 2 v. Prince Hugo 2 v. Cara Roma 2 v.

M. Gray: The Silence of Dean Maitland 2 v. The Reproach of Annesley 2 v.

Ethel St. Clair Grimwood: My Three Years in Manipur (with Portrait) 1 v.

Grohman: Tyrol and the Tyrolese 1 v.

Gunter: Mr. Barnes of New York 1 v.

"Guy Livingstone," Author of—Guy Livingstone 1 v. Sword and Gown 1 v. Barren Honour 1 v. Border and Bastille 1 v. Maurice Dering 1 v. Sans Merci 2 v. Breaking a Butterfly 2 v. Anteros 1 v. Hagarene 2 v.

J. Habberton: Helen's Babies & Other People's Children 1 v. The Bowsham Puzzle 1 v. One Tramp: Mrs. Mayburn's Twins 1 v.

H. Rider Haggard: King Solomon's Mines 1 v. She 2 v. Jess 2 v. Allan Quatermain 2 v. The Witch's Head 2 v. Maiwa's Revenge 1 v. Mr. Meeson's Will 1 v. Col. Quaritch, V. C. 2 v. Cleopatra 2 v. Allan's Wife 1 v. Beatrice 2 v. Dawn 2 v. Montezuma's Daughter 2 v. The People of the Mist 2 v. Joan Haste 2 v. Heart of the World 2 v. The Wizard 1 v.

The price of each volume is 1 Mark 60 Pfennig.

H. Rider Haggard and Andrew Lang: The World's Desire 2 v.

Hake: *vide* "Gordon's Journals."

Mrs. S. C. Hall: Can Wrong be Right? 1 v. Marian 2 v.

Philip Gilbert Hamerton: Marmorne 1 v. French and English 2 v.

Thomas Hardy: The Hand of Ethelberta 2 v. Far from the Madding Crowd 2 v. The Return of the Native 2 v. The Trumpet-Major 2 v. A Laodicean 2 v. Two on a Tower 2 v. A Pair of Blue Eyes 2 v. A Group of Noble Dames 1 v. Tess of the D'Urbervilles 2 v. Life's Little Ironies 1 v. Jude the Obscure 2 v.

Beatrice Harraden: Ships that pass in the Night 1 v. In Varying Moods 1 v. Hilda Strafford, etc. 1 v.

Agnes Harrison: Martin's Vineyard 1 v.

Bret Harte: Prose and Poetry (Tales of the Argonauts; Spanish and American Legends; Condensed Novels; Civic and Character Sketches; Poems) 2 v. Idyls of the Foothills 1 v. Gabriel Conroy 2 v. Two Men of Sandy Bar 1 v. Thankful Blossom, etc. 1 v. The Story of a Mine 1 v. Drift from Two Shores 1 v. An Heiress of Red Dog, etc. 1 v. The Twins of Table Mountain, etc. 1 v. Jeff Briggs's Love Story, etc. 1 v. Flip and other Stories 1 v. On the Frontier 1 v. By Shore and Sedge 1 v. Maruja 1 v. Snow-bound at Eagle's and Devil's Ford 1 v. The Crusade of the "Excelsior" 1 v. A Millionaire of Rough-and-Ready, etc. 1 v. Captain Jim's Friend, etc. 1 v. Cressy 1 v. The Heritage of Dedlow Marsh, etc. 1 v. A Waif of the Plains 1 v. A Ward of the Golden Gate 1 v. A Sappho of Green Springs, etc. 1 v. A First Family of Tasajara 1 v. Colonel Starbottle's Client, etc. 1 v. Susy 1 v. Sally Dows, etc. 1 v. A Protégée of Jack Hamlin's, etc. 1 v. The Bell-Ringer of Angel's, etc. 1 v. Clarence 1 v. In a Hollow of the Hills, etc. 1 v. The Ancestors of Peter Atherly, etc. 1 v.

Sir H. Havelock: *vide* Rev. W. Brock.

G. Hawthorne: *vide* "Miss Molly."

Nathaniel Hawthorne: The Scarlet Letter 1 v. Transformation 2 v. Passages from the English Note-Books 2 v.

"Heir of Redclyffe," Author of—*vide* Yonge.

Sir Arthur Helps: Friends in Council 2 v. Ivan de Biron 2 v.

Mrs. Hemans: Select Poet. Works 1 v.

Admiral Hobart Pasha: Sketches from my Life 1 v.

John Oliver Hobbes: The Gods, some

Mortals and Lord Wickenham 1 v.

Mrs. Cashel Hoey: A Golden Sorrow 2 v. Out of Court 2 v.

Annie E. Holdsworth: The Years that the Locust hath Eaten 1 v.

Oliver Wendell Holmes: The Autocrat of the Breakfast-Table 1 v. The Professor at the Breakfast-Table 1 v. The Poet at the Breakfast-Table 1 v. Over the Teacups 1 v.

Hope: Mr. Witt's Widow 1 v. A Change of Air 1 v. Half a Hero 1 v. The Indiscretion of the Duchess 2 v. God in the Car 1 v. Chronicles of Count Antonio 1 v. Comedies of Courtship 1 v. The Heart of Princess Osra 1 v. Phroso 2 v.

E. William Hornung: A Bride from the Bush 1 v. Under Two Skies 1 v. Tiny Luttrell 1 v. The Boss of Taroomba 1 v.

Household Words: conducted by Charles Dickens. 1851-56. 36 v. NOVELS and TALES reprinted from Household Words by Charles Dickens. 1856-59. 11 v.

How to be Happy though Married 1 v.

Miss Howard: One Summer 1 v. Aunt Serena 1 v. Guenn 2 v. Tony, the Maid, etc. 1 v. The Open Door 2 v. A Fellowe and His Wife 1 v.

W. D. Howells: A Foregone Conclusion 1 v. The Lady of the Aroostook 1 v. A Modern Instance 2 v. The Undiscovered Country 1 v. Venetian Life (w. Portrait) 1 v. Italian Journeys 1 v. A Chance Acquaintance 1 v. Their Wedding Journey 1 v. A Fearful Responsibility, etc. 1 v. A Woman's Reason 2 v. Dr. Breen's Practice 1 v. The Rise of Silas Lapham 2 v.

Hughes: Tom Brown's School Days 1 v.

Mrs. Hungerford: Molly Bawn 2 v. Mrs. Geoffrey 2 v. Faith and Unfaith 2 v. Portia 2 v. Loÿs, Lord Berresford, etc. 1 v. Her First Appearance, etc. 1 v. Phyllis 2 v. Rossmoyne 2 v. Doris 2 v. A Maiden all Forlorn, etc. 1 v. A Passive Crime, etc. 1 v. Green Pleasure and Grey Grief 2 v. A Mental Struggle 2 v. Her Week's Amusement, etc. 1 v. Lady Branksmere 2 v. Lady Valworth's Diamonds 1 v. A Modern Circe 2 v. Marvel 2 v. The Hon. Mrs. Vereker 1 v. Under-Currents 2 v. In Durance Vile. etc. 1 v. A Troublesome Girl, etc. 1 v. A Life's Remorse 2 v. A Born Coquette 2 v. The Duchess 1 v. Lady Verner's Flight 1 v. A Conquering Heroine, etc. 1 v. Nora Creina 2 v. A Mad Prank, etc. 1 v. The Hoyden 2 v. The Red House Mystery 1 v. An Unsatisfactory Lover 1 v. Peter's Wife 2 v. The Three Graces 1 v. A Tug of War 1 v. The Professor's Experiment 2 v.

The price of each volume is 1 Mark 60 Pfennig.

A Point of Conscience 2 v. A Lonely Girl 1 v. Lovice 1 v. The Coming of Chloe 1 v.

Jean Ingelow. Off the Skelligs 3 v Poems 2 v. Fated to be Free 2 v. Sarah de Berenger 2 v. Don John 2 v.

Lady Inglis. The Siege of Lucknow 1 v.

John H. Ingram. *vide* E. A. Poe.

Iota A Yellow Aster 1 v. Children of Circumstance 2 v.

Washington Irving: The Sketch Book (with Portrait) 1 v. The Life of Mahomet 1 v. Successors of Mahomet 1 v. Oliver Goldsmith 1 v. Chronicles of Wolfert's Roost 1 v. Life of Washington 5 v.

Helen Jackson (H. H.): Ramona 2 v. W. W. Jacobs: Many Cargoes 1|v The Skipper's Wooing 1 v.

Charles T. C. James: Holy Wedlock 1 v

G. P. R. James: Morley Ernstein (with Portrait) 1 v. Forest Days 1 v. The False Heir 1 v. Arabella Stuart 1 v. Rose d'Albret 1 v. Arrah Neil 1 v. Agincourt 1 v. The Smuggler 1 v. The Step-Mother 2 v. Beauchamp 1 v. Heidelberg 1 v. The Gipsy 1 v. The Castle of Ehrenstein 1 v. Darnley 1 v Russell 2 v The Convict 2 v. Sir Theodore Broughton 2 v.

H. James: The American 2 v. The Europeans 1 v. Daisy Miller, etc 1 v. Roderick Hudson 2 v. The Madonna of the Future, etc. 1 v. Eugene Pickering, etc. 1 v Confidence 1 v. Washington Square, etc. 2 v. The Portrait of a Lady 3 v. Foreign Parts 1 v. French Poets and Novelists 1 v. The Siege of London, etc. 1 v. Portraits of Places 1 v A Little Tour in France 1 v.

J Cordy Jeaffreson: A Book about Doctors 2 v. A Woman in Spite of Herself 2 v. The Real Lord Byron 3 v.

Mrs. Jenkin: "Who Breaks—Pays" 1 v. Skirmishing 1 v. Once and Again 2 v. Two French Marriages 2 v Within an Ace 1 v. Jupiter's Daughters 1 v

Edward Jenkins: Ginx's Baby, etc 2 v. "Jennie of 'the Prince's,'" Author of —*vide* B. H. Buxton.

Jerome K. Jerome: The Idle Thoughts of an Idle Fellow 1 v. Diary of a Pilgrimage 1 v. Novel Notes 1 v. Sketches in Lavender, Blue and Green 1 v.

Douglas Jerrold: History of St. Giles and St James 2 v. Men of Character 2 v. "Halifax," Author of—*v* Mrs. Craik. "Johnny Ludlow," Author of—*vide* Mrs. Henry Wood.

Johnson. Lives of the English Poets 2 v Emily Jolly: Colonel Dacre 2 v.

"Joshua Davidson," Author of—*vide* E. Lynn Linton.

Miss Kavanagh. Nathalie 2 v Daisy Burns 2 v. Grace Lee 2 v. Rachel Gray 1 v. Adèle 3 v. The Two Sicilies 2 v. Seven Years, etc. 2 v. French Women of Letters 1 v. English Women of Letters 1 v Queen Mab 2 v. Beatrice 2 v. Sybil's Second Love 2 v. Dora 2 v. Silvia 2 v. Bessie 2 v. John Dorrien 3 v. Two Lilies 2 v. Forget-me-nots 2 v.

A. Keary: Oldbury 2 v. Castle Daly 2 v.

Elsa D'Esterre-Keeling: Three Sisters 1 v. A Laughing Philosopher 1 v. The Professor's Wooing 1 v. In Thoughtland and in Dreamland 1 v. Orchardscroft 1 v. Appassionata 1 v. Old Maids and Young 2 v

Kempis: *vide* Thomas a Kempis.

R B. Kimball: Saint Leger 1 v. Romance of Student Life abroad 1 v. Undercurrents 1 v. Was he Successful? 1 v. To-Day in New-York 1 v.

A. W. Kinglake: Eothen 1 v. The Invasion of the Crimea 14 v.

Charles Kingsley: Yeast 1 v. Westward ho ! 2 v. Two Years ago 2 v. Hypatia 2 v. Alton Locke 1 v. Hereward the Wake 2 v. At Last 2 v.

Charles Kingsley: His Letters and Memories of his Life, ed. by his Wife 2 v.

H. Kingsley. Ravenshoe 2 v. Austin Elliot 1 v The Recollections of Geoffry Hamlyn 2 v. The Hillyars and the Burtons 2 v. Leighton Court 1 v. Valentin 1 v. Oakshott Castle 1 v. Reginald Hetherege 2 v. The Grange Garden 2 v.

Kipling. Plain Tales from the Hills 1 v. Second Jungle Book 1 v. Seven Seas 1 v. "Captains Courageous" 1 v.

May Laffan. Flitters, Tatters, and the Counsellor, etc. 1 v.

Lamb Essays of Elia and Eliana 1 v.

A. Lang *vide* H. R. Haggard.

Mary Langdon: Ida May 1 v

"The Last of the Cavaliers," Author of—The Last of the Cavaliers 2 v. The Gain of a Loss 2 v.

The Hon. Emily Lawless: Hurrish 1 v. Leaves from the Journal of our Life in the Highlands from 1848 to 1861 1 v. More Leaves from the Journal of a Life in the Highlands from 1862 to 1882 1 v.

Holme Lee: *vide* Miss Parr.

S. Le Fanu: Uncle Silas 2 v. Guy Deverell 2 v.

Mark Lemon: Wait for the End 2 v. Loved at Last 2 v. Falkner Lyle 2 v. Leyton Hall, etc. 2 v. Golden Fetters 2 v.

The price of each volume is 1 Mark 60 Pfennig.

Charles Lever: The O'Donoghue 1 v. The Knight of Gwynne 3 v. Arthur O'Leary 2 v. Harry Lorrequer 2 v. Charles O'Malley 3 v. Tom Burke of "Ours" 3 v. Jack Hinton 2 v. The Daltons 4 v. The Dodd Family Abroad 3 v. The Martins of Cro' Martin 3 v. The Fortunes of Glencore 2 v. Roland Cashel 3 v. Davenport Dunn 3 v. Confessions of Con Cregan 2 v. One of Them 2 v. Maurice Tiernay 2 v. Sir Jasper Carew 2 v. Barrington 2 v. A Day's Ride 2 v. Luttrell of Arran 2 v. Tony Butler 2 v. Sir Brook Fossbrooke 2 v. The Bramleighs of Bishop's Folly 2 v. A Rent in a Cloud 1 v. That Boy of Norcott's 1 v. St. Patrick's Eve; Paul Gosslett's Confessions 1 v. Lord Kilgobbin 2 v.

G. H. Lewes: Ranthorpe 1 v. Physiology of Common Life 2 v. On Actors and the Art of Acting 1 v.

E. Lynn Linton: Joshua Davidson 1 v. Patricia Kemball 2 v. The Atonement of Leam Dundas 2 v. The World well Lost 2 v. Under which Lord? 2 v. With a Silken Thread, etc. 1 v. Todhunters' at Loanin' Head, etc. 1 v. "My Love!" 2 v. The Girl of the Period, etc. 1 v. Ione 2 v.

L. W. M. Lockhart: Mine is Thine 2 v.

Lord Augustus Loftus, Diplomatic Reminiscences of—, 1837-1862 (w. Portr.) 2 v.

Longfellow: Poetical Works (w. Port.) 3 v. The Divine Comedy of Dante Alighieri 3 v. The New-England Tragedies 1 v. The Divine Tragedy 1 v. Flower-de-Luce, etc. 1 v. The Masque of Pandora 1 v.

Margaret Lonsdale: Sister Dora (with a Portrait of Sister Dora) 1 v.

A Lost Battle 2 v.

Sir J. Lubbock: The Pleasures of Life 1 v. The Beauties of Nature (w. Illust.) 1 v. The Use of Life 1 v. Scenery of Switzerland (w. Illust.) 2 v. [by Eastwick 1 v.

Lutfullah: Autobiography of Lutfullah,

Edna Lyall: We Two 2 v. Donovan 2 v. In the Golden Days 2 v. Knight-Errant 2 v. Won by Waiting 2 v. Wayfaring Men 2 v.

Lord Lytton: *vide* Bulwer.

Robert Lord Lytton (Owen Meredith): Poems 2 v. Fables in Song 2 v.

Maarten Maartens: The Sin of Joost Avelingh 1 v. An Old Maid's Love 2 v. God's Fool 2 v. The Greater Glory 2 v. My Lady Nobody 2 v.

Lord Macaulay: History of England (w. Port.) 10 v. Critical & Historical Essays 5 v. Lays of Ancient Rome 1 v. Speeches 2 v. Biographical Essays 1 v. William Pitt, Atterbury 1 v. (See also Trevelyan).

Justin McCarthy: The Waterdale Neighbours 2 v. Dear Lady Disdain 2 v. Miss Misanthrope 2 v. A History of our own Times 5 v. Donna Quixote 2 v. A short History of our own Times 2 v. A History of the Four Georges vols. 1 & 2. A History of our own Times vols. 6 & 7 (supplemental).

George Mac Donald: Alec Forbes of Howglen 2 v. Annals of a Quiet Neighbourhood 2 v. David Elginbrod 2 v. The Vicar's Daughter 2 v. Malcolm 2 v. St. George and St. Michael 2 v. The Marquis of Lossie 2 v. Sir Gibbie 2 v. Mary Marston 2 v. The Gifts of the Child Christ, etc. 1 v. The Princess and Curdie 1 v.

Mrs. Mackarness: Sunbeam Stories 1 v. A Peerless Wife 2 v. A Mingled Yarn 2 v.

E. Mackay: Love Letters of a Violinist 1 v.

Chas. M\^{c\}Knight: Old Fort Duquesne 2 v.

Ian Maclaren: Beside the Bonnie Brier Bush 1 v. The Days of Auld Langsyne 1 v.

Norman Macleod: The old Lieutenant and his Son 1 v.

Mrs. Macquoid: Patty 2 v. Miriam's Marriage 2 v. Pictures across the Channel 2 v. Too Soon 1 v. My Story 2 v. Diane 2 v. Beside the River 2 v. A Faithful Lover 2 v.

"Mademoiselle Mori," Author of— Mademoiselle Mori 2 v. Denise 1 v. Madame Fontenoy 1 v. On the Edge of the Storm 1 v. The Atelier du Lys 2 v. In the Olden Time 2 v.

Lord Mahon: *vide* Stanhope.

E. S. Maine: Scarscliff Rocks 2 v.

L. Malet: Colonel Enderby's Wife 2 v.

Lord Malmesbury: Memoirs of an Ex-Minister 3 v.

Mary E. Mann: A Winter's Tale 1 v.

R. Blachford Mansfield: The Log of the Water Lily 1 v.

Mark Twain (Samuel L. Clemens): Tom Sawyer 1 v. The Innocents Abroad; or, the New Pilgrim's Progress 2 v. A Tramp Abroad 2 v. "Roughing it" 1 v. The Innocents at Home 1 v. The Prince and the Pauper 2 v. The Stolen White Elephant, etc. 1 v. Life on the Mississippi 2 v. Sketches (w. Portrait) 1 v. Huckleberry Finn 2 v. Selections from American Humour 1 v. A Yankee at the Court of King Arthur 2 v. The American Claimant 1 v. The Million Pound Bank-Note, etc. 1 v. Tom Sawyer Abroad 1 v. Pudd'nhead Wilson 1 v. Personal Recollections of Joan of Arc 2 v. Tom Sawyer, Detective 1 v. More Tramps Abroad 2 v.

Marmone: *v.* Philip G. Hamerton.

The price of each volume is 1 Mark 60 Pfennig.

Capt. Marryat: Jacob Faithful (w. Port.) 1 v. Percival Keene 1 v. Peter Simple 1 v. Japhet, in Search of a Father 1 v. Monsieur Violet 1 v. The Settlers 1 v. The Mission 1 v. The Privateer's-Man 1 v. The Children of the New-Forest 1 v. Valerie 1 v. Mr. Midshipman Easy 1 v. The King's Own 1 v.

Fl. Marryat: Love's Conflict 2 v. For Ever and Ever 2 v. Confessions of Gerald Estcourt 2 v. Nelly Brooke 2 v. Véronique 2 v. Petronel 2 v. Her Lord and Master 2 v. The Prey of the Gods 1 v. Life of Captain Marryat 1 v. Mad Dumaresq 2 v. No Intentions 2 v. Fighting the Air 2 v. A Star and a Heart 1 v. The Poison of Asps, etc. 1 v. A Lucky Disappointment, etc. 1 v. "My own Child" 2 v. Her Father's Name 2 v. A Harvest of Wild Oats 2 v. A Little Stepson 1 v. Written in Fire 2 v. Her World against a Lie 2 v. A Broken Blossom 2 v. The Root of all Evil 2 v. The Fair-haired Alda 2 v. With Cupid's Eyes 2 v. My Sister the Actress 2 v. Phyllida 2 v. How They Loved Him 2 v. Facing the Footlights (w. Portrait) 2 v. A Moment of Madness, etc. 1 v. The Ghost of Charlotte Cray, etc. 1 v. Peeress and Player 2 v. Under the Lilies and Roses 2 v. The Heart of Jane Warner 2 v. The Heir Presumptive 2 v. The Master Passion 2 v. Spiders of Society 2 v. Driven to Bay 2 v. A Daughter of the Tropics 2 v. Gentleman and Courtier 2 v. On Circumstantial Evidence 2 v. Mount Eden. A Romance 2 v. Blindfold 2 v. A Scarlet Sin 1 v. A Bankrupt Heart 2 v. The Spirit World 1 v. The Beautiful Soul 1 v. At Heart a Rake 2 v. Hannah Stubbs 1 v. The Dream that Stayed 2 v. A Passing Madness 1 v. The Blood of the Vampire 1 v.

Mrs. Marsh: Ravenscliffe 2 v. Emilia Wyndham 2 v. Castle Avon 2 v. Aubrey 2 v. The Heiress of Haughton 2 v. Evelyn Marston 2 v. The Rose of Ashurst 2 v.

Emma Marshall: Mrs. Mainwaring's Journal 1 v. Benvenuta 1 v. Lady Alice 1 v. Dayspring 1 v. Life's Aftermath 1 v. In the East Country 1 v. No. XIII; or, The Story of the Lost Vestal 1 v. In Four Reigns 1 v. On the Banks of the Ouse 1 v. In the City of Flowers 1 v. Alma 1 v. Under Salisbury Spire 1 v. The End Crowns All 1 v. Winchester Meads 1 v. Eventide Light 1 v. Winifrede's Journal 1 v. Bristol Bells 1 v. In the Service of Rachel Lady Russell 1 v. A Lily among Thorns 1 v. Penshurst Castle 1 v. Kensington Palace 1 v. The White King's Daughter 1 v. The Master of the Musicians 1 v. An Escape

from the Tower 1 v. A Haunt of Ancient Peace 1 v. Castle Meadow 1 v.

Helen Mathers (Mrs. Henry Reeves): "Cherry Ripe!" 2 v. "Land o' the Leal" 1 v. My Lady Green Sleeves 2 v. As he comes up the Stair, etc. 1 v. Sam's Sweetheart 2 v. Eyre's Acquittal 2 v. Found Out 1 v. Murder or Manslaughter? 1 v. The Fashion of this World (80 Pf.) Blind Justice, etc. 1 v. What the Glass Told, etc. 1 v.

Colonel Maurice: The Balance of Military Power in Europe 1 v.

George du Maurier: Trilby 2 v. The Martian 2 v.   [Gould.

"Mehalah," Author of—*vide* Baring-Whyte-Melville: Kate Coventry 1 v. Holmby House 2 v. Digby Grand 1 v. Good for Nothing 2 v. The Queen's Maries 2 v. The Gladiators 2 v. The Brookes of Bridlemere 2 v. Cerise 2 v. The Interpreter 2 v. The White Rose 2 v. M. or N. 1 v. Contraband; or A Losing Hazard 1 v. Sarchedon 2 v. Uncle John 2 v. Katerfelto 1 v. Sister Louise 1 v. Rosine 1 v. Roys' Wife 2 v. Black but Comely 2 v. Riding Recollections 1 v.

G. Meredith: The Ordeal of Richard Feverel 2 v. Beauchamp's Career 2 v. The Tragic Comedians 1 v. Lord Ormont and his Aminta 2 v. The Amazing Marriage 2 v.

Owen Meredith: *v.* R. Lord Lytton.

L. Merrick: The Man who was good 1 v. This Stage of Fools 1 v. Cynthia 1 v. One Man's View 1 v.

Merriman: Young Mistley 1 v. Prisoners and Captives 2 v. From One Generation to Another 1 v. With Edged Tools 2 v. The Sowers 2 v. Flotsam 1 v. In Kedar's Tents 1 v.

Merriman & Tallentyre: The Money-Spinner 1 v.

Milton: The Poetical Works 1 v.

"Miss Molly," Author of—Geraldine Hawthorne 1 v.   [Hungerford.

"Molly Bawn," Author of—*vide* Mrs.

Miss Montgomery: Misunderstood 1 v. Thrown Together 2 v. Thwarted 1 v. Wild Mike 1 v. Seaforth 2 v. The Blue Veil 1 v. Transformed 1 v. The Fisherman's Daughter, etc. 1 v. Colonel Norton 2 v.

Frank Frankfort Moore: "I forbid the Banns" 2 v. A gray Eye or so 2 v. One Fair Daughter 2 v. They call it Love 2 v. The Jessamy Bride 1 v.

George Moore: Celibates 1 v.

Moore: Poet. Works (w. Portr.) 5 v.

Lady Morgan's Memoirs 3 v.

Henry Morley: Of English Literature

The price of each volume is 1 Mark 60 Pfennig.

in the Reign of Victoria. With Facsimiles of the Signatures of Authors in the Tauchnitz Edition [v. 2000].

William Morris: Poems. Edited with a Memoir by Francis Hueffer 1 v.

Morrison: Tales of Mean Streets 1 v. A Child of the Jago 1 v.

D. Christie Murray: Rainbow Gold 2 v.

E. C. Grenville: Murray: The Member for Paris 2 v. Young Brown 2 v. The Bondoir Cabal 3 v. French Pictures in English Chalk (1st Series) 2 v. The Russians of To-day 1 v. French Pictures in English Chalk (2nd Series) 2 v. Strange Tales 1 v. That Artful Vicar 2 v. Six Months in the Ranks 1 v. People I have met 1 v.

"My Little Lady," Author of—*vide* E. Frances Poynter.

The New Testament [v. 1000].

Mrs. Newby: Common Sense 2 v.

Dr. J. H. Newman: Callista 1 v.

"Nina Balatka," Author of—*vide* Anthony Trollope.

"No Church," Author of—No Church 2 v. Owen:—a Waif 2 v.

Lady Augusta Noel: From Generation to Generation 1 v. Hithersea Mere 2 v.

W. E. Norris: My Friend Jim 1 v. A Bachelor's Blunder 2 v. Major and Minor 2 v. The Rogue 2 v. Miss Shafto 2 v. Mrs. Fenton 1 v. Misadventure 2 v. Saint Ann's 1 v. A Victim of Good Luck 1 v. The Dancer in Yellow 1 v. Clarissa Furiosa 2 v. Marietta's Marriage 2 v.

Hon. Mrs. Norton: Stuart of Dunleath 2 v. Lost and Saved 2 v. Old Sir Douglas 2 v. Not Easily Jealous 2 v.

Novels & Tales *v.* Household Words.

Laurence Oliphant: Altiora Peto 2 v. Masollam 2 v.

Mrs. Oliphant: The Last of the Mortimers 2 v. Margaret Maitland 1 v. Agnes 2 v. Madonna Mary 2 v. The Minister's Wife 2 v. The Rector and the Doctor's Family 1 v. Salem Chapel 2 v. The Perpetual Curate 2 v. Miss Marjoribanks 2 v. Ombra 2 v. Memoir of Count de Montalembert 2 v. May 2 v. Innocent 2 v. For Love and Life 2 v. A Rose in June 1 v. Valentine and his Brother 2 v. Whiteladies 2 v. The Curate in Charge 1 v. Phœbe, Junior 2 v. Mrs. Arthur 2 v. Carità 2 v. Young Musgrave 2 v. The Primrose Path 2 v. Within the Precincts 3 v. The greatest Heiress in England 2 v He that will not when he may 2 v. Harry Joscelyn 2 v. In Trust 2 v. It was a Lover and his Lass 3 v. The Ladies Lindores 3 v. Hester 3 v. The

Wizard's Son 3 v. A Country Gentleman and his Family 2 v. Neighbours on the Green 1 v. The Duke's Daughter 1 v. The Fugitives 1 v. Kirsteen 2 v. Life of Laurence Oliphant 2 v. The Little Pilgrim in the Unseen 1 v. The Heir Presumptive and the Heir Apparent 2 v. The Sorceress 2 v. Sir Robert's Fortune 2 v. The Ways of Life 1 v. Old Mr. Tredgold 2 v.

Ossian: Poems 1 v.

Ouida: Idalia 2 v. Tricotrin 2 v. Puck 2 v. Chandos 2 v. Strathmore 2 v. Under two Flags 2 v. Folle-Farine 2 v. A Leaf in the Storm, etc. 1 v. Cecil Castlemaine's Gage, etc. 1 v. Madame la Marquise, etc. 1 v. Pascarèl 2 v. Held in Bondage 2 v. Two little Wooden Shoes 1 v. Signa (w. Port.) 3 v. In a Winter City 1 v. Ariadnê 2 v. Friendship 2 v. Moths 3 v. Pipistrello 1 v. A Village Commune 2 v. In Maremma 3 v. Bimbi 1 v. Wanda 3 v. Frescoes, etc. 1 v. Princess Napraxine 3 v. Othmar 3 v. A Rainy June (60 Pf.). Don Gesualdo (60 Pf.). A House Party 1 v. Guilderoy 2 v. Syrlin 3 v. Ruffino, etc. 1 v. Santa Barbara, etc. 1 v. Two Offenders 1 v. The Silver Christ, etc. 1 v. Toxin, etc. 1 v. Le Selve, etc. 1 v. The Massarenes 2 v. An Altruist, etc. 1 v.

The Outcasts: *vide* Roy Tellet.

Miss Parr (Holme Lee): Basil Godfrey's Caprice 2 v. For Richer, for Poorer 2 v. The Beautiful Miss Barrington 2 v. Her Title of Honour 1 v. Echoes of a Famous Year 1 v. Katherine's Trial 1 v. Bessie Fairfax 2 v. Ben Milner's Wooing 1 v. Straightforward 2 v. Mrs. Denys of Cote 2 v. A Poor Squire 1 v.

Mrs. Parr: Dorothy Fox 1 v. The Prescotts of Pamphillon 2 v. The Gosau Smithy, etc. 1 v. Robin 2 v. Loyalty George 2 v.

G. Paston: A Study in Prejudices 1 v. A Fair Deceiver 1 v.

"Paul Ferroll," Author of—Paul Ferroll 1 v. Year after Year 1 v. Why Paul Ferroll killed his Wife 1 v.

James Payn: Found Dead 1 v. Gwendoline's Harvest 1 v. Like Father, like Son 2 v. Not Wooed, but Won 2 v. Cecil's Tryst 1 v. A Woman's Vengeance 2 v. Murphy's Master 1 v. In the Heart of a Hill, etc. 1 v. At Her Mercy 2 v. The Best of Husbands 2 v. Walter's Word 2 v. Halves 2 v. Fallen Fortunes 2 v. What He cost Her 2 v. By Proxy 2 v. Less Black than we're Painted 2 v. Under one Roof 2 v. High Spirits 1 v. High Spirits (2nd Series) 1 v. A Confidential Agent 2 v. From Exile 2 v. A Grape

The price of each volume is 1 Mark 60 Pfennig.

from a Thorn 2 v. Some Private Views 1 v. For Cash Only 2 v. Kit. A Memory 2 v The Canon's Ward (with Port.) 2 v. Some Literary Recollections 1 v. The Talk of the Town 1 v. The Luck of the Darrells 2 v. The Heir of the Ages 2v. Holiday Tasks 1 v. Glow-Worm Tales (1st Series) 1 v. Glow-Worm Tales (2nd Series) 1 v. A Prince of the Blood 2 v. The Mystery of Mirbridge 2 v. The Burnt Million 2 v. The Word and the Will 2 v. Sunny Stories 1 v. A Modern Dick Whittington 2 v. A Stumble on the Threshold 2 v. A Trying Patient 1 v. Gleams of Memory 1 v. In Market Overt 1 v. George Driffell 1 v. Another's Burden 1 v.

Miss Peard: One Year 2 v. The Rose-Garden 1 v. Unawares 1 v. Thorpe Regis 1 v. A Winter Story 1 v A Madrigal, etc. 1 v. Cartouche 1 v Mother Molly 1 v. Schloss and Town 2 v. Contradictions 2 v. Near Neighbours 1 v. Alicia Tennant 1 v. Madame's Grand-Daughter 1 v.

Pemberton. The Impregnable City 1 v. A Penitent Soul 1 v.

Bishop Percy: Reliques of Ancient English Poetry 3 v.

F. C Philips: As in a Looking Glass 1 v. The Dean and his Daughter 1 v. Lucy Smith 1 v. A Lucky Young Woman 1 v. Jack and Three Jills 1 v. Little Mrs. Murray 1 v. Young Mr. Ainslie's Courtship 1 v. Social Vicissitudes 1 v. Extenuating Circumstances, etc 1 v. More Social Vicissitudes 1 v. Constance 2 v. That Wicked Mad'moiselle, etc 1 v. A Doctor in Difficulties 1 v. Black and White 1 v. "One Never Knows" 2 v. Of Course 1 v. Miss Ormerod's Protégé 1 v. My little Husband 1 v. Mrs. Bouverie 1 v. A Question of Colour 1 v. A Devil in Nun's Veiling 1 v. A Full Confession, etc. 1 v. The Luckiest of Three 1 v. Poor Little Bella 1 v.

F. C. Philips & P. Fendall. A Daughter's Sacrifice 1 v. Margaret Byng 1 v.

F. C. Philips & C. J. Wills: The Fatal Phryne 1 v. Scudamores 1 v A Maiden Fair to See 1 v Sybil Ross's Marriage 1 v.

E. Phillpotts: Lying Prophets 2 v.

Edgar Allan Poe: Poems and Essays, edited with a new Memoir by J H Ingram 1 v. Tales, edited by J. H. Ingram 1 v.

Pope. Select Poet. Works (w. Port) 1 v.

E. Frances Poynter. My Little Lady 2 v. Ersilia 2 v. Among the Hills 1 v. Madame de Presnel 1 v.

Praed. *vide* Campbell-Praed.

E. Prentiss Stepping Heavenward 1 v.

The Prince Consort's Speeches and Addresses (with Portrait) 1 v.

Richard Pryce. Miss Maxwell's Affections 1 v. The Quiet Mrs. Fleming 1 v. Time and the Woman 1 v.

Horace N. Pym: *vide* Caroline Fox.

Q.: Noughts and Crosses 1 v I Saw Three Ships 1 v. Dead Man's Rock 1 v. Ia and other Tales 1 v.

W. F. Rae: Westward by Rail 1 v. Miss Bayle's Romance 2 v. The Business of Travel 1 v.

The Rajah's Heir 2 v.

Charles Reade "It is never too late to mend" 2 v. "Love me little, love me long" 1 v. The Cloister and the Hearth 2 v. Hard Cash 3 v. Put Yourself in his Place 2 v. A Terrible Temptation 2 v. Peg Woffington 1 v. Christie Johnstone 1 v. A Simpleton 2 v. The Wandering Heir 1 v. A Woman-Hater 2 v. Readiana 1 v. Singleheart and Doubleface 1 v. "Recommended to Mercy," Auth. of— Recomm. to Mercy 2 v. Zoe's "Brand" 2 v.

James Rice: *vide* W. Besant.

A. Bate Richards: So very Human 3 v.

Richardson: Clarissa Harlowe 4 v.

Mrs. Riddell (F. G Trafford): George Geith of Fen Court 2 v. Maxwell Drewitt 2 v. The Race for Wealth 2 v. Far above Rubies 2 v. The Earl's Promise 2 v. Mortomley's Estate 2 v. [Thackeray.

Anne Thackeray Ritchie: *vide* Miss

Rev. F. W. Robertson: Sermons 4 v.

Charles H. Ross. The Pretty Widow 1 v. A London Romance 2 v.

Dante Gabriel Rossetti: Poems 1 v. Ballads and Sonnets 1 v.

Roy Tellet: The Outcasts 1 v. A Draught of Lethe 1 v. Pastor & Prelate 2 v.

J. Ruffini: Lavinia 2 v. Doctor Antonio 1 v Lorenzo Benoni 1 v. Vincenzo 2 v. A Quiet Nook in the Jura 1 v. The Paragreens on a Visit to Paris 1 v Carlino, etc. 1 v.

Russell A Sailor's Sweetheart 2 v. The "Lady Maud" 2 v. A Sea Queen 2 v.

Sala. The Seven Sons of Mammon 2 v.

John Saunders: Israel Mort, Overman 2 v. The Shipowner's Daughter 2 v. A Noble Wife 2 v.

Katherine Saunders: Joan Merryweather, etc. 1 v. Gideon's Rock, etc. 1 v. The High Mills 2 v. Sebastian 1 v.

Col R H. Savage: My Official Wife 1 v. The Little Lady of Lagunitas (w. Port.) 2 v. Prince Schamyl's Wooing 1 v. The Masked Venus 2 v Delilah of Harlem 2 v. The Anarchist 2 v A Daughter of Judas

The price of each volume is 1 Mark 60 Pfennig.

1 v. In the Old Chateau 1 v. Miss Devereux of the Mariquita 2 v. Checked Through 2 v. A Modern Corsair 2 v.

Olive Schreiner: Trooper Peter Halket of Mashonaland 1 v.

Sir Walter Scott: Waverley.(w. Port.) 1 v. The Antiquary 1 v. Ivanhoe 1 v. Kenilworth 1 v. Quentin Durward 1 v. Old Mortality 1 v. Guy Mannering 1 v. Rob Roy 1 v. The Pirate 1 v. The Fortunes of Nigel 1 v. The Black Dwarf; A Legend of Montrose 1 v. The Bride of Lammermoor 1 v. The Heart of Mid-Lothian 2 v. The Monastery 1 v. The Abbot 1 v. Peveril of the Peak 2 v. The Poetical Works 2 v. Woodstock 1 v. The Fair Maid of Perth 1 v. Anne of Geierstein 1 v.

Prof. Seeley: Life and Times of Stein (with a Portrait of Stein) 4 v. The Expansion of England 1 v. Goethe 1 v.

Miss Sewell: Amy Herbert 2 v. Ursula 2 v. A Glimpse of the World 2 v. The Journal of a Home Life 2 v. After Life 2 v. The Experience of Life 2 v.

Shakespeare: Plays and Poems (with Portrait) *(Second Edition)* compl. 7 v.

Shakespeare's Plays may also be had in 37 numbers, at *M* 0,30. each number. Doubtful Plays 1 v.

Shelley: A Selection from his Poems 1 v.

Nathan Sheppard: Shut up in Paris *(Second Edition, enlarged)* 1 v.

Sheridan: The Dramatic Works 1 v.

J. H. Shorthouse: John Inglesant 2 v. Blanche, Lady Falaise 1 v.

Slatin Pasha: Fire and Sword in the Sudan (with two Maps in Colours) 3 v.

Smollett: Roderick Random 1 v. Humphry Clinker 1 v. Peregrine Pickle 2 v.

Society in London 1 v.

Somerville & Martin Ross: Naboth's Vineyard 1 v.

The Spanish Brothers 2 v.

Earl Stanhope (Lord Mahon): The History of England 7 v. The Reign of Queen Anne 2 v.

Sterne: Tristram Shandy 1 v. A Sentimental Journey (with Portrait) 1 v.

Robert Louis Stevenson: Treasure Island 1 v. Dr. Jekyll and Mr. Hyde, etc. 1 v. Kidnapped 1 v. The Black Arrow 1 v. The Master of Ballantrae 1 v. The Merry Men, etc. 1 v. Across the Plains 1 v. Island Nights' Entertainments 1 v. Catriona 1 v. Weir of Hermiston 1 v. St. Ives 2 v.

"Still Waters," Author of—Still Waters 1 v. Dorothy 1 v. De Cressy 1 v.

Uncle Ralph 1 v. Maiden Sisters 1 v. Martha Brown 1 v. Vanessa 1 v.

M. C. Stirling: Two Tales of Married Life 2 v. Vol. II. A True Man, Vol. I. *vide* G. M. Craik.

Stockton: The House of Martha 1 v. "The Story of Elizabeth," Author of —*vide* Miss Thackeray.

Mrs. H. Beecher Stowe: Uncle Tom's Cabin (with Portrait) 2 v. A Key to Uncle Tom's Cabin 2 v. Dred 2 v. The Minister's Wooing 1 v. Oldtown Folks 2 v.

"Sunbeam Stories," Author of—*vide* Mrs. Mackarness.

Swift: Gulliver's Travels 1 v.

John Addington Symonds: Sketches in Italy 1 v. New Italian Sketches 1 v.

Tasma: Uncle Piper of Piper's Hill 2 v.

Baroness Tautphoeus: Cyrilla 2 v. The Initials 2 v. Quits 2 v. At Odds 2 v.

Colonel Meadows Taylor: Tara: A Mahratta Tale 3 v.

H. Templeton: Diary and Notes 1 v.

Alfred (Lord) Tennyson: The Poetical Works of, 8 v. Queen Mary 1 v. Harold 1 v. Becket; The Cup; The Falcon 1 v. Locksley Hall, etc. 1 v.

W. M. Thackeray: Vanity Fair 3 v. Pendennis 3 v. Miscellanies 8 v. Henry Esmond 2 v. The English Humourists 1 v. The Newcomes 4 v. The Virginians 4 v. The Four Georges; Lovel the Widower 1 v. The Adventures of Philip 2 v. Denis Duval 1 v. Roundabout Papers 1 v. Catherine 1 v. The Irish Sketch Book 2 v. The Paris Sketch Book (w. Portrait) 2 v.

Miss Thackeray: Story of Elizabeth 1 v. The Village on the Cliff 1 v. Old Kensington 2 v. Bluebeard's Keys 1 v. Five Old Friends 1 v. Miss Angel 1 v. Out of the World 1 v. Fulham Lawn 1 v. From an Island 1 v. Da Capo 1 v. Madame de Sévigné 1 v. A Book of Sibyls 1 v. Mrs. Dymond 2 v. Chapters from some Memoirs 1 v.

Thomas a Kempis: The Imitation of Christ 1 v.

A. Thomas: Denis Donne 2 v. On Guard 2 v. Walter Goring 2 v. Played Out 2 v. Called to Account 2 v. Only Herself 2 v. A Narrow Escape 2 v.

Thomson: Poetical Works (w. Port.) 1 v.

Thoth 1 v.

Tim 1 v.

F. G. Trafford: *vide* Mrs. Riddell.

G. O. Trevelyan: The Life and Letters of Lord Macaulay (w. Portrait) 4 v. Selections from the Writings of Lord Macaulay 2 v.

Trois-Etoiles: *vide* Murray.

The price of each volume is 1 Mark 60 Pfennig.

Anthony Trollope: Doctor Thorne 2 v. The Bertrams 2 v. The Warden 1 v. Barchester Towers 2 v. Castle Richmond 2 v. The West Indies 1 v. Framley Parsonage 2 v. North America 3 v. Orley Farm 3 v. Rachel Ray 2 v. The Small House at Allington 3 v. Can you forgive her? 3 v. The Belton Estate 2 v. Nina Balatka 1 v. The Last Chronicle of Barset 3 v. The Claverings 2 v. Phineas Finn 3 v. He knew he was right 3 v. The Vicar of Bullhampton 2 v. Sir Harry Hotspur of Humblethwaite 1 v. Ralph the Heir 2 v. The Golden Lion of Granpere 1 v. Australia and New Zealand 3 v. Lady Anna 2 v. Harry Heathcote of Gangoil 1 v. The Way we live now 4 v. The Prime Minister 4 v. The American Senator 3 v. South Africa 2 v. Is He Popenjoy? 3 v. An Eye for an Eye 1 v. John Caldigate 3 v. Cousin Henry 1 v. The Duke's Children 3 v. Dr. Wortle's School 1 v. Ayala's Ange 3 v. The Fixed Period 1 v. Marion Fay 2 v. Kept in the Dark 1 v. Frau Frohmann, etc. 1 v. Alice Dugdale, etc. 1 v. La Mère Bauche, etc. 1 v. The Mistletoe Bough, etc. 1 v. An Autobiography 1 v. An Old Man's Love 1 v.

T. Adolphus Trollope: The Garstangs of Garstang Grange 2 v. A Siren 2 v.

Twain: *vide* Mark Twain.

The Two Cosmos 1 v.

Venus and Cupid 1 v.

"Vèra," Author of—Vèra 1 v. The Hôtel du Petit St. Jean 1 v. Blue Roses 2 v. Within Sound of the Sea 2 v. The Maritime Alps, etc. 2 v. Ninette 1 v.

Victoria R. I.: *vide* Leaves.

Virginia 1 v.

L. B. Walford: Mr. Smith 2 v. Pauline 2 v. Cousins 2 v. Troublesome Daughters 2 v.

D. Mackenzie Wallace: Russia 3 v.

Lew. Wallace: Ben-Hur 2 v.

Eliot Warburton: The Crescent and the Cross 2 v. Darien 2 v.

Mrs. Humphry Ward: Robert Elsmere 3 v. David Grieve 3 v. Miss Bretherton 1 v. Marcella 3 v. Bessie Costrell 1 v. Sir George Tressady 2 v.

S. Warren: Passages from the Diary of a late Physician 2 v. Ten Thousand a-Year 3 v. Now and Then 1 v. The Lily and the Bee 1 v.

"The Waterdale Neighbours," Author of—*vide* Justin McCarthy.

Hugh Westbury: Acte 2 v.

Wells: The Stolen Bacilius, etc. 1 v. The War of the Worlds 1 v.

Miss Wetherell: The wide, wide World 1 v. Queechy 2 v. The Hills of the Shatemuc 2 v. Say and Seal 2 v. The Old Helmet 2 v.

Stanley J. Weyman: The House of the Wolf 1 v. Francis Cludde 2 v. A Gentleman of France 2 v. The Man in Black 1 v. Under the Red Robe 1 v. My Lady Rotha 2 v. From the Memoirs of a Minister of France 1 v. The Red Cockade 2 v.

A Whim and its Consequences 1 v.

Walter White: Holidays in Tyrol 1 v.

Whitby: The Awakening of Mary Fenwick 2 v. In the Suntime of her Youth 2 v.

Richard Whiteing: The Island 1 v.

S. Whitman: Imperial Germany 1 v. The Realm of the Habsburgs 1 v. Teuton Studies 1 v.

"Who Breaks—Pays," Author of—*vide* Mrs. Jenkin.

K. D. Wiggin: Timothy's Quest 1 v. A Cathedral Courtship, etc. 1 v.

Mary E. Wilkins: Pembroke 1 v. Madelon 1 v. Jerome 2 v.

C. J. Wills: *vide* F. C. Philips.

J. S. Winter: Regimental Legends 1 v.

H. F. Wood: The Passenger from Scotland Yard 1 v.

Mrs. Henry Wood: East Lynne 3 v. The Channings 2 v. Mrs. Halliburton's Troubles 2 v. Verner's Pride 3 v. The Shadow of Ashlydyat 3 v. Trevlyn Hold 2 v. Lord Oakburn's Daughters 2 v. Oswald Cray 2 v. Mildred Arkell 2 v. St. Martin's Eve 2 v. Elster's Folly 2 v. Lady Adelaide's Oath 2 v. Orville College 1 v. A Life's Secret 1 v. The Red Court Farm 2 v. Anne Hereford 2 v. Roland Yorke 2 v. George Canterbury's Will 2 v. Bessy Rane 2 v. Dene Hollow 2 v. The foggy Night at Offord, etc. 1 v. Within the Maze 2 v. The Master of Greylands 2 v. Johnny Ludlow 2 v. Told in the Twilight 2 v. Adam Grainger 1 v. Edina 2 v. Pomeroy Abbey 2 v. Court Netherleigh 2 v. (The following by "J. Ludlow"): Lost in the Post, etc. 1 v. A Tale of Sin, etc. 1 v. Anne, etc. 1 v. The Mystery of Jessy Page, etc. 1 v. Helen Whitney's Wedding, etc. 1 v. The Story of Dorothy Grape, etc. 1 v.

M. L. Woods: A Village Tragedy 1 v. The Vagabonds 1 v.

Wordsworth: The Poetical Works 2 v.

Lascelles Wraxall: Wild Oats 1 v.

Edm. Yates: Land at Last 2 v. Broken to Harness 2 v. The Forlorn Hope 2 v. Black Sheep 2 v. The Rock Ahead 2 v. Wrecked in Port 2 v. Dr. Wainwright's Patient 2 v. Nobody's Fortune 2 v.

Castaway 2 v. A Waiting Race 2 v. The yellow Flag 2 v. The impending Sword 2 v. Two, by Tricks 1 v. A silent Witness 2 v. Recollections and Experiences 2 v.
S. Levett-Yeats: The Honour of Savelli 1 v. The Chevalier d'Auriac 1 v.
Miss Yonge: The Heir of Redclyffe 2 v. Heartsease 2 v. The Daisy Chain 2 v. Dynevor Terrace 2 v. Hopes and Fears 2 v. The young Step-Mother 2 v. The Trial 2 v. The clever Woman 2 v. The Dove in the Eagle's Nest 2 v. The Danvers Papers, etc. 1 v. The Chaplet of Pearls 2 v. The two Guardians 1 v. The caged Lion 2 v. The Pillars of the House 5 v. Lady Hester 1 v. My young Alcides 2 v. The three Brides 2 v. Womankind 2 v. Magnum Bonum 2 v. Love and Life 1 v. Unknown to History 2 v. Stray Pearls (w. Port.) 2 v. The Armourer's Prentices 2 v. The two Sides of the Shield 2 v. Nuttie's Father 2 v. Beechcroft at Rockstone 2 v. A reputed Changeling 2 v. Two penniless Princesses 1 v. That Stick 1 v. Grisly Grisell 1 v. The Long Vacation 2 v.
"Young Mistley," Author of—*vide* Henry Seton Merriman.

Collection of German Authors.

Berthold Auerbach: On the Heights, (Second Edition) 3 v. Brigitta 1 v. Spinoza 2 v.
Georg Ebers: An Egyptian Princess 2 v. Uarda 2 v. Homo Sum 2 v. The Sisters [Die Schwestern] 2 v. Joshua 2 v. Per Aspera 2 v.
Fouqué: Undine, Sintram, etc. 1 v.
Ferdinand Freiligrath: Poems (Second Edition) 1 v.
Wilhelm Görlach: Prince Bismarck (with Portrait) 1 v.
Goethe: Faust 1 v. Wilhelm Meister's Apprenticeship 2 v.
Karl Gutzkow: Through Night to Light 1 v.
F. W. Hackländer: Behind the Counter [Handel und Wandel] 1 v.
Wilhelm Hauff: Three Tales 1 v.
Paul Heyse: L'Arrabiata, etc. 1 v. The Dead Lake, etc. 1 v. Barbarossa, etc. 1 v.

Wilhelmine von Hillern: The Vulture Maiden [die Geier-Wally] 1 v. The Hour will come 2 v.
Salomon Kohn: Gabriel 1 v.
G. E. Lessing: Nathan the Wise and Emilia Galotti 1 v.
Fanny Lewald: Stella 2 v.
E. Marlitt: The Princess of the Moor [das Haideprinzesschen] 2 v.
Maria Nathusius: Joachim v. Kamern, and Diary of a poor young Lady 1 v.
Fritz Reuter: In the Year '13 1 v. An old Story of my farming Days [Ut mine Stromtid] 3 v.
Jean Paul Friedrich Richter: Flower, Fruit and Thorn Pieces 2 v.
J. Victor Scheffel: Ekkehard. A Tale of the tenth Century 2 v.
George Taylor: Klytia 2 v.
H. Zschokke: The Princess of Brunswick-Wolfenbüttel, etc. 1 v.

Series for the Young.

Lady Barker: Stories about 1 v.
Louisa Charlesworth: Ministering Children 1 v.
Mrs. Craik (Miss Mulock): Our Year 1 v. Three Tales for Boys 1 v. Three Tales for Girls 1 v.
Miss G. M. Craik: Cousin Trix 1 v.
Maria Edgeworth: Moral Tales 1 v. Popular Tales 2 v.
Bridget and Julia Kavanagh: The Pearl Fountain 1 v.
Charles and Mary Lamb: Tales from Shakspeare 1 v.
Captain Marryat: Masterman Ready 1 v.
Emma Marshall: Rex and Regina 1 v.
Florence Montgomery: The Town-Crier; to which is added: The Children with the Indian-Rubber Ball 1 v.
Ruth and her Friends. A Story for Girls 1 v.
Mrs. Henry Wood: William Allair 1 v.
Miss Yonge: Kenneth; or, the Rear-Guard of the Grand Army 1 v. The Little Duke. Ben Sylvester's Word 1 v. The Stokesley Secret 1 v. Countess Kate 1 v. A Book of Golden Deeds 2 v. Friarswood Post-Office 1 v. Henrietta's Wish 1 v. Kings of England 1 v. The Lances of Lynwood; the Pigeon Pie 1 v. P's and Q's 1 v. Aunt Charlotte's Stories of English History 1 v. Bye-Words 1 v. Lads and Lasses of Langley, etc. 1 v.